When
Prophets
Die

SUNY Series in Religious Studies

Harold Coward, Editor

When Prophets Die

The Postcharismatic Fate
of New Religious Movements

Edited by
Timothy Miller

With an Introduction
by J. Gordon Melton

State University of New York Press

Published by
State University of New York Press, Albany

© 1991 State University of New York

For information, address State University of New York
Press, State University Plaza, Albany, N.Y., 12246

Production by Diane Ganeles
Marketing by Bernadette LaManna

Library of Congress Cataloging-in-Publication Data

When prophets die : the postcharismatic fate of new religious
    movements / edited by Timothy Miller.
        p.   cm. — (SUNY series in religious studies)
    ISBN 0-7914-0717-9 (alk. paper). — ISBN 0-7914-0718-7 (pbk. :
alk. paper)
    1. Cults.   2. Sects.   I. Miller, Timothy, 1944-   . II. Title:
Postcharismatic fate of new religious movements.   III. Series.
BP603.W43   1991
291—dc20   90-44859
                                                               CIP

10 9 8 7 6 5 4 3 2 1

Contents

v

99 825

Preface

At the opening reception of the 1986 annual meeting of the American Academy of Religion, Steven J. Gelberg and I found ourselves in a relatively quiet corner of a huge roomful of religion professors discussing recent events in the history of religious movements in America, and in particular that of the International Society for Krishna Consciousness (ISKCON), Gelberg's own spiritual home for many years. The founder of that movement in America, A.C. Bhaktivedanta Swami Probhupada, had died in 1977; he had appointed a board of directors to oversee ISKCON's future course, but many problems had ensued notwithstanding. Still, ISKCON was alive and, in the eyes of some of its members, recovering from its problems, poising itself to resume adding its Vaishnavite Hindu spice to the American spiritual stew.

As our conversation continued we began trying to compare ISKCON's recent history to that of other movements whose leaders had died. The conventional wisdom has long been that most new religious movements are so heavily dependent on a single dominant personality that they cannot long survive that leader's passing. But the examples we could come up with on that evening kept pointing in the other direction: We could think of many movements that had survived for some time, albeit with struggle and conflict in some cases, and we were hard pressed to think of many that had indeed dissolved on the heels of the leader's demise.

From that conversation came this book. Gelberg here tells the most fascinating tale of ISKCON after 1977, reflecting on the larger issue of the problems involved in transplanting a religion from one culture to another. Eleven other chapters similarly track the courses taken by other religious movements.

A comprehensive analysis of the fate of new religions after the departure of their founding-era charismatic leaders awaits a major monograph that to the best of my knowledge no one has yet undertaken. This book approaches the question through a series of case studies. After some consultation with other scholars of new or marginal religions, most of them participants in the New Religious Movements Group of the American Academy of Religion, I composed a list of substantial alternative religions, mainly American, and sought out persons who had studied those movements in depth. The majority agreed to contribute chapters to the present volume; in every case the contributors are ranking experts on the movements they present here, familiar with the latest and best scholarship on their groups as well as with, in many cases, situations and source materials that have heretofore received little attention from scholars. J. Gordon Melton has used the extensive resources of his Institute for the Study of American Religion as a basis for his introduction that outlines the book's basic finding.

The study of new religious movements is a relatively young and tentative field. It is clear that many who have written about new religions in the past, and even some in the present, have done so from other than empirical bases. The authors of the present volume hope that we may help in putting one old myth to rest.

Acknowledgments

Some of the chapters in this book have been delivered as papers at meetings of the American Academy of Religion and other professional societies. The discussions that have followed such presentations have helped to sharpen several of the papers; we are grateful to the community of scholars for collegial criticism and support.

As editor I have tried to learn on my own about the groups discussed in this volume. Several individuals have provided various kinds of direct support in that pursuit. Ravindra Svarupa Dasa deserves special mention in that regard; he was very generous with time and documents as he helped me try to sort my way through the events of the last few years in the International Society for Krishna Consciousness. Robert Minor, my chairperson, arranged for considerable support in the form of photocopying, mailing, and telephone expenses, despite the exigencies of a tight departmental budget. Our support staff here at Kansas and at the institutions of the various chapter authors also helped greatly in a variety of practical chores, and we all appreciate their efforts.

Introduction: When Prophets Die: The Succession Crisis in New Religions

J. Gordon Melton

It is a common assumption among social scientific observers of new religions (popularly termed "cults") that the period immediately following the death of the founder/leader of a group is critical, a period that generally leads to major disruption and often fatal consequences for the group itself. This widely held assumption is not so much a finding derived from the observation of the phenomenon in specific situations as it is a conclusion drawn from early definitions of the term "cult" and lists of the characteristics of cults. According to the traditional wisdom in the field, among the most important characteristics of a cult (and the one most relevant to understanding the role of the founder) is that its leadership is invested in the person of a "charismatic" individual. That assumption ties cults to Max Weber's classic discussion of charismatic leaders.

Weber, in an oft quoted passage, defined charisma as ". . . a certain quality of an individual personality, by virtue of which [s/]he is set apart from ordinary [people] and treated as endowed with supernatural, superhuman, or at least specifically exceptional powers or qualities. These are such as are not accessible to the ordinary person, but are regarded as of divine origin or as exemplary, and on the basis of them the individual concerned is treated as a leader."[1]

Charismatic religious leaders may appear in the center of culture; for example, Methodist evangelist/healer Oral Roberts is a prominent example of an American Christian charismatic leader. However, founders of new religions have been especially singled out as examples

1

of charismatic leaders since they often not only possess some marked natural ability in either leadership, teaching, or speaking, but also have followers who ascribe to them special "supernatural" or "paranormal" powers.[2] The nature of such special powers varies enormously. Some leaders might be seen as incarnations of the divine, such as the average Hindu guru to whom may be given any one of a set of divine titles such as avatar, bhagwan, or lord. Some might be seen as being in special contact with the supernatural realms such as a spiritualist medium, a Wiccan priestess, or the bearer of a new revelation (for example, the prophet Joseph Smith, Jr. or Mary Baker Eddy). Others might be viewed as the channel for a spiritual or psychic power. Most, however, seem to be "charismatic" only in a weaker sense of having been discoverers of new truth or insight as a result of their hard work and/or specialized research. Most founders who have been labeled "cult" leaders, but who have actually founded new Christian sects, fall into this latter category: Victor Paul Wierwille, founder of the Way International; Charles Taze Russell, founder of what today is called the Jehovah's Witnesses; and Herbert W. Armstrong of the Worldwide Church of God.

Among the most influential attempts to bring together Weber's insights about charismatic leaders and the concept of cult was made by J. Milton Yinger in his important 1957 textbook, *Religion, Society and the Individual*. Concluding his oft discussed typology of religious groups is a lengthy paragraph discussing "The Cult." He says,

> The term cult is used in many different ways, usually with the connotations of small size, search for a mystical experience, lack of an organizational structure, and presence of a charismatic leader. Some of these criteria (mysticism, for example) emphasize cultural characteristics that are inappropriate in our classification scheme; yet there seems to be the need for a term that will describe groups that are similar to sects, but represent a sharper break, in religious terms, from the dominant religious tradition of a society. By a cult, therefore, we will mean a group that is at the farthest extreme from the "universal church" with which we started. It is small, short-lived, often local, frequently built around a dominant leader (as compared with the greater tendency toward widespread lay participation in the sect). Both because its beliefs and rites deviate quite widely from those that are traditional in a society (there is less of a tendency to appeal to "primitive Christianity," for example) and because the problems of succession following the death of a charismatic leader are often difficult, the cult tends to be small, to break up easily, and is relatively unlikely to develop into an established sect or a denomination. The cult is concerned almost wholly with problems of the individual, with little regard for questions of social order; the implications for anarchy

are even stronger than in the case of the sect, which is led by its interest in "right behavior" (whether the avoidance of individual sin or the establishment of social justice) back to the problem of social integration. The cults are religious "mutants," extreme variations on the dominant themes by means of which men try to solve their problems. Pure type cults are not common in Western society; most groups that might be called cults are fairly close to the sect type. Perhaps the best examples are the various Spiritualist groups and some of the "Moslem" groups among American Negroes.[3]

This paragraph lists the essential characteristics of a cult, as social scientists understood them in the 1960s. Most importantly, a cult makes a sharp break religiously from the mainstream of any given culture's religious life. It is small, short-lived, and built around a dominant charismatic leader. Yinger suggests both by the brevity and placement of his discussion of cults that they are ephemeral and hence less than serious religious phenomena. They do not share the full religious life of a church or even a sect, but are instead built around the drama of life with the leader. While the leader lives, the group lives for the leader and follows his/her direction. When the leader dies, the group will probably die, since its life was dependent upon his/her presence.[4]

In the 1970s, of course, this sociological definition of a cult was turned against the new religions by anticultists who tried to characterize the new religions as something different from genuine religion. They said the new religions were led by charismatic leaders who were devoid of spiritual motives and whose actual agenda was the accumulation of power, money, and fame through the manipulation of duped followers who gave their leader their blind allegiance.

Yinger's definition of "cult" was challenged in the 1960s by the work of various researchers, most definitively by Geoffrey Nelson, whose work on British Spiritualism[5] demonstrated that cults can be quite large and very long-lived (Spiritualism was over a century old at that point and showed no signs of dying). More recently Stark and Bainbridge[6] have been able to summarize the findings of new religious movement scholars and note that the essential distinction of cults is their radical religious break with the dominant culture. In the generation between Yinger and Stark/Bainbridge, sociologists were somewhat confused and confusing in their writings about cults. They were seeking to establish a typology of religious groups that ignored the important theological-ideological dimension that most precisely defines the nature of "cult." That is to say, a cult is a religious body with a distinctive religious pattern. It does more than simply vary somewhat more from dominant religious patterns than do sects. It offers a completely different religious gestalt.[7]

The work of Nelson, Stark and Bainbridge, and the host of recent scholars of new religions has called into question the collection of ideas that reduced new religions to ephemeral marginal groups finding their total life in the extraordinary career of a charismatic leader. Increasingly, new religions are being seen in more mundane terms as a vital part of the total spectrum of diverse religious offerings in a pluralistic society. While different, at times radically different, from mainstream groups, new religions offer followers a full religious vision and a serious religious program. In spite of the changing understanding of new religions, however, the assumption that there are usually serious succession problems following the death of the founder as something of special significance has been separated from the ongoing discussion and has survived as an independent remnant of the earlier definition of "cult." While only rarely mentioned in print, that assumption is frequently dropped in conversations on new religions as assumed truth.[8]

It will not be the task of this essay to review the lengthy and continuing process of the changing assessment of new religions, a process in which this volume participates. Rather, what follows will be an attempt to summarize a perspective on cults and cult leaders and then speak to the issue of what happens to the followers when their prophet dies. The chapters on the demise and aftermath of various new religions serve as fitting examples of the range of responses of first generation religions to the loss of their founders.

Toward an International Perspective on New Religions

Much of the literature on new religions (especially the sociological material) has treated them primarily as a strange new phenomenon that has suddenly emerged in a fresh context and hence is in need of analysis. For example, the famous Glock/Bellah study in the 1970s focused upon centers of the new religions whose presence they had discovered in the San Francisco Bay Area in the early 1970s.[9] From the series of case studies, supplemented with some broad surveys, this most significant work attempted to draw conclusions about the larger religious context of the commuity and other similar American communities in which they were appearing. However, the analysis offered began with the assumption that it was the presence of the new religions that needed explanation, rather than, for example, that it was the absence of new religions in earlier decades that was the odd phenomenon. The research then was directed to speculation about (1) the nature of the American cultural context (the changes in the 1960s) that seemed to have opened the country to hosting such exotic new religions, and (2) the sociological and psychological predisposition of those people who deviated from their normal course in life to convert. However helpful such analysis may be, without additional probing of the historical and legal background of the Bay Area new religions, and without some understanding of the larger international movement of people and ideas in which these new religions were participating, the impression was often created that the new religions were nothing more than a more or less interesting product of the social upheavals of the 1960s. This impression was reinforced by the rather slow growth experienced by the new religions relative to the total population and older churches.

As new groups have emerged in the last half of the twentieth century, examination of them on the local level presents a picture of numerous, small, barely stable centers, many struggling to keep a minimum critical mass in membership and attendance, and others coming and going. As a group, the new religions have shown themselves no meaningful threat to take over the religious life in the West or any part thereof. On the other hand, the groups have permeated the culture geographically. If one moves from the Bay Area to Los Angeles, the same groups appear, and in like measure, the same or very similar groups show up in Denver and Chicago and New York and Miami. Moreover, the same groups can be found in Vancouver, Toronto, and Montreal. And, equally importantly, the same story is also true in city after city in Europe. Be it London, Geneva, or Copenhagen, the very same array of groups appears. What happened in Berkeley in the 1970s also happened in every major urban center in the West, and Berkeley was by no means the most extreme example.

But if we begin an examination of new religions in Berkeley with some broad understanding of the emergence of new religions all over the West, where might it lead us? Let us, for example, launch a probe from the Berkeley center of the Unification Church or the Hare Krishna temple or the Church of Scientology or the local Soka Gakkai center. Regardless of their local strength, we would quickly discover that the local group is in fellowship with other similar local centers around the country. These centers are associated in a more or less hierarchical organization with a national headquarters and auxiliary national offices. In addition, each group is affiliated with local centers in other countries, each of the four mentioned above having centers in a majority of the world's countries. These additional centers are associated under the direction of an international headquarters. In the case of the Unification Church that international direction comes from Seoul, Korea, and New York. The Hare Krishna Movement is under the direction of an international governing council that operates through a number of regional centers that have responsibility for various parts of the world. The Church of Scientology International is centered in Los Angeles. The Soka Gakkai International is directed out of Tokyo.

In light of the international headquarters office, the little centers in Berkeley, Chicago, or London take on a completely different character. They now appear as end points of a vast international missionary network. From Los Angeles, the Church of Scientology has developed centers across North America, in most countries of Europe, and to a lesser extent around the world. From Tokyo, Soka Gakkai International missionaries spread the teaching of Nichiren Shoshu Buddhism to all parts of the world. From its several regional centers, the Hare Krishna Movement has reached into over one hundred countries. From Korea, the Unification church is now established worldwide on every continent. And what has been said about these four movements can be repeated for hundreds of others. Thus what we see locally as the opening of a new religious center in our town is, when viewed globally, but one more step in the spread of a vast worldwide movement and the further diffusion of its teachings and practices internationally.

Further, while new religions may seem to be a strange and different innovation, only rarely are they actually that. The overwhelming majority of the "new" religions are variations of an old religious tradition that somewhere in the world, usually in the country of origin, is part of the mainstream. Thus the Hare Krishna Movement is part of the larger Chaitanya Movement in Bengal, and in India it is honored as very much a part of the majority culture. Soka Gakkai is one of a hundred sects of Buddhism, the largest religious grouping in Japan. The Unification Church perspective synthesizes insights from the three major religious traditions of Korea—Christianity, Buddhism, and ancient shamanism. Scientology, one of the few "new" innovative religions, nevertheless draws major elements of its teachings from Buddhism, the occult, and trditional psychology.

The majority of the new centers of the "new" religions currently functioning in the urban areas throughout the West are usually outposts of large religious organizations that are many decades, if not centuries, old. And most of the remaining groups are schisms from these older groups. The old Asian religions are now in the process of spreading throughout the world from a home base in Asia or the Middle East, just as Christianity has spread from the West into the rest of the world during the last century and a half. This process of spreading began in the late nineteenth century, but was markedly increased following World

War II, primarily due to improved commercial transportation and legal changes in Japan (religious freedom), India (independence), and the United States (removal of immigration restrictions in 1965). The spread of new religions can thus be seen as a by-product of the vast human population shifts that have changed the demographics of most of the world's countries. And in encountering a local center of the new religions, westerners are confronted, as a whole, not so much by new revelations and immature theology as by very sophisticated, time-tested religious phenomena, however different and strange they might seem.

Meanwhile, adding to the intensity of the changes being experienced in the encounter with the new religions from Asia are the several new innovations in religious life that emerged in the West. In the nineteenth century, the distinctly new religious traditions of the Latter Day Saints, Spiritualism, Christian Science, New Thought metaphysics, and Theosophy appeared to challenge Christianity's exclusive hegemony over the religious experience of Western culture. During its first generation, though maligned and held up to ridicule, each offered an attractive and sophisticated religious vision and spread across the continent and to Europe. During its first generation, each grew into a stable organization, and each became, however unwillingly, the ground upon which variations could emerge. Over the decades of the twentieth century, the five new religions of the nineteenth century became five new families of religious organizations. As of 1990, there are over fifty Mormon churches, over thirty metaphysical denominations, over one hundred Spiritualist organizations, and over one hundred separate groups that can be traced directly to the Theosophical Society (though few bear that name). In the postwar period of religious mobility, aside from the older Asian and Western traditions, these new nineteenth-century religions are now spreading into new territory. Seicho-No-Ie, one of the largest of the "new" religions of Japan, developed out of the Church of Religious Science, an American metaphysical denomination. Theosophy gave birth to the New Age Movement that is now present, in strength, in such far away places as Australia and South Africa.

And the new American groups have been bolstered by the emergence of new European traditions. For example, in England, Neo-Pagan Wicca emerged soon after World War II and began what has been a spectacularly rapid diffusion in the 1960s. Within one generation it has spread throughout Europe and North America and through the avenues offered by the British Commonwealth to distant parts of the earth. In like manner, Rosicrucianism emerged in Germany several centuries ago. It has spread worldwide, with no fewer than nine different Rosicrucian groups operating in North America.

This seemingly lengthy digression into the nature of the new religions has direct implications for our understanding of the role of leaders and the effect their deaths might have on their movements. The leader/founder of the average group to which reference is made when speaking of new religions is (or was) more than likely the leader/founder of a vast international organization that has developed an appropriate bureaucracy and organization that has in turn adapted to the numerous differing legal restraints in the many countries in which it has begun missions. In the process many hundreds, if not thousands, of people have found in the particular group enough spiritual depth to devote their lives to the spread of ideas and practices while many tens of thousands, if not hundreds of thousands, have found enough spiritual depth to adhere to the movement.

In simple terms, the average founder of a new religion, especially one that shows some success during the first generation, is obviously an important factor in the growth and development of his/her movement. The movement is initially an extension of the founder's ideas, dreams, and emotional makeup. The leader may be valued as a teacher and/or venerated as a cosmic being or even divine entity. However, once the founder articulates the group's teachings and practices, they exist independently of him/her and can and do develop a life of their own. Once the follower experiences the truth of the religion, that experience also exists independently. Once a single spokesperson for the founder arises, the possibly of transmitting the truth of the religion independently of the founder has been posited. If a leader has developed a religious vision with the depth to gain a significant following during his/her lifetime, it will be a religion in which the role of the individual who created the religion, however important, will be but one element, not the overwhelming reality. Just as the disconfirmation of a prophecy rarely alters the direction of a group,[10] so the death of the founder rarely proves fatal or leads to drastic alteration in the group's life. But what does happen when the founder dies? Generally the same thing that happens in other types of organizations, that is, very simply, power passes to new leadership with more or less smoothness depending upon the extent and thoroughness of the preparation that has been made ahead of time.

Consider, for example, two very different groups. Siddha Yoga Dham (see chapter 11) had been built into an international organization by its founder, Swami Muktananda. Prior to the time of his death in 1982, he formally installed his successors and introduced them to the movement. After his death a short time later, a smooth transition of power followed, though it was disturbed by a scandal involving charges of Muktananda's illicit sexual encounters. The new leaders worked well together for a few years; then one stepped down (or was pushed aside, depending upon which story is believed), and Swami Chidvilasananda became the sole head of the vast empire. Swami Nityananda went on to found a rival organization, but once the break was made, he took too few followers to essentially disturb the life of the Siddha Yoga Dham.

In sharp contrast was Psychiana, founded in 1929 by Frank B. Robinson. Robinson ran Psychiana out of his office in Moscow, Idaho. He wrote all of the materials, kept the mail order organization at a size he could control, and made little provision for a successor. At one time he began to form groups, out of which a new generation of leadership could have emerged, but he soon disbanded them. There being no one in place to assume his duties, the organization died with him in 1948. Psychiana is exceptional, and other examples of such nonconventional groups that died as a result of their founder's death are extremely hard to discover.

One of these rare examples is provided by the Spirit Fruit Society (see chapter 8). A relatively small community, still in the first years of life, it was traumatized by the death of its leader who was taken suddenly and unexpectedly. Only three years after the society found some stability in a permanent home in Ingleside, Illinois, founder Jacob Beilhart was stricken with appendicitis from which he died five days later. He had not had time to build the group to a critical mass and the society ceased to grow. It remained in existence for several decades but Beilhart's death essentially sealed its fate. Had he had more time with his followers, even his sudden death might not have proved fatal, as the survival of the Mormons after Joseph Smith's assassination demonstrates.

In the long run, the Spirit Fruit Society is illustrative of the many new religions that come and go having never found enough response to gain a stable life or following. When a new religion dies, it usually has nothing to do with the demise of the founder; it is from lack of response of the public to the founder's ideas or the incompetence of the founder in organizing the followers into a strong group. Most new religions will die in the first decade, if they are going to die.

In the overwhelming majority of cases, however, if a new religion finds some response and survives its initial phases of organization to attain a relative stability (the more so if it becomes fairly successful, with multiple centers and a mature leadership), the death of the founder will be experienced as a sad event but not a fatal or even traumatic one. In years past, the passing of a founder has often led to a power struggle, with the loser breaking away and taking some supporters to establish a rival organization. Such power struggles are a clear sign that leader-ship was allowed to develop in the group, though the final choice among several possible successors was postponed until after the founder's death.

Such power struggles, while momentarily important, are no more significant than any other issues that threaten schism. The more prepara-tion is made for a smooth transition, the more likely an orderly succession is to occur. We have seen such orderly transfers of power following the deaths of a number of founders who passed away in recent years: L. Ron Hubbard (Scientology), Victor Paul Wierwille (the Way), and Herbert W. Armstrong (Worldwide Church of God), not to mention the earlier examples of Mary Baker Eddy (see chapter 7), Charles Fillmore (Unity School of Christianity), Ernest Holmes (Religious Science), Baha'u'llah (the Baha'i Faith), and the founders of the several hundred other nonconventional religions whose founders have died and whose organizations continue to this day.

One important factor that has served to further lessen the impact of succession problems on new religions is the control of property. In past years, the single leader of a group could have complete control of the group's assets. If no clear successor was named, the property was the bounty to be won by rivals. However, that concern has increas-ingly become a nonissue, as movements in the United States (and many other countries) have moved to develop corporate structures. In the United States, almost all new religions are organized as corporations under the leadership of boards of directors who have formal legal control of the corporate assets. Generally, the corporate constitution and bylaws include specific provisions to cover the death (or removal from office by other means) of a leader and the method of his/her replacement. Given the collective nature of the board leadership, it is not subject to the disturbances caused by the death of any single person, including a founder, in a leadership position. Imposed for tax purposes, the corporate structure has as a by-product given new religious groups an additional stability that no single leader could bequeath.

In Conclusion

As we rid ourselves of the myths about new religions, we lose our naivete about their seriousness and the fullness of their religious life. We also can discard the inappropriate list of superlatives frequently used to describe new religions as totalistic societies under the absolute con-trol of their charismatic leaders. Such talk is more rhetoric than reality and more polemic than analysis. While we observe the adulation of religious leaders in ritual setting, we also experience the ability of members to distance themselves emotionally when away from the presence of the guru. As the myths drop away, we become free to explore the rich storehouse of data available to us in the experience and operation of first-generation religion. Normal, creative people form new religious structures, and the continued generation of new religions is to be expected as a sign of health in any open society.

New religions as first-generation religions, whether a new orthodox Christian movement such as eighteenth-century Methodism or a new Hindu group built around a recently arrived guru, share many characteristics. During the first generation, the founder, whose new ideas led to the formation of the group, places a definitive stamp upon it. The first members are self-selected because of their initial confidence in the leader and/or their agreement with the leader's program. The first generation is also a time of experimentation and rapid change. The leader must discover the right elements to combine in a workable program, generate solutions to unexpected obstacles, choose and train capable leaders, and elaborate upon the initial ideas or vision that motivated the founding of the group in order to create a more complete theology. The group formally or informally gives feedback in the form of approval or disapproval of the leader's actions. The most successful leaders are continually adjusting and reacting to that feedback.

Over time, the choices open to the leader are narrowed. Structures (and expectations) develop. As the movement grows, and especially as branches are established, the leader has to work through intermediaries, and the lines of authority and communication become more impersonal. The leader's real ability to change structures, should s/he desire such adjustments, meets greater and greater resistance. Though the leader may retain some important pieces of control, the real task of managing the organization and administering the organization's affairs increasingly passes to the second and third echelon leadership. The analogy between religious and secular corporations, however much it offends religious sensibilities, is both appropriate to and informative of religious group dynamics.

Just as different religious groups will believe and act differently when their founders are alive, different groups will bring all of their unique experiences as new religions to bear in their responses to the leaders' deaths and to filling the vacuums created by those losses. Rather than anticipate the many ways they have of dealing with their founders' deaths, I will leave that task to the essays below. This essay has a much more modest task, merely pointing out that the problem of succession is not the determinative trauma it has often been considered to be and that it in no way cuts off options limiting the group's determination of its own future course. Groups will tend to react to their leaders' deaths as they have previously reacted to other situations, and will make the necessary decisions in much the same way they have made decisions in the past.

Starting from this new assumption, the essays below can be seen as providing a fresh opening upon an old problem as the authors initiate an exploration of what really happened when the prophet died, and what can it teach us about religion in general and new religions in particular.

1

The Shakers:
The Adaptation of Prophecy

Diane Sasson

For over two centuries, the persistence of the Shakers, a religious group founded by the eighteenth-century charismatic Ann Lee, has fascinated Americans. The longest lived communal society in America, the Shakers are today the subject of lavishly illustrated books, scholarly articles, public television films, and Elder Hostel classes. Their endurance has intrigued the public as well as the scholar. Over the last fifty years, periodic news reports have announced the demise of Shakerism, as the movement's members dwindle.[1] Yet, the lives of contemporary Believers testify to the stability and viability of Shakerism as a religious movement.

Within thirteen years after the first Shakers landed on American soil, the movement's entire British leadership was gone. Yet, when the nineteenth century opened, Shakers had established eleven communal societies in New England and New York, and they were dispatching missionaries westward to participate in the religious excitement of the Second Great Awakening. Why and how did the Shakers survive the death of their charismatic leaders? How was the succession of leadership determined? What turned individual converts, who were scattered across several states, into a communally structured and enduring religious organization?

Ann Lee

Shakerism, like many new religious movements, originated in the special "gnosis" received by its leader. Ann Lee, while in prison in

13

England in 1770[2], proclaimed that sexual abstinence was necessary for salvation. Subsequently, she assumed prophetic leadership of a group of radical dissenters who accepted her claims to divine inspiration, acknowledged her as "the first visible leader of the church of God upon earth," and caller her "Mother."[3] In August 1774, Mother Ann led eight British followers to the New World. Among them was the young James Whittaker, whose own visions had confirmed the decision to emigrate and who would assume leadership of the Society after Ann Lee's death.

During the early years in America, the Shakers were an unstructured group, connected loosely by family ties and united primarily by the desire to reinstate the apostolic age. In the first Shaker settlement at Niskeyuna, New York,[4] Ann Lee supervised domestic chores, urging industry, prudence, and economy. Like a mother, she nurtured both the physical and spiritual needs of her followers. There is, however, little evidence that she proposed any social or religious organization beyond that modeled on the extended family.[5] The movement centered on Ann Lee's personal charisma,[6] and Believers cited her extraordinary visions, prophecies, glossolalia, healing gifts, and insight into the inmost secrets of those around her as evidence that the new apostolic age had arrived. The touch of her hand or the "heavenly melody" of her voice aroused the emotions of her followers. Charisma was not routinized, and the manifestations of the spirit took unpredictable forms.[7] Leadership was determined by "spiritual gifts" that took precedence over social status, educational level, or gender distinctions, and authority was neither static nor vested in a single person. Instead, it was shared by several members of the "little family." John Hocknell—who provided the financial resources both for the transatlantic crossing and, eventually, for the purchase of land—was the leader in "temporal" concerns. Ann Lee shared spiritual leadership, always contingent on personal purity and charismatic gifts, with her brother William, and James Whittaker.

William Lee and James Whittaker

William Lee, the prophet's brother, considered himself "next in the lead" and was so recognized by later Believers. *A Summary View of the Millennial Church* published by the Shakers in 1823 lauds Father William's clear, sonorous voice, his courage in facing persecution, and his "feeling soul."[8] Even this hagiography, however, casts some doubt on his leadership ability, admitting that William Lee was "not gifted in public speaking" and suggesting that he was hot-tempered and emotionally volatile.

Articulate and attractive, James Whittaker was considerably younger than William Lee. Since his childhood, Whittaker had been closely attached to Mother Ann and was almost young enough to be her son. In contrast to William Lee and Mother Ann, Whittaker claimed that sexually he was as innocent as an infant, asserting that he had not only avoided sexual experience, but that he had overcome all sexual desire. The appeal to superior personal purity may have increased Whittaker's stature among Believers; it was his way with words, however, that gave him a leadership advantage over William Lee. During the short period of time when Mother and the "Elders" spread the Shaker gospel throughout New England and eastern New York, James Whittaker emerged as the chief spokesman for Shaker doctrine. He assumed authority not only for interpreting Ann Lee's message to other Believers, but he also began to instruct converts to support the Society with their property and their labor.

A Summary View presents Whittaker as a charismatic figure. A tall man, with a fair complexion and straight dark hair, he possessed "an inexpressible something which could not but impress the feelings of a stranger with confidence and respect." Sometimes assuming a "mild, gentle and forebearing" disposition,[9] at other times Whittaker fiercely and vividly denounced sin and sinners. Believers recalled that, like Mother Ann, he had almost magical power over some followers. The picture of Whittaker that emerges from Shaker sources is one of an energetic leader who possessed the vigor of mind and strength of personality to shape an emerging religious movement.

Yet despite his popularity and public visibility as a preacher, Whittaker took care not to upstage Ann Lee, deferring to her wishes. In an 1785 tract, apostate Daniel Rathbun faults Whittaker for failing to assert himself as the Shaker chief religious teacher.[10] However, Whittaker willingly accepted the role of a dutiful son, never challenging Ann Lee's leadership of the Society. Nevertheless, by the summer of 1783, Whittaker had gained such prominence that he came into conflict with William Lee over leadership of the Society. While not preserved in Shaker documents, apostates Thomas Brown and Reuben Rathbone record this rivalry. In Brown's account:

> For sometime past William Lee and James Whittaker had been called
> Fathers by the believers; and they had always understood that Lee stood

in the lead next to the Mother, and Whittaker next to him. But as
Whittaker had been the principal instrument in gaining proselytes,
there arose a dispute between them in the latter part of the year 1783,
which should be first, and Mother Ann interfered to settle the controversy—and the contention arose to such a height that it was the cause
of several losing their faith.[11]

According to Rathbone who claimed to be an eyewitness to the
dispute, Mother's attempt to settle the conflict resulted in a physical
scuffle between the sister and brother.[12] In neither of these sources,
however, is it clear that Mother had chosen either William Lee or
Whittaker to succeed her. Only the fact that Father William passed away
on 21 July, 1784—just weeks before Mother Ann's death—may have
prevented a destructive power struggle within the Society. There seems
no doubt, however, that William Lee, beloved as he was in the memory
of later Shakers, could not have provided leadership needed to survive
the trauma of the death of the prophet.

The First American Converts

After witnessing the ecstatic worship of the Shakers in the spring
of 1780, two travelers returned to New Lebanon, New York, and
recounted their experiences to Joseph Meacham, a New Light minister
who had led a revival there the previous year.[13] Intrigued by the description of Shaker worship and belief, Meacham sent Calvin Harlow, one
of his trusted associates, to further investigate the "woman in the
wilderness" and to ask her to justify female religious leadership.
Impressed by Ann Lee's responses to his questions, Meacham himself
visited the Shakers and was converted, as was Harlow.

Revolutionary New England afforded a "favorable ecology"[14] for
the establishment of new sects. "New Lights" such as Meacham and
Harlow had previously accepted the need to separate themselves from
the world and to build a church composed of "saints" who could give
evidence of personal religious experience and who sought to live
perfect, sinless lives. Already seeking to reinstate the apostolic age, they
were troubled by the decline of ecstatic experiences in their own
worhsip and by the delay in the coming of the millennium.[15] Thus,
Joseph Meacham and the "New Light" inquirers were prepared to heed
Ann Lee's charismatic claims. The Shakers offered simple answers to
their questions: No one, asserted the Shakers, can become perfect
without "taking up the cross" against the flesh. Pentecostal gifts, they

told inquirers, are granted to those who live a pure life. The redeemed need wait no longer for the coming of the millennium: They live in it every day. Such reasoning made sense to the "separates," as it did in coming years to other radical millenarians.

Much of the success of Shakerism after Ann Lee's death depended on these first converts, especially on the leadership of men and women like Joseph Meacham, Calvin Harlow, and Lucy Wright. Shakerism was fortunate to attract not only leaders of splintered religious groups, but also to bring into the fold members of their families and their congregations.[16] Family networks were especially important to the development of Shakerism as an organized religious movement. For example, during the first "gathering" of Shaker converts, twenty-four members of the Goodrich family joined Shaker communities in Hancock and Lebanon.[17] Although Shakerism challenged the structure of the biological family, it effectively used the institution of the family to spread its gospel. At the same time, the Shakers reinterpreted the meaning of "family," offering converts a spiritual family of mothers, fathers, brothers, and sisters to replace the biological family that they had relinquished.

Contrary to the implication of much scholarly writing, most early Shakers were neither economically "dispossessed" nor psychologically crippled. Instead, they were generally representative of the social and economic spectrum of New England frontier society. The religious separatists, from whom the Shakers drew most of their converts, included a number of leading citizens, many of whom belonged to the middle classes,[18] and several were exceptionally well educated.[19] What set potential converts to Shakerism apart, however, was the intensity of their religious concerns and their expectation of a new millennial age.

The Beginnings of Communal Organization

About 1782, James Whittaker began to translate Mother's inspirational but vague visions of Believers living together and sharing a common life into specific demands that followers "sell their possessions and give to the poor." In one of the earliest Shaker documents, dated 1782, Whittaker wrote to Josiah Talcott, a Believer in Hancock, admonishing him for sloth and idleness. You must, Whittaker wrote: "Put up fences, haul out your dung, plow your land when the season comes. . . . Get up early and in a lively active manner put things in order." Whittaker asserts that if Talcott will improve his land, he has holdings "enough to maintain three families or more. . . . The time has come for you to give up yourselves and your all to God—your substance, your temporal property—to possess as though you possessed not."[20] William Deming Andrews thus concludes that James Whittaker "was the original promulgator of the commuity principle."[21]

Shakers had originally implemented these principles on a small scale out of necessity. Calvin Harlow recalled that at Niskeyuna, Believers "gave what they gained by their industry, with the use & improvement of their farm, for the good & benefit of the whole Society." They provided a "free table" to all inquirers, and they expected visitors of means to contribute beyond their own "table expenses." "For," writes Harlow, "if none were to do more than support themselves, the poor could not have equal privilege of the gospel with the rich. . . ."[22] Thus, at its earliest stage, Shaker communalism grew out of two convictions: that the gospel must be equally available to rich and poor alike, and that everyone—whether temporary guests or permanent residents—must freely contribute their assets and their labor. Even during the movement's most charismatic phases, Shakers insisted on the importance of physical labor and of improving "temporal" and material gifts. Religious ecstasy was never enough by itself and sloth was never tolerated.

The Death of the Prophet

After the death of William Lee in July 1784, Mother Ann's health declined visibly and rapidly. She died at Niskeyuna on 8 September. *A Summary View of the Millennial Church* recounts that shortly before her death she spoke to Job Bishop, a young Believer: "Be not discouraged, nor cast down: for God will not leave his people without a leader. Elder James and Elder Joseph will be left, and there will be a great increase of the gifts of God to all who are faithful and obedient."[23]

Ann Lee's untimely death severely tried the faith of many of her followers. Some converts had presumed that since Mother and the Elders were free from sin, they were also free from its wages: death. If Mother had, as Believers claimed, initiated the millennial age, then should death not also be overcome? Such, it seems, was the reasoning of some early Shakers, a number of whom subsequently left the movement. Detractors, such as Benjamin West, author of an early attack on the Shakers, asserted that the Shakers had once believed themselves immortal, but that they had later "grown ashamed of their doctrine of immortality . . . [and] began to deny that they ever held to any such things."[24] Thomas Brown also indicates that Mother Ann may have given "some such intimations" of immortality; he notes that "Whittaker never inculcated such a belief."[25] Thus, early on Whittaker seems to have interpreted Ann Lee's prophecies spiritually, not literally. At the time of her death, Believers looked to him for an explanation of their loss. Both those who remained committed to the faith and those who subsequently left the Shakers agreed that it was Whittaker who helped Believers reconcile themselves to Ann Lee's death by reinterpreting her mission.

In fall 1784, Shakerism consisted of an indeterminate number of converts (perhaps as many as two thousand persons) who were widely scattered throughout New England.[26] Leadership was still primarily charismatic. Although rudimentary institutional structures in the form of communal households were in place, communalism was not yet a tenet of faith. Shaker theology was largely undeveloped. Most converts still lived with their biological families, and some may have considered themselves Shakers while still engaging in conjugal relations.

Crucial questions about the future direction of the movement needed answers: Was celibacy a requirement for all Believers or only for those most advanced in the faith? Must converts donate all their wordly goods to the Society? Was belief in Ann Lee essential to conversion to Shakerism? If so, what did such belief entail? Could Shakerism survive "in the world" or must converts be segregated into isolated enclaves? On these and other important issues, Ann Lee's statements had been ambiguous or contradictory; it was up to the next generation of leaders to select and interpret her words.

Although years later Believers recalled that Mother Ann had designated Whittaker and Joseph Meacham to lead the Society, there is no evidence that she had made any formal provision for the succession of leadership. *A Summary View* suggests that she looked primarily to Joseph Meacham to ensure the continuation of the movement, and it quotes her as saying: "It will not be my lot, nor the lot of any that came with me from England, to gather and build up the church; but it will be the lot of Joseph Meacham and others. . . . Joseph Meacham is my first-born son in America; he will gather the church into order; but I shall not live to see it."[27] Such statements ascribed to Ann Lee must be used with caution, however, since they were penned many years after Meacham had institutionalized the Shaker church. They give the sanction of the prophet to his leadership, but they tell us little about whether Meacham was an active contender for leadership after Mother's death.

According to Shaker sources, James Whittaker preached so powerfully at Ann Lee's funeral that it was evident he would be the next leader of the Society: "So solemn and impressive were his words at this time, and so evident the power of God that appeared in him, that it produced a great impression upon the mind of every feeling believer. It was clearly seen and felt that Mother's mantle had fallen upon him, and that God had chosen him to lead and protect his people."[28] In no account did Whittaker proclaim himself Mother's successor: Instead, he humbly sought divine guidance and waited for Believers to call him to leadership. Not all Shakers were happy when Whittaker gained control of the Society. John Partington and James Shephard, who had followed Ann Lee from England to America, opposed Whittaker and left the movement rather than accept his leadership. Thus, some scholars have concluded that the "American faction, probably supported by the Shakers' English patron, John Hocknell, . . . carried the day."[29] It is undoubtedly the case that after Ann Lee's decease American converts increasingly influenced the movement, determining to a large extent its developing theology and social organization.

Father James Whittaker and the Interpretation of Prophecy

Ann Lee's death occasioned considerable confusion and bewilderment about the future direction of the Society. Realizing the danger, Whittaker responded on several levels to retain converts as the nucleus of an ongoing religious organization. *A Summary View* recounts that "with tears in his eyes," Whittaker pleaded with Believers to "be faithful and persevering."[30] According to Thomas Brown's account, he also placed "judgments" on those who abandoned the faith: "His words were these—'Whosoever from this time forsakes the blessed work of God, will never prosper in this world nor in the world to come, nor die the natural death of other men; if they do, God never spake by my mouth!' "[31] One of Whittaker's major tasks was to institutionalize the Shaker message, detaching it from the person of Ann Lee. Shakerism, Whittaker preached, does not consist in "belief" in Mother Ann; rather he asserted that Shakers acknowledge the power of God manifest through her. This same power was now passed to those who wore the "mantle " of leadership: The power would continue to be transmitted through the Society's leaders and to be displayed in the lives of the faithful.

On the important question of celibacy, Ann Lee's position was not clear-cut. On one occasion she graphically described sinners who were punished in hell "in those same parts" in which they had taken sexual pleasure. But in another instance, she stated that those who were unable to adopt celibacy should marry and live with their lawful spouses. Given different leadership after Mother's death, Shakerism might well have developed two orders, one celibate and more spiritually advanced, another composed of married couples who agreed to strictly regulate the "times and seasons" of sexual relations.[32]

Whittaker, however, took an adamant position: No one polluted by the flesh could be a Shaker, since spiritual regeneration required a complete renunciation of the natural life. Later Shakers acknowledged that "it was the peculiar gift" of his "ministry to wean the affections of the Believers from their natural and earthly ties."[33] The most prominent characteristic of Whittaker's leadership was thus his unwillingness to make any concessions to the weakness of the flesh. Whittaker's attitude is clearly revealed in a letter that he wrote to his own family in England the year after Mother Ann's death: "All earthly profits and pleasures; all earthly generation, and propagation which are the delights of all men in their natural birth . . . all these, I say, have I forsaken for CHRIST'S sake." He goes on to assert that he has received "redemption from the bondage of corruption; which is that sordid propensity to, or ardent desire of copulation with women," and he excoriates members of his family in terms that are shocking to the contemporary reader: "Why tell ye me of your increasing and multiplying after the flesh? Your vessels are marred in the potter's hand, and they must be made over again by regeneration; or go down to the pit. . . . I hate your fleshly lives, and your fleshly generation, and increasing, as I hate the smoke of the bottomless pit. . . ."[34] He refuses to give any material support to his relatives or to help them emigrate to America, for he says, "You are a stink in my nostrils." The letter undoubtedly echoes central themes of Whittaker's preaching, and it is significant that in it Whittaker never once mentions Ann Lee. He proclaims that a new era of regeneration, the "Day of the Second Appearance of the Son of Man," is at hand: The life of a particular prophet is not central to his message. It is clear, therefore, why Whittaker became a controversial leader whose relentless zeal and demands for strict obedience could both inspire great devotion while alienating some who had been among the first converts to Shakerism.

Although converts continued to live with their natural families and to manage their own temporal affairs, they nevertheless vowed to live celibate lives.[35] However, since Shakers believed that the sin of sexual intercourse had affected the very structure of society—resulting in a host of sins, including violence, greed, and war—only a celibate community, they argued, in which all relationships were restructured and that preserved strict boundaries between itself and the world could redeem society.[36] From the time of Whittaker's leadership, only those who were willing to completely renounce their sexuality and their ties to the biological family were accepted as Shakers.

In addition to his refusal to modify the essence of the Shaker message, Whittaker framed it within a familiar millennial context. Whittaker may have learned much of the language through which he interpreted Ann Lee's prophetic utterances from the American converts to Shakerism. Whether or not Whittaker brought with him from England notions of a final "dispensation" that would usher in a millennial age, in the New World he began to interpret Ann Lee's revelation as a new and final dispensation offered to sinners. There is little evidence that Mother Ann herself ever thought or spoke in such terms. To be sure, she occasionally referred to "Christ within her," or envisioned herself as the bride of Christ. Such was—and is—the common language of religious mysticism. However, it was quite a leap from such visionary experience to an interpretation of Ann Lee as the "second appearing of Christ," the last and final dispensation, and humankind's last chance for salvation. Scanty though the evidence is, early sources strongly suggest that James Whittaker was among the first to understand Shakerism in these terms. In such terms James Whittaker preached, and in such terms, particularly after Mother's death, early Believers accepted Shakerism. Thus, James Whittaker might be viewed as the Paul of Shakerism. Both during Ann Lee's lifetime and especially after her death, he translated and interpreted her prophetic utterances and developed around them a theory of history and a theology.

On 29 January 1786, James Whittaker dedicated the first Shaker meeting house at Lebanon proclaiming the first "orders" for behavior in the Society:

> These are the orders that ye are to observe and keep that ye shall Come In & go oute of this House with Reverence & Godly fear that all men Shall come in & go oute at the west Doors & gates & all women at the East Doors & Gates that man & woman shall not intermix in this House or yard nor sit together that there shall not be any whispering or talking or Laughing or unnecessary going out & in time of Publik worship That there shall be no buying or selling or bargaining Done in this House or yard for ye shall not make this House a Place of merchandize for it was Built to worship God in & to Repent in. Furthermore ye shall do no servile labour in this House Except it be to wash & Clean the House and Keep it in order.[37]

The construction of a house of worship was an important step toward routinization: It established a central physical location for Shakerism at Lebanon, a location from which the authority of the Church would emanate. It was a visible symbol of the new society, creating both physical and psychological boundaries between the world of the redeemed and those outside. And within its walls, the Shakers instituted ritualized behavior and worship to express their world view.

In his last public address to Believers at New Lebanon in January 1787, Whittaker revealed a premonition of his premature death: "I am going to leave you; I feel that my work is done here, and I do not know that I shall ever see you again in this world; but I leave those with you who are able to teach you the way of God."[38] Whittaker became ill in March while at Enfield, Connecticut, where he died on 20 July 1787, at age thirty-eight. Writing in 1812, Thomas Brown commented: "Thus the church had lost its three principal leaders, who had nurtured it in its infant state, and whose fostering care had protected it through all its imbecilities and various trials, and had raised it to a degree of maturity. They had been the principal pillars to support its fabric, which more than once has been threatened by the rage of opposition and persecution to be annihilated."[39]

However, after only three years, Whittaker had established Shakerism as a religious movement able to survive the death of its prophet. He had organized a rudimentary communal structure, he had built a meeting house for worship, he had instituted regulations governing the separation of the sexes. And, he bequeathed the Shakers a theology centered less on the person of Ann Lee and focused more on the expectations of frontier millennialism.

Father Joseph Meacham Brings Order

At the time of Whittaker's death, three American converts—Joseph Meacham, David Meacham, and Calvin Harlow—vied for leadership in the Society of Believers. More than a century later, Anna White and Leila Taylor described the scene at Whittaker's funeral when all three men addressed Believers: "For a time Elder Joseph felt the silent opposition of the people of the place who were in attendance. The oppression was so great that at the grave he shook and trembled from head to foot, and then spoke under the influence of the Spirit with such power that even Believers marveled. He declared that the work of God would increase and the power of God would overcome all things."[40]

Despite the fact that Meacham had displayed great spiritual power, sole leadership of the Society was not immediately conferred on him.

Instead, for two months, he shared that role with David Meacham and Calvin Harlow. While they were away on a journey to the eastern societies, Joseph Meacham began to organize the Society, demonstrating his considerable administrative skills. As Thomas Brown observed: "Elder Meacham was indefatigable in his exertions to collect the believers into families, to support a joint interest and union and to hold all things in common, (for Whittaker had begun to make some preparations previously to his death.) . . . [H]e laboured to convince the believers of the necessity of travailing out of a fleshly relation . . . and of being gathered into a church or spiritual relation. . . ."[41]

Few historians of Shakerism would disagree with Edward Deming Andrews's statement: "Eliminate the influence of Joseph Meacham, and the church would probably not long have survived the death of its founder, or merited more than a footnote in the social, economic, or religious history of America."[42] While James Whittaker made crucial decisions about the ideological direction of the movement, Meacham created an organizational structure that sacralized ideology and assured its perpetuation. Meacham's accomplishments are so numerous that space does not permit a detailed account. Shortly after Father James's death, he began "gathering" converts to Lebanon, where the first communal organization was institutionalized. He appointed Lucy Wright to head the "female line," thus creating a dual order of leadership. He conceptualized a structure for the Society based on the biblical description of Solomon's temple with three courts: He established an inner sacred order (or court) composed of unmarried persons of middle age who were able to cut off all ties with the world and who had "the greatest faith and abilities in things spiritual;" a second court of younger persons who performed agricultural work and who were deemed "second in their faith and abilities;" and a third court of older members designated to deal with "the world."[43] From this organization of the Lebanon Church, the Shaker system of "families" emerged. When Believers were first gathered into communities, they made an oral convenant. In 1795, however, just before his death, Meacham initiated the first written covenant that delineated the obligations and privileges of membership. With the establishment of written covenants, Shakerism had evolved from a charismatic sect into an institutionalized religion.

By the late 1780s it was clear that the Kingdom on Earth would not come rapidly. Meacham realized that if they remained among the "world's people" most Believers would be unable to lead the pure life demanded by Shakerism. At the same time, he understood—as perhaps Whittaker did not—the difficulty of weaning men and women away from the ties of the natural family. Some Believers did not have so far to "travel," having never lived in the flesh. But others, particularly those who had lived the married life for many years, must conquer ingrained ways of thinking and living. Consequently, not all Believers would reach the same level of spiritual perfection. Rather than looking for an instant change in the lives of converts, Meacham was content to acknowledge that change occurred gradually and progressively. In reading his instructions to Believers, one cannot help but be struck by Meacham's common sense and his ability to hold in creative tension a belief in perfection with a deep appreciation of the imperfect nature of humankind. His emphasis on progress was an important contribution to Shakerism, one that brought the religious movement more closely in line with the American cultural milieu.

Convinced that steady "travel" toward perfection would occur if the faithful were protected and nourished within a community separated from the norms of the "world," in September 1887, Meacham began to "gather" Believers to Lebanon. Unlike Whittaker who dreamed of outfitting a ship to take the gospel across the oceans, Meacham turned his entire energy to the creation of a social and economic order that exemplified the righteous kingdom. Drawing upon a deep-seated American image, Meacham saw that Shaker communities could become as the "city set on a hill" whose light could not be hid.

In a religious movement that never ceased valuing charismatic gifts, Meacham faced the challenge of creating a structure that would not be undermined by individual religious inspiration. Although he asserted that all Shakers had abandoned the "Old Adam," Meacham was nevertheless aware of the dangers of individuals who, believing themselves perfect, might look to their own "lead" rather than to the hierarchy for guidance. Thus, he affirmed that in each stage of spiritual development, obedience to those at a higher stage was the key to progress. He created two levels of authority, one governing temporal concerns, the other spiritual. All decisions should be in "union" with the decisions of previous leaders; at the same time, they should be in "union" with those of the hierarchical chain. It was under his guidance that the governing offices of the Society were established whereby ministers of the Church were appointed by their predecessors and their authority was confirmed by the unanimity of the members.[44] Since Believers were constantly enjoined to express their "union" with their leaders and since dissent from "union" was unacceptable, leaders, in effect, appointed their own successors. In the system of Elders and Deacons, Meacham utilized the terminology and functions familiar to Shakers from their experiences as members of other religious organizations. "The titles and the division of functions recalled the Congregational and Baptist polities from which nearly all the Shakers had come, but their authority was enormously extended."[45] Through promulgating the notion of the progressive character of Shakerism and the need for "union," Joseph Meacham reconciled an emphasis on pentecostal gifts with the need for hierarchical authority that bound the community together.

Father Joseph also recognized that individuals possessed a variety of talents and that the organization must utilize all members—male and female—for maximum effectiveness. Thus, he required conformity in the external details of life, but at the same time offered opportunities for members to use their diverse abilities—whether their talents be in the material or the spiritual realm. He fostered inventiveness among the Shakers and kept them open to more efficient ways of performing everyday activities. Meacham's reorientation of the Society had profound ramifications: It shaped not only theological attitudes, but also directed them toward material progress and creativity.

Meacham was also the first Shaker leader to explicitly address the issue of sexual equality and to confront the social implications of Ann Lee's message. He established parallel and equal orders of male and female leaders, ensuring that the institution of the Society would express "a perfect equality of Rights between male and female."[46] Since the founder of the Society was female, and since celibacy profoundly altered the relationship between the sexes, Meacham's institutionalization of female leadership was a logical, but nevertheless daring step. Some early Shakers, although accepting female charismatic leadership, were uneasy with the institutionalization of female authority. Clearly, there was some resistance to the appointment of Lucy Wright to an equal position of leadership with Meacham, although the degree is difficult to gage. Reuben Rathbone, writing in 1800, commented that ". . . it was doubtless without any difficulty [the Shakers] acknowledged Elder Joseph to be their father in the Gospel; but as to a mother, it was such a new thing and so unexpected that there was something of a labor before the matter was finished."[47] Such comments make us aware that religious celibacy, in itself, did not ensure that male and female would share power and authority. Without Joseph Meacham's personal willingness to share authority, Shaker organization might not have embodied a commitment to sexual equality.

If James Whittaker was a zealot who kept the fires of faith burning during the first three years after Ann Lee's death, Joseph Meacham was a pragmatist with the skills of a corporate manager. Like a good manager, Meacham consolidated Shaker converts, established clear lines of authority, and as Shakers would say, brought the "church into order."

Under his administration, much of daily life was organized; the economy of the community was structured; worship was ritualized. In contrast to the unpredictable pentecostal gifts that characterized earlier Shaker worship, under Meacham's lead the Shakers developed controlled forms of song and dance that reflected specific religious meanings. However, Joseph Meacham's greatest contribution was his ability to envision and to create organizational structures and ritualized forms of worship that concretely embodied Shaker belief. Organization itself was sacralized, and participation in all aspects of the community became a religious act.

Shaker historians have rightly noted that withdrawal from the world lessened the conflicts between Shakerism and the surrounding society. By the time of Meacham's death, Shakers had gained the respect of their neighbors who admired their hard work and economic success and who complimented them on their "solemn" worship of God. Likewise, some admired the Shaker commitment to sexual equality. The order, the peace, and the organization of the Shaker communities that impressed even the casual visitor contributed to a revision of the "world's" opinion of the Shakers. Throughout the nineteenth century, the Shakers were decreasingly viewed as a dangerous cult, and increasingly judged an eccentric, albeit admirable, religious movement.

Contemporary scholars are vigorously debating the reasons for the dramatic numerical decline in Shaker membership in the second half of the nineteenth century. Demographic studies that point to the aging and increasing female membership of Shaker communities, particularly in the post–Civil War period, describe the symptoms, not the causes, of decline. Certainly as the nineteenth century progressed, Shakers gained few members who matched the religious zeal of the early converts; many of those joining did so for economic or practical reasons. Social and economic dislocation contributed more members to the community in the nineteenth century than during the formative years, including numerous youngsters who seldom became permanent members of the Society.

However, it would be a mistake to gauge the "success" of Shakerism at any given historical period by the number of members in the Society. Indeed, the major accomplishment of early Shakerism was not so much the conversion of large numbers as it was the institutionalization of a integral religious vision. In fact, during the entire span of Joseph Meacham's leadership the Shakers, eschewing evangelical activity, focused their energy on the attainment of individual perfection and the creation of a workable communal organization. It is possible to argue that the second half of the twentieth century has been one of the most "successful" periods of Shaker history; for, even though fully committed Shakers are few, we are currently witnessing a recognition of the Shaker way as a model of religious and communal living.

2

Postcharismatic Authority in the Amana Society: The Legacy of Christian Metz

Jonathan G. Andelson

The phenomenon of "postcharismatic collapse" has been observed frequently enough in various kinds of religious movements that many observers have come to expect such movements to fall apart upon the death or departure of the charismatic leader. Of particular interest in this regard are the so-called "utopian" religious communities. Many religious utopias have precisely those characteristics that are thought to undermine their ability to make a successful transition to postcharismatic leadership. They are founded by highly charismatic individuals who are believed by their followers to possess divine favor if not supernatural gifts; the communities break fundamentally from the wider society over one or more issues, have well defined boundaries, and remain relatively small while developing steeply hierarchical structures. If it were true, as many believe, that strong leaders attract weak followers and that orthodoxy will out in the end, then such groups would usually be reabsorbed by the wider society following their leaders' deaths. In point of fact, many religious utopias do not fall apart upon their prophet/founder's death.

The Amana Society of Amana, Iowa, is an example of a religious utopia that survived the death of its charismatic founder. Amana was settled in 1855 by members of a German radical pietist sect led by the highly charismatic Christian Metz. For a total of fifty years, first in

Europe and then in America, Metz was the spiritual and temporal head of the group. Beginning about 1820, he proselytized widely in Germany and Switzerland, later gathered his scattered followers together into communities, presided over their arduous transatlantic journey, forged a successful communal economic order among them, planned their relocation from New York State, where they had first settled, to Iowa, and supervised the building there of Amana, which by 1862 comprised seven villages with a population of twelve hundred members.

Christian Metz's death on 24 July 1867 left his followers aggrieved and shaken. Yet his passing precipitated no crisis in the community, nor did it leave a power vacuum that others rushed to fill. The economic, social, and political system Metz helped to create persisted for another sixty-five years with only minor modifications. And although the Amana Society was reorganized in 1932 as a joint-stock corporation and thrives today as a prominent Iowa tourist attraction, Metz's memory and many of the values he promoted are still honored.

Why did Amana not founder or fall apart after the death of its charismatic leader? To answer this question we will first examine the context of Metz's status as a charismatic leader in the community. Then we will consider the events surrounding his death and in the decade afterward, which indicate the members' interpretation of his role and the institutional and individual responses to his absence. Their responses reveal the nature of the political and social order that Metz forged, an order that was able to survive without him.

Metz and the Role of *Werkzeug*

The Community of True Inspiration, the sect to which Christian Metz belonged, actually originated in 1714 in Hessen, Germany. Its members sought to live simple and pious lives according to Christ's teachings and the will of God. The group took its name from its members' belief that certain individuals among them were divinely selected to proclaim "the word of the Lord" to the Community. The Inspirationists, as they were known, called such individuals *Werkzeuge*, or "instruments" of God, and attributed to their inspired pronouncements, or testimonies, a sanctity comparable to that of Scripture. In many ways, these *Werkzeuge* resembled the prophets of the Old Testament, itinerant ministers to scattered congregations of the faithful.

The Inspirationists have recognized eleven *Werkzeuge* in their 275 years of existence. Eight were active during the first decade of the sect's history, but only one of these, Johann Friedrich Rock, for more than a few years. After Rock died in 1749, the movement was without inspired leadership for sixty-eight years. Then, on the verge of total eclipse, three new prophets led a revitalization. The first, Michael Krausert, joined an Inspirationist congregation in 1817. Stirred by a spiritual power that some of the older elders recognized as evidence of inspiration, Krausert was accepted as a *Werkzeug* by many of the Inspirationists, and the "reawakening" was under way. A few months later, an illiterate Alsatian serving maid named Barbara Heinemann arrived in the community seeking an explanation for the powerful inner promptings she felt. Krausert pronounced her to be divinely inspired, and she too was accepted as a *Werkzeug*, despite the reservations of some of the members and elders. At about the same time, in 1818, a young carpenter born in the community, Christian Metz, was "awakened" under Krausert and Heinemann's influence and became the third new *Werkzeug*.

The first years of the reawakening were volatile. Krausert confessed doubts about his own inspiration and apostatized. Several false prophets rose and fell. Then in 1823, Heinemann, ignoring the warnings of the community's elders, married Br. Georg Landmann "against the will of God" and spontaneously lost the power of inspiration. There remained Christian Metz, who after a wavering of faith at the time of Krausert's fall went on to become unquestionably the greatest Inspirationist leader of the nineteenth century.

Under Metz's leadership the Inspirationist community grew to the point of becoming the object of persecution, not only from church authorities because of the group's nonconformity, but also from state officials upset by the members' refusal to swear oaths, participate in military service, or send their children to the state schools. The decision to emigrate followed a "hidden prophecy" by Metz, and in 1843 the Inspirationists arrived in America and established their first settlement at Ebenezer, near Buffalo, New York. There, Metz prophesied that Barbara Heinemann Landmann would again receive the "gift of inspiration," a prophecy that was fulfilled in 1849. Landmann remained inspired until her death in 1883.

Thus, although Christian Metz was a brilliant, innovative, and successful leader, and founder of the Inspirationists' communitarian and communal form of organization, he stepped into an already defined role, that of an inspired *Werkzeug*. He was charismatic, but not in the purest Weberian sense, as his gift was not unique. Furthermore, his death did not leave the community without charismatic leadership. While Landmann was neither as accomplished nor as popular as Metz, she filled the same traditional role. These facts are part, but only part, of the explanation for Amana's survival after Metz's death.

The Death of Christian Metz: An Inspirationist Account

The Inspirationists' reaction to Metz's death is recorded in his obituary, which was written by Gottlieb Scheuner, Metz's scribe as well as a school teacher, and later a church elder and the community's historian. The obituary is the longest in Inspirationist history and was published as an addendum to Metz's own diary.[1] Metz's obituary does not present a comprehensive account of his life's work; in fact, his career in the community is covered in one short paragraph. Instead, it goes into great detail about the last few months of his life, his death, and his funeral service, but in doing so provides as true a measure of the man's stature among his followers as would a lengthy recitation of his life's accomplishments.

Metz's health had been wavering for several years. He frequently missed church services and often could not leave his quarters for days at a time. On 30 May 1867 he gave his last inspired testimony. His strength continued to decline perceptibly, and by mid-July it became apparent to most that his end was near. Scheuner wrote:

> Lately, there had been so many different opinions and judgments about his condition. Many believed . . . that he would recover . . . but those who knew more about his spiritual inner life held no hope for improvement. They could see that the time of his work and labor had come to an end. Therein they could also see the wondrous leading and wisdom of God, how this liberation and the freeing from all the things for which our dear brother had worked and labored for so many years gradually, step by step, came to pass.[2]

In other words, Metz's followers viewed him as a leader who had successfully fulfilled his mission. The Inspirationist world view thus allowed Scheuner to interpret Metz's inarticulate end in a positive way:

> His last days of life were so different from many other persons' who, often in their last days, get a vision or insight into eternity and relate that through words of admonition. With him it was a "dying before death." Everything was already done that had to be done through him. The time of his work was over, so that he had no more orders or admonitions, nor said what was going on in his mind, or inside of him, but waited in silence for his end to come.[3]

On July 21, Scheuner sounded a note of hope, as the shoulder abscess that had bothered Metz seemed to be healing and he appeared a little stronger. Three days later, however, and despite a morning in which he "felt good in mind and spirit," an acute spasm of coughing brought Metz to the brink of death, and at ten o'clock that night he expired. "The next morning," Scheuner wrote, "the report of Br. Christian's death spread rapidly to the other communities, and after the initial consternation about it was over, a feeling of pain and sorrow overcame everyone, and yet also one of joy, because of the final release from the suffering he endured and the persistence of it."[4] The prolonged physical distress and decline that Metz endured at the end of his life helped his followers, and doubtless Metz himself, see his death as a release to a better existence.

Metz's funeral in the village of Amana (also called Main Amana) followed the usual pattern for Inspirationist funerals, except that it was attended by many more people than was typical. The more than two hundred members present from the other villages were expressing an extra measure of respect and affection for Metz, since memorial services were held in all seven villages simultaneously at two o'clock in the afternoon. Throughout the Colonies, work was suspended for several hours.

The service itself was led by the First Elder of the church. It included prayers, the singing of three hymns, and a reading of chapter 11 in Hebrews about faith. Consolation was the central theme in the inspired testimony delivered by Barbara Heinemann Landmann, the sole remaining *Werkzeug*:

> Be consoled, my people . . . ; You have a strong arm and good advocates, and the fathers who have passed into eternity before you and from you are assistants who maintained the union and the faith, and today their testimony is exercising its entire influence upon you, oh community; and your concern and distress—about the Work of God and if it will be lost or will close itself off—is their concern and distress as well.[5]

It is significant that Landmann, who had never enjoyed a status as elevated as Metz's in the community, would call attention to the members' apprehension concerning the continuance of inspiration. We will return to this point later.

At the conclusion of the service, Metz's simple coffin was carried to the cemetery by twelve elders, an honor accorded to all of that company. Scheuner reported, "The procession of those accompanying [the coffin] was so long that, as the first ones arrived at the grave site the last ones were leaving the village."⁶ Three verses of a hymn were sung, and everyone went home in silence.

The monument erected on Metz's grave was identical to the others in Amana's cemeteries. All graves were identified by simple markers bearing only the name, date of death, and age at death of the deceased. Even for their beloved leader, the Inspirationists would not break the symbolic equality of that sameness. One subtle expression only did they allow their special regard for Metz: Unique among the graves in all of the villages, his occupies a double plot.

Institutional Adjustments Following Metz's Death

One of the indicators of a charismatic leader's prominence in a community, and at the same time a measure of the community's resilience, is the number and variety of institutional rearrangements that are made following the leader's death. The changes reflect the extent of the need for new sources of structure in the leader's absence, as well as the group's willingness and ability to innovate. In Amana, the changes came primarily in the institutions of government and church.

Metz had been very involved in the community's temporal affairs. Not only did he play the key role in winning the members' acceptance for the communal economic order adopted in Ebenezer; testimonies he gave in Amana urged completion of a mill race and authorized the construction of new businesses. He generally approved the admission of new members and not infrequently made job assignments through inspiration. He also named all church elders through inspiration.

But governance in Amana was never based exclusively on a charismatic principle. A formal constitution, in terms of which the Amana Society was recognized under state law as a not-for-profit religious association, vested general powers in a thirteen-member board of trustees (*Grosser Bruderrath*, or Great Council) elected annually from among the elders of the community by voting members of the Society. The trustees were empowered to admit new members, to reprimand those who broke the rules (by expulsion, if necessary), and to settle accounts with those who withdrew from the Society. In the economic sphere, the trustees had authority to develop and manage the Society's businesses, to acquire or dispose of property, to buy and to sell goods, to borrow and lend money, to erect and take down buildings, and to transact any and all necessary legal matters. The constitution did not specify how often the board should meet. Before 1867, it met between four and nine times a year.⁷ The board's decisions were recorded and announced in the form of *Bruderraths Beschluesse* [Trustees' Resolutions].[8]

Eleven days after Metz's funeral the board of trustees met in Amana. For the first time, Barbara Landmann met with them. As a woman, she could not become an elder and hence could not be elected to the board. Nor, so far as the records show, had she joined them previously in her capacity as *Werkzeug*. Possibly they thought that as long as Metz was alive the Lord's will would be represented. Whether the initiative for the change came from Landmann or from the board is uncertain. We do know that on this occasion she addressed the board in inspiration, and presumably she continued to meet with them, since in the next fifteen years she gave nearly twenty testimonies at board meetings.

The board's first decision at its first meeting after Metz's death stated that "from now on there shall be a Trustee meeting the first Thursday of every month."[9] This was the first of several instances of routinization in Amana following Metz's death. Does it imply a recognition that in his absence the board would have more to do? Does it imply a lack of confidence in Landmann? Whatever motivated the trustees to make this declaration, their behavior fell short of the intention; in the subsequent decade they actually met between eight and eleven times a year, though still more regularly than when Metz lived.

The board's second action was to appoint someone to fill Metz's term as trustee. The unembellished account of this given in the records may mask debate or uncertainty among the trustees, but they appear to have followed a procedure no different than if any other board member had died. Furthermore, the board did not appreciably alter the character of its decisions or the operation and organization of the Society after 1867. Businesses appear to have been managed as before, kitchen and garden activities did not change, and the Amana schools continued to offer a basic and practical curriculum through the eighth grade. The members continued to receive medical and dental care from the Society's physicians and dentists, and the communal system of ownership was not modified. The board must have felt that Metz was replaceable in his role as trustee and saw no need to alter the Society's effective secular operation.

Metz's position as head of the Inspirationist church was another matter, as can be seen from changes in church routine following his death. One of the first of these was the special emphasis the board began to place on Metz and his testimonies. Two weeks after his death, the trustees announced that the teachers in each village should provide books of printed testimonies to any member who wanted them.[10] In October, the board directed that in church services the elders read only

Metz's most recent testimonies, "because we have to consider them very highly, and these testimonies shall also be read by the members at home."[11] The directive did not indicate how long this procedure should continue. It was surely temporary, though the records do not contain any later announcement rescinding it. The board further stipulated that the Society's print shop print "without delay" those of Metz's testimonies still in manuscript.

Another homage to Metz was the institution of a memorial service to commemorate his death. The first mention of such a service is in the *Bruderraths Beschluss* from 1 July 1872, though given the sometimes incomplete record of decisions it may have been instituted earlier. The significance of the service can be seen from the fact that Metz is the only figure in Inspirationist history to be so honored.[12]

Changes also occurred after 1867 in the scheduling of certain church rituals. In addition to the eleven regular weekly worship services, the Inspirationists had always observed a number of special rites, including Holy Communion (*Liebesmahl,* or Love-Feast) the especially sacred Renewal of the Covenant (*Bundesschliessung* or *Bundeserneuerung*), the members' yearly Spiritual Examination (*Unterredung,* or *Untersuchung*), and a special service for children and young people called *Kinderlehre.* While he lived, Metz had determined the timing of these services, and it tended to be unpredictable. Between 1843 and 1867, for example, the Inspirationists held Communion only three times. Renewal of the Covenant was equally infrequent, Metz ordering it half a dozen times in forty-five years. The Spiritual Examination, although conducted annually in each village in turn, began at Metz's direction and was occasionally suspended if he judged a village's inhabitants to be spiritually unprepared. The *Kinderlehre* service also appears to have been held irregularly.[13]

The first change in these services actually came two years before Metz's death. In 1863, President Abraham Lincoln revived the notion of a national day of thanksgiving, and in 1865 the Inspirationists responded to the call with a special *Danktag* in December, at the conclusion of the yearly Spiritual Examination. (Earlier that year, Metz had ordered a Renewal of the Covenant, which was held in April.) The following year, in keeping with Washington's instruction, the Inspirationists had planned another *Danktag* for Thursday, 29 November. The Sunday before the *Danktag* was to occur, Metz became inspired during a church service and proclaimed that henceforth the Inspirationists' annual Renewal of the Covenant be held in conjunction with the national thanksgiving day.[14] Although Metz cannot be presumed to have known he was then near death, it is tempting to believe that, in addition to the symbolic link this plan established with the national culture, he anticipated a need for more regularized worship services once he was gone.

The elders routinized other church activities after Metz died. In their Resolution from November 1867, after reiterating Metz's injunction to observe a combined Thanksgiving and Covenant service, the trustees announced that the *Kinderlehre* would be conducted four times a year.[15] Similarly, Holy Communion began to be held in alternate years beginning in 1868.[16] No apparent reason emerges for the particular schedules, and nothing explicit is recorded that would explain why Landmann did not undertake the scheduling of ritual after Metz died (or, for that matter, why she did not share this task with him while he lived), especially when she did assume the important duties of appointing elders through inspiration and advising the trustees.

The institutional changes in church and governance that followed Christian Metz's death were few but significant. His death did not elicit new religious doctrines or alter the basic character of worship in Amana's churches, and it did not require or lead to any fundamental restructuring of Amana's decision-making apparatus. The most obvious changes, including the routinization of board meetings and of certain religious services, were in the timing rather than in the nature of institutional functions; that is, the changes were in procedure rather than content. This suggests that a central feature of Metz's leadership had been his authority to regulate ritual and sacred time and to activate the community's highest level executive and legislative body. He was able to call or cancel an assembly (religious or political) in response to need and to conditions in the community. After Metz's death, other leaders either would not or could not assume this authority. Instead, they regularized the occurrence of both ritual and political assemblies, preserving the structures but altering the processes.

Individual Responses to Metz's Death

Institutional adjustments to change are, by definition, planned, formal, and corporate in nature. We must also examine the responses of individuals to change, for these reveal dimensions of a different, more personal and psychological kind.

Virtually no documents have come to light from the time of Christian Metz's death that directly reveal the personal feelings or reactions of members of the Amana community to his passing. To some extent, however, personal responses can be inferred from official

records. We will examine the impact of Metz's death on Barbara Landmann's position in the community, the reactions of other members as
revealed in the testimonies and Scheuner's history, and finally the
insights that demographic evidence can provide about the reaction of
individuals in the aggregate.

Barbara Landmann

Though recognized as a *Werkzeug*, Barbara Landmann's position
in the Community of True Inspiration had never been as secure as
Christian Metz's. Doubtless many members of the community wondered
what would happen to Landmann after Metz died. Some may have
believed that her authority depended on Metz's and that, deprived of
his support, she would lose her position. Others perhaps feared that
she would assert her leadership too strongly. Neither extreme came to
pass. Instead, Landmann's role in the community expanded to fill most,
but not all, of Metz's.

In the months after Metz's death, Landmann set to work dealing
with various problems that had been ignored due to Metz's illness. She
settled a dispute between two families in South Amana that had been
simmering for some time. She resumed the interrupted work of the
Annual Spiritual Examination. She ordered the observance of the
Kinderlehre, which had not been held in two years. She also gave dozens
of inspired testimonies before the year was over, far more than her
previous output, causing Gottlieb Scheuner to observe at the time:

> One cannot fail to appreciate that, since our dear Br. Chr. Metz departed
> from us, a greater and higher mercy and godly strength has descended
> on the *Werkzeug* Sister B. Landmann and the first brethren connected
> with her. She has now also established her residence here in Amana
> without, however, giving up her home in Homestead completely, and
> now dedicates herself fully at her age to the service and work of the
> Lord in the Community. . . .[17]

Despite her increased activity, Landmann never addressed herself in
inspiration to decisions as monumental as emigration, the adoption of
communal property, or resettlement. During her time as sole *Werkzeug*,
the community underwent no major changes. From this perspective,
her contribution to life in Amana was more or less one of maintenance
rather than of innovation.

A careful examination of the timing and occasion of Landmann's
testimonies confirms this in another way and echoes changes in the
community discussed earlier. Quantitative analysis reveals that Land-

mann's inspirations became strikingly patterned after 1867, a consistent number of testimonies being given in particular years, in particular villages, and on particular occasions. The pattern in Landmann's testimonies contrasts markedly with the irregularity in the occurrence of Metz's, which varied in number, location, and occasion from year to year. Furthermore, Landmann's testimonies during Metz's lifetime were less patterned than those she gave later.[18]

This evidence suggests that not only did aspects of Amana's institutional life become routinized after Metz's death, but inspired revelation did as well. It can be hazarded that the two are connected and ultimately derive from Barbara Landmann's different status in the community compared to that of Christian Metz. This is not to say that Landmann was totally committed to precedent, or totally unable to innovate. In fact, she was quite capable of postponing church services or calling for a general fast in the community when she felt the membership was not spiritually prepared for a particular ritual. Nor does it mean that in Metz's absence Landmann's authority waned. We have already noted that her output of testimonies increased after his death. She also reprimanded recalcitrant members of the group more often, and she was secure enough in her position to issue statements proscribing the use of photography, the making of homemade wine, and the planting of "purely decorative" evergreen trees rather than "useful" fruit trees in the Amana villages; and to authorize the construction of a railroad through Amana land.[19] Landmann became a more assertive leader after Metz died than she was beforehand, a fact that at first seems difficult to reconcile with the routinization of ritual and governance that occurred after 1867. A likely explanation is that the trustees routinized aspects of the church because they were unwilling to believe that Landmann was capable of filling Metz's role completely. Landmann never challenged their action, and in retrospect her own leadership style appears to justify it.

Other Members of the Community

No new claimants to special authority appeared in Amana either during Christian Metz's lifetime or after his death. If anyone had claimed to have the power of inspiration, that person would have needed to be acknowledged by Metz or later by Landmann. Furthermore, none of the elders or trustees ever attempted to aggrandize his position and assert himself. Landmann and the traditional authority structure would probably have opposed it, and in any case the community's ethos of humility and equality would have militated against it.

Although there was no power struggle following Metz's death, there does appear to have been a temporary breakdown of unity, especially among the elders. Barbara Landmann spoke of this situation in several inspired testimonies. On 4 August 1867, at High Amana, she said: "I see, and have seen, the hard-heartedness among your Elders. . . . Oh, you Elders, draw together in love and concord, lest you not be able to be helpers in the Lord's vineyard."[20] On 10 August, in the village of Homestead, she repeated the same theme: "I also see among your Elders how they do not stand in one spirit and [do not] carry out and do work of the Lord. But I often see the opposite: how Satan walks about [in order] to devour, and how one lets oneself be taken in so that the evil spirit disgraces the honor of God here and there. . . ."[21] In his history for 1867, Scheuner wrote about the village of Homestead: "According to both the announcement of the Lord and the understanding of the First Brethren [Trustees], something should and must happen in that community, for particularly the Council of Elders appeared torn apart and divided in its exterior. . . ."[22]

One can also glean from the records evidence of disunity and selfishness among ordinary members. On 5 August, Landmann delivered a harsh message to the congregation in Main Amana:

> How anguished I am, speaks the Spirit of Grace, which is the Spirit of the Community, when I look into this pit of murderers and see the assassin, the hater of brothers, and the slanderer ravage, for no love lives [here] except self-love. . . . Shall I not say: you are not a Community of the Lord; you are a collection and a gathering of the wicked, who want to tear and bite, throttle and oppress one another.[23]

On 8 August, in East Amana, she warned of those who "want to make their own judgment and want to instigate feud between brother and brother, and between community and community."[24] Two days later she told the Homestead congregation, "I see the evil spirit, the independent spirit, the high-handed spirit and see how he will tear you apart and hurl one hither, the other thither. I see the murderer between brother and brother; I see the snake, how it divides the hearts so that true love is lacking."[25]

The linked dangers of selfishness and disunity pointed to the even more fundamental threat of disobedience. At one point, Landmann seemed to fear that the gossip sparked by her chastisements of the elders might undermine their authority, for in a testimony on 4 August 1867, she rebuked the members for their prattle:

The members should not be allowed to open their big mouths [*das Maul aufzureissen*] when I scold my servants, but rather they should turn inward and learn to recognize how wrong it is that like a vindictive person they so often look around and like a slanderer and telltale have their mouths open. They should recognize the great self-love . . . and how one so hard-hearted is often against his neighbor. . . . And they still want to be and be called a Community of God![26]

Landmann also had to remind the congregation in East Amana to submit to the scrutiny of the elders, who "are there for when one sees or suspects danger. They shall walk a wise path and examine [matters in the commumity]."[27] She then turned to the elders: "And this is a great mistake, that the first [elders] in this community are not sufficiently awake and do not take their calling and their duty seriously enough."[28] Her words in Amana on 5 August seem to sum up her view of the situation: "This chaos cannot and must not remain standing among the members and the Elders, and they [all] shall stand subordinated in their actions and enterprises, so that the great Spirit, the independent Spirit, finds reason to descend."[29]

The last statement contains a hint of what must have seemed for Landmann the ultimate threat: disobedience from the elders. A more certain indication that serious problems of this kind existed comes from 1868, when Landmann reprimanded the elders for ignoring an inspired directive she had given:

The suffering, working, and creating grace of your God speaks: how it hurts me so, that human opinions are set before me, and they believe that I will submit to them! How it hurts me, and how I must stand back when I do not want to submit! I want to wait about it, until it is found out, until they can recognize it, what opposition and resistance they lay in the way and with that prevent the opening.[30]

The almost plaintive tone of these words seems to reflect the stance that Landmann adopted to deal with these problems.

To judge from Landmann's testimonies, dissension and disunity were fairly common in Amana following Metz's death. Were the members, and perhaps even the elders, more content under Metz's leadership, or uneasy with Landmann's elevation in status? Alternatively, did long-standing differences and resentments that Metz had held in check surface after his death? How prevalent, in fact, was the dissension? Do these testimonies, which are the only direct evidence for the problems, simply betray Landmann's self-consciousness or insecurity in her new position of authority?

The only other clue as to the level of disunity in Amana lies in the rate of apostasy before and after Metz's death. The relevance of numbers to the question of the community's response to Metz's death was established by Landmann herself. In inspiration at Metz's funeral, she reassured the memberhip about the future of the community, telling them that the work of God would continue, and that God promised an increase in their numbers, "including by those whom He finds in the big world and leads to you, so that you may receive them as a mother cares for and protects her own children."[31] In fact, the years after 1867 do show sizeable annual increments to membership from outside the community, with a net gain of 245 members for the decade 1867 to 1876.[32] It was not until after 1877 that net migration began to shift toward negative values. Therefore, although some members did withdraw from the community shortly after Metz's death, there was no surge in emigration, and for the next ten years more people joined than left the community. It may be that the growing number of apostates after 1877 simply reveals a delayed negative reaction to Landmann's leadership, but other factors, particularly economic ones, are likelier explanations for their departure.

To summarize what is known about the reactions of individual members to Metz's death: A period of readjustment occurred as Barbara Landmann assumed a new, more central role in the community. Her leadership became more forceful, but also more routinized and predictable. The transition was accomplished with little overt strife; however, there is evidence of a temporary increase in disunity among the elders and members. Emigration from Amana in the 1860s and 1870s cannot be clearly linked to disenchantment with the authority system in the community once Metz died.

Interpretation: Why Did Amana Survive?

Having reviewed the evidence concerning the collective and individual responses to Metz's death, we are in a better position to suggest some explanations as to why Amana not only did not collapse when Metz died, but survived for sixty-five years without undergoing any substantial changes in its economic, political, and social organization.

First, Christian Metz was not the founder of Inspirationism. Others laid down the tenets of the group's creed early in the eighteenth century. Nor was he the instigator of the group's nineteenth-century revival. If he was the greatest *Werkzeug* of the nineteenth century, he nevertheless followed Michael Krausert and Barbara Heinemann in the reawakening.

In short, Metz did not create the position of charismatic leadership that he held. Rather, he stepped into a role that already had well-defined expectations associated with it and filled it in an especially admirable way.

It is also significant that the Inspirationists experienced a prolonged period without a *Werkzeug*. Between 1749 and 1817, the group lacked inspired leadership. Despite Metz's long tenure as *Werkzeug*, the Inspirationists knew they had existed as a religious association apart from him, and in fact apart from any *Werkzeug*. Experience reassured them that their association would not collapse without Metz.

Finally, Metz was not the last *Werkzeug*. Barbara Heinemann Landmann continued to lead the community through inspiration until her death in 1883. Therefore, the community cannot truly be said to have entered a "postcharismatic" phase until that year. The Inspirationist case is perhaps atypical, yet it reminds us to be cautious of overly simple distinctions such as "charismatic" and "postcharismatic." The facts of Inspirationist history and culture make Metz's position in his community different from that of the charismatic leaders of many other separatist or communitarian groups. Although gifted, capable, and much beloved by his followers, he was neither the first nor the last charismatic leader in the community. Furthermore, Inspirationist culture could interpret his life's mission as amply fulfilled at the time of his death, could rejoice at his transition "from faith into knowledge," and could turn with only minor disruption to the succeeding leadership.

Nevertheless, Metz's leadership was special. The political and economic order he helped to establish in Ebenezer and Amana was a major achievement without which it is doubtful the community could have survived. The system's strength lay in the fact that authority did not revolve wholly around Christian Metz. Although his opinions doubtless counted for a good deal in the board's various deliberations, only when he spoke in inspiration were his words considered incontrovertible. Metz's personal modesty, amply revealed in numerous testimonies in which, imparting God's message, he reprimanded himself for his shortcomings and failings, underscored the Inspirationist ethos of humility and showed the members that he was not a stainless patriarch but a supportive brother. As a further evidence of this, he continued to practice his trade—carpentry—until advanced age and infirmity prevented it.

Metz's qualities as a leader also attracted other self-effacing men and women to the community. Among them were several who combined personal piety and a lack of arrogance with genuine leadership ability. This was true not only of Barbara Landmann, but of a surprising number of the principal elders. One could say that at the time of Metz's death Amana possessed "leadership in depth." Virtually without exception, the other leaders were resolutely community-minded. As a group they never constituted a cabal. Although most had been with the community for some time, talented newcomers were readily incorporated into the authority structure at the highest levels. While some transgenerational nepotism occurred, none of the principal elders were related to Metz (though he did have siblings and cousins in the community), and never was any elder, or indeed any member of the community, egotistical or ambitious enough to head a dissident faction.

Amana did not collapse when Christian Metz died because of the nature of the community's authority system, which in turn depended largely on the qualities of Christian Metz's leadership. Metz was a gifted leader whose vision and charisma brought the Inspirationists to America and helped them create a settlement with a sound economic base. His humble character attracted followers of similar temperament. It also meant that Metz was disposed that others participate in decision-making. This led not only to the development of an effective system of institutionalized authority in which to a great extent Metz subsumed himself, but to his sanctioning of a second charismatic leader in the community in the midpoint of his career. Metz's leadership style also set an example for the other leaders to follow. When he died, these trusted "pillars of the community" continued to guide the Inspirationists in the ways Christian Metz had counseled.

Epilogue: The Community After the Death of Landmann

By the time of Metz's death, the Community of True Inspiration had existed under the authority of one or more *Werkzeuge* for fifty years, and most members had come to expect the presence of an inspired instrument. As late as 1874, the Inspirationists were predicting that a new *Werkzeug* would appear to take Landmann's place.[33] However, none appeared, and Landmann was the "seal of inspiration in the Community."

Landmann died on 21 May 1883, at the age of eighty-eight. Her funeral in Amana was attended by two hundred fifty members from the other villages, including twenty-seven church elders. In the sixteen years following Metz's death, the population of Amana had grown from 1288 to 1774, and her funeral procession was the longest ever seen in the colonies. At her funeral service, the elders read the testimony she had given at Metz's funeral in 1867, as well as her own final testimony, which she presented on 23 April 1883. They also read chapters 21 and 22 from the Revelation of John, the final chapters in the Bible that depict the millennium and the second coming of Christ. But apart from these expressions, Landmann's death received less special recognition than had Metz's. Although Scheuner referred to her as the "dear Mother of the Community," her obituary was only six pages compared to Metz's twenty-five.[34] She was not buried in a double plot. The church did not hold an annual service to commemorate the anniversary of her death.

With Landmann's death, not Metz's, did Amana actually enter its "postcharismatic" phase, but in light of all that has been said above, it is not surprising that very little changed in Amana when she died. The authority structure continued to operate as before. The economic system was not modified. The church, though now deprived of new inspired testimonies, remained the same in all other ways. The community settled into a routine existence, and there was nothing of consequence that needed to be rearranged once Landmann was gone, and for half a century nothing was changed. Yet demographics inexorably set the stage for the abandonment of the theocratic, communal order. Although an unusually large contingent of over 250 newly recruited members arrived from Germany in 1879, 1880, and 1881, virtually no new members were accepted into the community after Landmann's death in 1883. Yet emigration continued, and over the next forty years, despite a slight preponderance of births to deaths, the population of Amana fell by four hundred (23 percent), due mostly to the departure of young people. The Society could not sustain such a loss and retain a healthy economy, and in 1932 the members accepted the need to reorganize the system created ninety years earlier by Christian Metz.

3

American Indian Prophets

James R. Lewis

> Long ago when the people were given these
> ceremonies, the changing began, if only in the aging
> of the yellow gourd rattle or the shrinking of the skin
> around the eagle's claw, if only in the different voices
> from generation to generation, singing the chants. You
> see, in many ways, the ceremonies have always been
> changing. . . . At one time, the ceremonies as they
> had been performed were enough for the way the
> world was then. But after the white people came,
> elements in this world began to shift; and it became
> necessary to create new ceremonies. I have made
> changes in the rituals. The people mistrust this greatly,
> but only this growth keeps the ceremonies strong.
> . . . Things which don't shift and grow are dead
> things.[1]

Until comparatively recently, a common misapprehension of tribal religions was that such traditions were—when left undisturbed by outsiders—largely unchanging, if not actually static, cultural forms.[2] The persistence of this view in the face of much disconfirming evidence seems to have been partially a function of a civilized-savage ideology that required a static, regressive counterimage for the West's self-image as dynamic and progressive.[3] A more contemporary view is that such religions are flexible traditions, quite capable of adapting to social and

47

environmental changes.[4] There are, nevertheless, limits to a culture's adaptability, as when the intrusion of colonialists radically disrupts the lifestyle of a tribal society.[5]

The religious life of a traditional culture is built around the most pressing concerns of the group, such as its economic concerns (e.g., a hunting society will usually have hunting myths and rituals). Thus a conquest situation in which a defeated people's economic base is shattered and radically reoriented (e.g., hunters who are forced to become farmers) can quite suddenly make irrelevant significant segments of a traditional religion. Conquest also transforms the contact situation itself into one of the more pressing concerns of the conquered group.

Such a state of affairs can lead to several different outcomes. If the intruding society is open to assimilation, one possible scenario is that the conquered group will abandon its traditions in favor of the conqueror's traditions. In the case of American Indians, Euro-American society, although professing an ideology of assimilation, was never really open to accepting native Americans as equals. After tribal groups such as the Cherokee, for example, had adopted Anglo-American culture in the early nineteenth century, they were rewarded with forced removal to western territories.[6]

With the possibility of full assimilation closed off and the alternative of violent warfare suicidal (particularly after the War of 1812, the last historical juncture at which there was a reasonable chance of turning the tide of conquest), defeated tribes had few options beyond getting by as best they could within the limitations imposed by the United States government. Bare existence is not, however, enough to fulfill a human community. Lacking a spiritual vision that could imaginatively transform their situation into a condition with ultimate meaning, postconquest life tended to be characterized by all of the various traits that one usually associates with demoralized social groups, such as alcoholism and a high suicide rate. While the religions of their ancestors might still have been relevant to many aspects of life, the received tradition did not address their oppressed state. And while Christianity contains many elements that speak to oppressed peoples, it was often rejected because of its association with the conquerors.

Situations such as these constitute ideal environments for the emergence of "new" religions in the form of millenarian movements (also termed messianic movements, nativistic movements, crisis cults, and so forth).[7] Characteristically, these movements begin with the religious experience of a single individual—a "prophet" for lack of a better term. While there was a fair amount of variability among the religious visions of different American Indian prophets, the central tendency of the new revelations was to speak to those aspects of the new environment that traditional religions did not address. Often these revelations provided divine sanctions for new lifestyles (e.g., the legitimation of male farming in communities that had customarily assigned farming activities to females). New religious visions also tended to address the presence of Euro-Americans in some manner (as in the well-known case of the Ghost Dance). At the level of ritual, the usual effect of prophet religions was to encourage religious practices—often modified versions of traditional dances and rituals—within groups that had partially or completely abandoned community ceremonials, thus providing native Americans with religio-social activities that helped to preserve group identity.[8]

On the whole, contemporary North Americans are unaware of these prophet religions beyond the so-called Ghost Dance of 1890 (originating with the Paiute prophet Wovoka), a movement that left a significant trace in the historical record because of the many tribes affected and because of the Ghost Dancers massacred at Wounded Knee. To convey some sense of how extensive the phenomenon of native American new religions is, it might be useful simply to list a few of the more important Indian prophets: Neolin (whose religious revelation inspired Pontiac's Rebellion), Handsome Lake (an Iroquois of the late eighteenth and early nineteenth centuries whose religion survives to this day), Tenskwatawa (whose vision of nativistic pan-Indianism lay behind his and his brother Tecumseh's efforts to halt the Euro-American advance), Smohalla (who is said to have been partially responsible for Chief Joseph's stand against Euro-American intrusion), and John Slocum (who founded the Indian Shaker Church over a century ago). Some other Indian prophets were Kenekuk, Main Poc, Josiah Francis, Wodziwob, Jake Hunt, Kolaskin, Isatal, and John Wilson. Even this list is not exhaustive, especially if one takes into consideration the various individuals who adapted the Ghost Dances of 1870 and 1890 to the needs of particular tribal groups.[9] These movements were distributed across the continent from New York to Washington State with no discernable (to the present writer) geographical pattern, beyond the obvious temporal sequence by which more westerly movements tended to arise in later periods corresponding to the later arrival of Euro-Americans.

Native American prophets were usually dissolute (e.g., alcoholic) individuals prior to their visions, and were thus people who had experienced the demoralized state of their group in a concrete, personal way. Prophets were also often drawn from the ranks of shamans, religious functionaries who naturally tended to cast problems in spiritual terms. Typically, these prophets seemed to die during their initial contact with the god who gave them their mission, so much so that sometimes—as in the cases of Tenskwatawa and John Slocum—the tribal group actually began preparing their funeral before they revived. As I have argued elsewhere,[10] the pattern of the prophetic call replicated the pattern of the shamanic call[11] fairly faithfully, although the content of the two visions diverged considerably.[12] The new revelations were more or less syncretic, with even the most nativistic movements adopting some elements of Euro-American culture. For example, the style of even the strongly antiwhite Neolin was clearly influenced by Evangelical Christianity in such areas as his emotional preaching, his notion of heavenly and hellish realms, his injunction to his followers to repeat a certain written prayer, and his map-like scripture "which He called 'the great Book or Writing.' "[13]

With remarkable consistency, the new revelations were emphatically moralistic, condemning in strong terms alcoholism, sexual promiscuity, lying, stealing, and so forth. To give this condemnation "teeth," the prophecies warned that a terrible punishment (most often in the form of postmortem residence in some sort of hell) would be meted out to individuals who failed to mend their ways. The new visions were remarkably similar on this point because the demoralized social conditions that they sought to redress were remarkably similar.

It is not until one examines the position that their revelations took on the topic of the non-Indian presence that native American prophets begin to diverge significantly from one another. On the one hand, a prophet like Kenekuk led his people to become adjusted to the new lifestyle imposed on them by Euro-American society. For instance, as in the case of other new religious leaders like Handsome Lake, the Kickapoo prophet taught that men should farm in a community where farming had been regarded as women's work.[14] Prophets like Tenskwatawa, on the other hand, encouraged their followers to reject the culture of the intruders. The Master of Life, the god of the Shawnee prophet's visions, went so far as to assert that Anglo-Americans were "not my child, but the children of the Evil Spirit. . . . I hate them."[15]

These divergent types of revelation correspond with Lanternari's analysis,[16] which groups American Indian messianic movements into two major categories, depending on their attitude toward Euro-Americans—hostile (e.g., Neolin and Tenskwatawa) or adaptive (e.g., Handsome Lake and John Slocum). These two types, to continue to follow Lanternari's discussion, arise at two different phases of native American history. Hostile movements arise in the first stage, and look back to a recovery of precontact conditions. Adaptive movements, which arise in the second stage, proceed to construct new worlds of meaning that accept the contemporaneous situation, including the ongoing Euro-American presence, as a given.

These categories are useful, although, for our present purposes, they need to be modified so as to include a third category that will distinguish movements that were simultaneously hostile and adaptive. In other words, a war revelation such as Tenskwatawa's was hostile without being adaptive. However, a movement like the Ghost Dance, which Lanternari classifies as hostile, in effect led many tribes to become more adjusted to their situation. Some of the potentially adaptive aspects of Wovoka's teachings are evident in certain passages of the so-called "Messiah Letter" recorded by James Mooney, for example: "Do not refuse to work for the whites and do not make any trouble with them. . . ."[17]

In fact, had it not been for the stupidity of a few key U.S. officials in the Dakotas, the only significant violence resulting from the Ghost Dance—the Wounded Knee Massacre—could easily have been avoided.[18] Thus modified, Lanternari's classification allows us to explain why a certain subset of native American prophet movements did not survive: Simply put, movements built around war visions (i.e., hostile *non*-adaptive movements) were defeated on the battlefield.[19] So that the reader can acquire a clearer sense of this phenomenon, it might be useful to outline representative movements for each of these three categories.

In early 1805, Tenskwatawa was a less than stunningly successful medicine man for a group of Shawnee living in eastern Indiana. In the wake of military defeat and an unfavorable treaty that had been imposed a decade earlier, many of the midwestern tribes had slid into a state of social and cultural demoralization. Tenskwatawa, a boastful alcoholic, fully embodied this demoralized state. In the wake of an epidemic of some European disease on which the healer's ministrations had little impact, he unexpectedly fell into a comalike state that the Shawnee interpreted as death. However, before the funeral arrangements could be completed, Tenskwatawa revived, to the amazement of his fellow tribesmen. Considerably more amazing were the revelations he had received during his deathlike trance.

Tenskwatawa had been permitted to view heaven, "a rich, fertile country, abounding in game, fish, pleasant hunting grounds and fine corn fields." But he had also witnessed sinful Shawnee spirits being tortured according to the degree of their wickedness, with drunkards (one of Tenskwatawa's principal vices) being forced to swallow molten lead. Overwhelmed by the power of his vision, Tenskwatawa abandoned his old ways. More revelations followed in the succeeding months— revelations that eventually added up to a coherent new vision of religion and society.[20]

Although the new revelation departed from tradition on many points (e.g., new songs and dances were introduced), its central thrust was a nativistic exhortation to abandon Euro-American ways for the lifestyle of earlier generations. According to Thomas Jefferson's account, the Master of Life instructed Tenskwatawa,

> To make known to the Indians that they were created by him distinct from the whites, of different natures, for different purposes, and . . . that they must return from all the ways of the whites to the habits and opinions of their forefathers; they must not eat the flesh of hog, of bullocks, of sheep, etc., the deer and the buffalo having been created for their food; they must not make bread of wheat, but of Indian corn; they must not wear linen nor wollen, but dress like their fathers, in the skins and furs of animals; [and] they must not drink ardent spirits.[21]

Tenskwatawa successfully extended his religion to other tribes. New rituals that reflected the Shawnee's contact with Catholicism were evolved in order to formalize conversions.[22]

While the new movement experienced its share of ups and downs, the promise of restored greatness was overwhelmingly appealing. Consequently, the religious leadership of the prophet remained strong until Tenskwatawa's prophecies failed at the battle of Tippecanoe:

> Assuring them that the Master of Life had provided him with medicine to gain a great victory over their enemies, the Prophet promised he would make them invulnerable to the Long Knives. He would send rain and hail to dampen the Americans' powder, but the weapons of his warriors would not be affected.[23]

Although from a purely military angle the battle was indecisive, Tenskwatawa's status as a leader was irreparably damaged. And while failed prophecies need not spell the doom of millenarian movements, in the present case the hopes that Tenskwatawa's vision addressed were transferred to the more secular efforts of Tecumseh (the prophet's brother) to unite the tribes in opposition to Euro-Americans. The Shawnee prophet lived until 1836, but his religious vision died at Tippecanoe in 1811.[24]

In the same way that Tenskwatawa almost perfectly exemplifies the "war prophet," the Iroquois prophet Handsome Lake exemplifies the "peace prophet." The parallels between these two men are striking. Like Tenskwatawa, Handsome Lake was somewhat of a healer (a herbalist, at the very least) and an alcoholic who encountered the Creator during a death vision. He was also given a vision of heaven and hell, and, in time, instructions for a new religious pattern that selectively revived and rejected parts of the religious tradition of the Iroquois. Like Tenskwatawa, Handsome Lake also preached a strong moral code and instituted formal confessions (his first vision in 1799 focused on the moral reclamation of his people).

Unlike the Shawnee, however, Handsome Lake did not condemn Euro-Americans as children of the Evil Spirit. The Iroquois prophet did not even condemn Christianity. Rather, Handsome Lake's visions made it clear that in the same way in which his revelations were directed to native Americans, Christianity was an appropriate religion for Euro-Americans. During one of his spirit journeys, for instance, the Iroquois prophet met Jesus with whom he discussed the relative success of their respective missions.[25]

Handsome Lake's teachings included all of the essential ingredients necessary to preserve the Iroquois as a people in the face of Euro-American encroachment. In addition to the points already mentioned, an important tenet of the new faith was the preservation of the tribal land base, while simultaneously maintaining peaceful relations with their non-Indian neighbors. Also important for surviving in the new political environment, the prophet advocated acculturation. For example, over and above promoting the nuclear family, "the prophet gave emphatic encouragement to the transformation of the Seneca economic system from a male-hunting-and-female-horticulture to a male-farming-and-female-housekeeping pattern."[26] As mentioned earlier, Handsome Lake's religion survives to the present day.

The Ghost Dance represents an intermediate category between the above two—hostile,[27] yet adaptive. The Paiute prophet Wovoka (also called Jack Wilson, not to be confused with the peyote prophet, John Wilson), unlike either Tenskwatawa or Handsome Lake, was not dissolute. However, like the earlier prophets, Wovoka was a healing shaman who experienced his revelation in a death vision during which God gave him strongly ethical teachings, although the usual pattern of heavenly and hellish realms was missing. Instead, Wovoka received a revelation of a millennium in which the earth would be renewed and the spirits of the dead return. The millennium would be preceded by a general catastrophe that would destroy Euro-Americans and their material culture. This would be a cosmic rather than a military-political catastrophe. Consequently, native Americans were instructed to keep the peace and wait.

Beyond remaining at peace and following Wovoka's ethical injunctions, American Indians were periodically to perform what Euro-Americans came to call the Ghost Dance:

> The Ghost dancers, women as well as men, paint their bodies to indicate the revelations they have received, and arrange themselves in concentric circles, the arms of each dancer resting on the shoulders of both neighbors, so that the vibrant rhythm of the dance sways the worshippers as if they were a single body. The mood quickly created by the dance is conducive to collective exaltation and trance, the dance being usually performed at night.[28]

Eventually some participants fell down into a trance during which they received revelations, usually from departed relatives. Performing the dance would hasten the advent of the new age.

Wovoka's revelation spoke powerfully to his contemporaries, and the dance was taken up by a wide variety of different tribes, such as the Shoshoni, Arapaho, Crow, Cheyㄴne, Pawnee, Kiowa, Comanche, and Sioux. As one might anticipate, relatively stable tribal groups that had adjusted successfully to changed conditions were least inclined to accept the new teaching.[29] The widespread excitement generated by Wovoka's vision declined rapidly in the wake of Wounded Knee (29 December 1890), so that the effective lifespan of the Ghost Dance as a mass movement was no more than a few years. The prophet himself died many years later, on 20 September 1932. Quite independently of the prophet, however, the Ghost Dance continued to be practiced. For example, as late as the 1950s the dance was still being performed by the Shoshonis in something like its original form.[30] Perhaps the most important adaptive responses were in tribal groups that partially adopted the Ghost Dance as a medium for reviving selected aspects of their traditional religion.[31]

The above discussion brings us to the issue being addressed by the present volume, which is the question of the unstable, ephemeral nature that has traditionally been attributed to "nonmainstream" religious movements. While American Indian movements belong in a somewhat different category from groups like the Unification Church, they have shared the imputed characterization of being ephemeral phenomena. It is thus relevant to the larger issue at hand to question the conventional wisdom about native American messianic movements.

To begin with, one should immediately note that no scholar with a reasonably broad knowledge of American Indian prophets would accept the attribution of instability as being a generally applicable trait. The movements initiated by Handsome Lake,[32] Kenekuk, [33] and John Slocum[34]—all founded over a hundred years ago—survive to the present day. Also, certain offshoots of the Ghost Dance, such as the Maru Cult,[35] as well as the Native American Church,[36] are still very much alive.

The impression of ephemerality appears to be the result of superficial acquaintance with the Ghost Dance of 1890, the one American Indian messiah movement with which there is widespread familiarity. There is a general awareness that the Ghost Dance led to a brief period of intense millenarian expectancy among native Americans, an expectancy that rapidly diminished in the wake of Wounded Knee. However, most people are not aware that the Ghost Dance continued to be practiced, especially in tribes where elements of the Dance became blended with the group's traditional religion. Even among academics, religion scholars without a background in native American studies often have no acquaintance with American Indian prophet religions beyond the short segment on the Ghost Dance of 1890 in *Black Elk Speaks*, a reading that reinforces the impression of prophet religions as ephemeral phenomena that flare up and then die.[37]

The picture presented by this narrow base of information dovetails nicely with the "common sense" view of messianic movements, which is that when predicted events do not occur, participants lose faith and the movement collapses. However, as the classic study *When Prophecy Fails* argued, the failure of prophecy can, in certain circumstances, actually serve to increase one's faith.[38] One might also recall that, if we accept the testimony of the synoptic gospels, Jesus predicted an imminent apocalypse that never occurred. The time frame he gave for the advent of the millennium was, "this generation will not pass away before all these things take place" (Mark 13:30). Despite this failed prophecy, the Christian Church went on to become one of the biggest "success stories" of all time.

The case of Christianity should also cause us to question the bit of conventional wisdom that views the death of the founding prophet as a crisis that usually leads more or less immediately to the death of the prophet's movement. As the introductory essay to this volume made clear, this "common sense" notion has almost no empirical foundation. The evidence supplied by the history of native American prophet religions only further serves to undercut the conventional wisdom on this point. If we set aside the nonadaptive visions of the war prophets, the majority of American Indian movements found in the ethnographic literature—almost all of which were initiated in the nineteenth century—either persist in some form to the present day, or at least persisted well after the deaths of their founders. Beyond these ongoing "success stories," we can find other demonstrations of the point that the demise of a prophet religion is rarely correlated with the founder's death.

For example, as far as can be determined, Wodziwob, the initiator of the Ghost Dance of 1870, lived well into the twentieth century, although his movement among the Paiute collapsed within a few years of its founding.[39] There is also the very unusual case of the prophet Kolaskin whose religion persisted not only after his death, but prior to his death it continued to exist even after the prophet himself abandoned the movement.[40] One of the few movements that seems to have adhered to the pattern predicted by the conventional wisdom was the so-called Feather Cult of the Pacific Northwest, a religion that declined rapidly in the wake of Jake Hunt's death, and which has long since died out as an active movement.[41] The Feather Cult was, however, the exception rather than the rule.

Beyond the ethnocentric attitude that leads one to perceive "eccentric" visions of the world as by nature unstable, a key factor in causing academics to attribute emphemerality to messianic movements is a mistaken theoretical perspective that portrays the personal charisma of the founder as the "glue" holding together alternative views of reality.[42] Such a perspective misconstrues the role of charisma. In the first place, no matter how charismatic the prophet, his message must somehow address the concerns of the community in a satisfactory manner if he is to convince more than a handful of close associates.[43] In other words, a contagious new vision has more going for it than merely the personality of the revealer.

In the second place, although the prophet's charisma may be necessary in giving life to the vision during the nascent stages of the new movement, the actual adoption of an emergent religion by a human community recruits the forces of social consensus to the side of the new revelation—forces that tend to maintain the alternate vision of reality independently of the charisma of the founder. To think of this in terms of the sociology of knowledge (as discussed by Berger and Luckmann),[44] the plausibility of a particular worldview and its accompanying lifestyle is maintained by the ongoing "conversation" that takes place among the members of a particular community. If an entire community is converted to a new vision of reality, as native American tribes frequently were, the possibility of encountering dissonance as a result of interaction with nonbelieving conversation partners is largely eliminated. (The unbelief of neighboring Euro-Americans would not have counted for much, given the general atmosphere of tension between the races.)

Because social consensus is the real glue that maintains the plausibility of any given worldview, potential sources of crisis in the life of a religious movement lie in the area of breakdowns of social consensus, not in the passing away of the founder. Thus as long as a new religion continues satisfactorily to address the concerns of the community, the prophet's death will not (under normal circumstances)[45] induce a crisis of faith.

4

The Latter Day Saint Movement: A Study in Survival

Steven L. Shields

Introduction

Few people would believe that a scarcely educated farm boy could found a religious movement that today is one of the fastest growing and most talked about movements in American society. Although the largest church in the movement, the Utah-based Mormon Church, is generally the focal point of attention, there have been more than one hundred church organizations since Joseph Smith's time. Almost without exception, each of these churches or religious organizations has claimed authority as the only legitimate Latter Day Saint church. More than fifty of these churches are functioning today.[1]

From its inception until the founder's death, the Latter Day Saint church was shaken from time to time by various individuals claiming to have a new interpretation of the scriptures, or a new and better "divine" authority. The reasons for this schismatic tendency are perhaps a matter for speculation, but Joseph Smith, Jr. had done something unique. He showed that education was not necessarily related to divine sanction; that poor farmers and frontierspeople had just as much claim on God as anyone else; and that the priesthood of all believers was a valid principle upon which a rational church organization could be established.[2]

During his fourteen-year administration of the church,[3] Joseph Smith's authority was challenged from within by at least ten identifiable

59

movements that disassociated themselves from Smith's leadership and attempted to form independent churches. None of these movements survived Smith's death. At least four of these groups claimed independent revelation that appointed their leader as prophet. Two of the groups appear to have renounced all scripture except the Bible.[4]

Two of these uprisings were very serious contenders for authority. The first was led by Warren Parrish in 1837[5] during a period of dissension within the church and economic crisis in the United States.[6] Parrish had been the cashier of the church's bank, the Kirtland Safety Society, and was accused by the church leadership of embezzlement. Within five years this movement had failed and Parrish was found preaching as a Baptist minister.[7]

The other dissident movement was established at Nauvoo, Illinois—then church headquarters—in 1844. William Law, a one-time counselor in the First Presidency,[8] along with several others established an opposition church with Law as the new prophet. This group was behind the publication of an alternative newspaper, the *Nauvoo Expositor*, of which only one issue was published. Through its pages the group intended to expose alleged wrongdoings on the part of Joseph Smith, Jr., particularly the rumored practice of "spiritual wifery" that was then apparently being practiced by only a small and select group of individuals within the ranks of the church leadership, and then only with the utmost of secrecy. The practice of polygamy and whether or not it was a legitimate doctrine of the church has been a point of contention among Latter Day Saints since Joseph Smith's death in 1844. That Smith sanctioned and practiced it has been ardently maintained by Brigham Young and the Latter Day Saints who follow his leadership. There are various fundamentalist groups, with roots in the Utah-based church, who continue the practice of polygamy in the present day by claiming special authority that was allegedly given them in the late 1800s by John Taylor, then president of the Utah church.[9] Other Latter Day Saint groups have been equally vociferous in the opposite contention. And there has been considerable speculation that what was practiced in Nauvoo may have been quite different from the practice as it emerged in Utah under Brigham Young's leadership.[10] But this was not the issue that caused the most serious divisions the church would ever be called upon to face.

The incidents surrounding the destruction of the *Expositor* press undoubtedly contributed to the strong public opinion against Joseph Smith. Smith, as mayor of Nauvoo, persuaded the city council to declare the *Expositor* a public nuisance and ordered the printing press to be destroyed. Neighboring journalists were outraged and called citizens to arms. The details of Smith's death are readily available in numerous resources.[11]

Joseph Smith's Provisions for Succession in the Presidency

The single most divisive issue the Latter Day Saint church has ever dealt with was the untimely death of its founder. Had Smith lived out his years, the church would have continued under whatever direction Smith led it, with assorted and small movements separating themselves from the mainstream from time to time as they had disagreement with policies, practices, or teachings. With Smith's death, however, the church had to deal with the matter of succession in its leadership. It is apparent that Smith did not really believe he was going to die when he went to Carthage, Illinois, that June of 1844. The instructions he left regarding his successor were vague. What had been a unified church with one leader was now about to be reborn into a movement with various leaders.

Between 19 April 1834 when Joseph Smith ordained his counselor Sidney Rigdon to "preside over the church in the absence of brother Joseph"[12] to the spring of 1844 when he is alleged to have conferred the full "keys of the kingdom to govern the church upon the Quorum of Twelve"[13] Smith provided for at least eight different methods of succession in the leadership of the church. On different occasions, Sidney Rigdon (as mentioned above), Oliver Cowdery, David Whitmer, Hyrum Smith, Samuel Smith, Joseph Smith III, and Joseph Jr.'s yet-unborn son David were all designated as potential leaders of the church.[14]

By the time of Joseph Smith's death in 1844, Oliver Cowdery and David Whitmer had left the church. Hyrum Smith was killed at Carthage, Illinois, with his brother Joseph. Samuel Smith, another brother, died from exposure incident to Joseph and Hyrum's assassination, about four weeks later. David was yet unborn. This left two individuals: Sidney Rigdon and Joseph Smith III, plus the Quorum of Twelve's claims in accordance with a revelation issued in 1835[15] and also the alleged designation of the spring of 1844.

Joseph Smith III had been designated as his father's successor on at least four different occasions.[16] Yet at the time of his father's death he was barely 12 years old. In addition, the church's law on succession was ambiguous. It was apparent to all that the church would need strong leadership in order to survive the crisis of its beloved founder's death. Some in Nauvoo were even suggesting that William Marks, president of the Nauvoo Stake,[17] should become the president of the church—a suggestion that was promoted during the latter part of July 1844.[18]

Sidney Rigdon's Claims

Sidney Rigdon, the last living member of the First Presidency, arrived in Nauvoo on 3 August. The preceding fall, Rigdon had left Nauvoo and was residing in Pittsburgh, Pennsylvania. In the fall of 1843, Joseph Smith attempted to have Rigdon expelled from the church. Rigdon's powerful oratory persuaded the saints in his favor, but so difficult were the relations between Smith and himself, Rigdon found it necessary to leave Nauvoo.[19]

By virtue of his ordination by Smith in 1834 to preside over the church in Smith's absence, Rigdon attempted to have the church at Nauvoo sustain him as a guardian over the church. Most of the members of the Quorum of Twelve were not in Nauvoo. Those who were in Nauvoo invited President Rigdon to meet with them, but he decided to take his case directly to the membership at the regular Sunday services. Rigdon proclaimed he had seen a vision in which he was called to take the leadership of the church. Rigdon asked stake president William Marks to call a special conference for Tuesday, 6 August, but instead Marks called it for 8 August. This allowed for a majority of the Twelve Apostles to be in town, having been en route from various missionary journeys since learning of Joseph's assassination.[20]

Brigham Young Takes Charge at Nauvoo

On 7 August the Twelve called the leaders of the church together to listen to Rigdon's proposal. Rigdon stated that "No man can be the successor of Joseph. . . . The martyred Prophet is still the head of this church. . . . I have been consecrated a spokesman to Joseph, and I was commanded to speak for him. The church is not disorganized though our head is gone."[21] In his journal, Wilford Woodruff wrote: ". . . we herd Sidney Rigdon tell his Story and message which he had to us and the Church. A long Story it was a kind of second Class vision."[22]

Brigham Young is quoted in the *History of the Church (LDS)* as having responded that "Joseph conferred upon our heads all the keys and powers belonging to the Apostleship which he himself held before he was taken away, and no man or set of men can get between Joseph and the Twelve in this world or in the world to come."[23] Since this quote was actually written several years after the fact for inclusion in the *History*, Brigham Young's words were undoubtedly much different when the issue of succession presented itself in June of 1844. In fact, the position as stated in the quote is at odds with contemporary documented statements made by Brigham Young. Upon learning of the Prophet's death, Young was worried about the continuity of the church. He is quoted in a more contemporary version as stating, "The first thing which I thought of was, whether Joseph had taken the keys of the kingdom with him from the earth."[24]

Rigdon, Young, and the other church leaders agreed to a meeting on 8 August, to which at least five thousand church members gathered to hear the various proposals and to make a decision for the future of the church. Various church leaders spoke to the claims of the Twelve, and when the vote was taken, the gathering voted to support the Twelve in their calling, as well as sustaining Rigdon as a counselor in the presidency of the church. In addition, they voted to continue to be tithed until the temple was completed, to allow the Twelve to regulate the business affairs of the church, and to permit the Twelve to select and ordain a new church patriarch.[25]

Rigdon was apparently not satisfied with this action, and began conducting private meetings throughout Nauvoo in an attempt to raise support for his claims. Within a month after this special conference, Brigham Young excommunicated Rigdon from the church. Rigdon returned to Pennsylvania and organized a church with himself as the head, in accordance with his claims and the 1834 ordination by Joseph Smith. This church organization lasted for a few years, fell apart, and then was revived a few years later, only to fall apart again. Rigdon's church is important in this discussion, because through this manifestation of the original church, William Bickerton became associated with the Latter Day Saint movement. His role will be discussed later.[26]

Brigham Young and the Twelve did not see themselves replacing Joseph Smith, even though Brigham Young was essentially president of the church by virtue of his position as president of the Twelve. In the regular October conference in 1844, the church sustained the Twelve as the presidency of the church. The following April, the conference went one step further and sustained Brigham Young as president of the church, by title,[27] but again, this was understood by virtue of the Twelve functioning in the role of presidency. A general epistle issued by the Twelve, dated 15 August 1844, clearly stated their position:

Let no man presume for a moment that his [Joseph Smith's] place will
be filled by another; for, remember he stands in his own place, and
always will; and the Twelve Apostles of this dispensation stand in their
own place and always will, both in time and in eternity, to minister,
preside and regulate the affairs of the whole church.[28]

One historian has concluded this about the August 1844 vote:

Some Mormon commentators about the August 1844 vote for the
Quorum of Twelve interpret the action as a vote for Brigham Young
as Joseph Smith's successor, and some RLDS commentators have
described the vote as a common consent "rejection of the church"
that ultimately required the church's reorganization. Neither position
is true. The Latter Day Saints voted on 8 August 1844 to preserve the
LDS Church from fragmentation by side-stepping the succession question: there were too many seemingly unresolvable succession claims
for various men to be the sole successor to Joseph Smith, and the
church membership simply voted to defer the question by turning to
the Quorum of Twelve to "act in its place" as the priesthood quorum
that had the full powers and authority of Joseph Smith.[29]

With the primary issue of divisiveness thus dealt with, the other
issue—that of doctrine and practice—came to the fore. Doctrinal
authenticity became the fuel for the fires of others who contended for
legitimate succession in the leadership of the church, and ultimately
this was what caused the original church to become fragmented into
several parallel organizations, each claiming to be "the" original church.
And that is when the Latter Day Saint church ceased to be a unified
body and became a movement. The challenge in attempting to determine one of the emerging church organizations as representing the continuation of the original church lies in the fact that it is extraordinarily
difficult, if not impossible, to clearly define what the original church
was.

In the last four years of his life, Joseph Smith began introducing
various doctrines and practices to a small group of selected individuals.
This was done under the veil of secrecy. Only a fraction of a percent
of the entire membership of the church knew anything about these
various secret practices. These included polygamy, endowments,[30] the
Council of Fifty, and the ordination of Smith to be a "king."[31] These
radical practices are further complicated by the fact that we have no
information about them by Joseph Smith himself. They are recorded
only by secondary alleged participants, and often months or years after
certain events were said to have taken place.[32] In the succession of the

leadership of the church whether or not these unusual developments took place became important issues. Brigham Young vowed both privately and publicly to carry out all of these ideas. Those members of the church who were aware of these practices and opposed to them found themselves also opposed to Brigham Young and his leadership.[33] Those who were unaware of the practices simply were unaware, except for the occasional rumor. When knowledge became public, through the efforts of Brigham Young and his followers promoting the practices as genuine teachings of the church, many found themselves opposed, but a significant number of the Saints who followed Young out of Nauvoo accepted them as legitimate. Later in Utah, when RLDS missionaries first began their work in 1863, several thousand returned to the East.

A further complication that has not been satisfactorily resolved is the manner by which a teaching becomes doctrine. The general consensus in the Utah church is that if a prophet (or president of the church) preaches an idea over the pulpit, or perhaps even proposes it to a select few, it automatically becomes doctrine of the church. The RLDS church takes the opposite view. Other Latter Day Saint churches have their own viewpoints as well.[34]

A Period of Fragmentation

A period of fragmentation in the church stretched essentially from the Prophet's death in 1844 to about 1865 when the rival church organizations finally settled down to six main expressions of the original church. During the twenty-year period, at least twenty-five different church organizations came directly out of the original church. In almost every case each of these groups saw itself as the legitimate expression of the original church. Generally, each was loyal to its own understanding of Joseph Smith as prophet and the work he had begun. Gradually, though, various smaller movements were caught up and absorbed into others—mostly into the RLDS[35] Church. The reasons for this are varied, but a few generalizations may be in order. First, there were some leaders who were simply looking for self-aggrandizement. Second, and perhaps the more common reason, was that the RLDS Church offered a viable movement and demonstrated through its several years of organizing (1851–1860) that it was attempting to be true to the public expression of the original church. In addition, the fact that the Prophet's son became the president provided many of the scattered groups a spiritual leader connected with the founder whom they highly revered. This essay will consider only those churches that emerged from the fragmentation period and have continued to the present. The six churches that survived the fragmentation period have also experienced their own fragmentation, almost from the time they themselves were identifiable as a separate church organization.

The six surviving churches that emerged from this period are those originally led by Brigham Young, James J. Strang, Alpheus Cutler, Joseph Smith III, William Bickerton, and Granville Hedrick. In a chronology I have adopted, Brigham Young is considered in apostolic continuity from the original church until 1847 when he established a new First Presidency. At that time the church under Brigham Young became a separate chronological organization to succeed the original church. Issues of doctrine, as stated, are strictly matters of personal faith and belief. This essay does not presume to address those matters.[36]

Ultimately, Young was the leader of the largest single body of church members, but there are literally thousands unaccounted for in the aftermath of Joseph Smith's death. Young and his followers eventually settled in what is now Salt Lake City, Utah, where they continued both the public teachings of the church and the esoteric practices they claimed were introduced to them by Smith before his death. Some writers, particularly those of the fundamentalist persuasion in Utah,[37] claim that Joseph Smith actually had established two separate church organizations: the external, or Church of Jesus Christ of Latter Day Saints, which maintained the public teachings; and the internal, or Church of the Firstborn, which was ordained to practice the various teachings that Joseph is said to have introduced in private, many of which were initially retained by Brigham Young, but have since been renounced by the Utah church.[38]

James J. Strang

Sidney Rigdon was the first to set up a rival church organization opposed to Brigham Young, but his church barely survived its first few years. James J. Strang, a virtually unknown and recently baptized church member from Wisconsin, on the other hand, presented a formidable challenge to Brigham Young in the summer of 1844.

James J. Strang had been baptized at Nauvoo by Joseph Smith himself early in 1844, and then sent to Wisconsin to scout a potential settling place for a group of Saints. At Joseph's death in June of that year, Strang produced a letter (known as the "Letter of Appointment") that bore the date of 18 June 1844, and bore the name "Joseph Smith" at the bottom.[39] Although Strang's faithful believe the letter to be authentic, historians cannot determine whose hand the letter is written in. Even the name at the bottom is not Joseph Smith's own signature, but in the same script as the rest of the document. The letter appoints Strang to be Smith's successor, and orders the Twelve Apostles and the church to move to Voree, Wisconsin (near Burlington) to gather. Strang went on to claim that at the very moment of Smith's death on 27 June 1844, an angel appeared and ordained him as prophet.

Strang produced his own translation of a set of ancient metal plates that he said were given him by an angel, he issued numerous revelatory documents, and he effected an elaborate church organization that saw him crowned as "king" in 1850. After Strang was killed in 1856 by two disaffected followers, the church disintegrated, but has maintained a small contingent still faithful to its teachings. Strang did not provide for a successor at his death, so the church has continued without benefit of the leadership of a "prophet"—maintaining that such would have to be provided for by angelic intervention. In the Latter Day Saint traditions, priesthood offices and ordinations can be passed on by others of the priesthood, and the leadership of a "prophet" would not be required.[40]

The Strangite view of the Restoration and Joseph Smith's work provides insight into the momentum that has perpetuated this segment of the Latter Day Saint movement:

> The office of the Angel is accomplished in committing a dispensation to the chosen of God, and preparing him for the work, by giving him a proper knowledge of the gospel, and the authority to administer in all the appointments of God. And this work was accomplished in the calling of Joseph Smith, and Oliver Cowdery, and in the Priesthood and revelations committed to them, for the beginning of the ministry. . . . They instituted the Church of Jesus Christ of Latter Day Saints, which alone, of all the Churches on earth, is possessed of the gospel of the Son of God. . . . As in the Church instituted by them alone, of all the Churches on earth, the doctrine of the gospel as it came from God is preached and believed, the conclusion is inevitable that this alone is the true Church of God. As the Priesthood derived in succession from Joseph Smith and Oliver Cowdery to understand the things of God and proclaim them according to God's word, unquestionably they are sent of God.[41]

The faithful have said of their prophet's work:

> The failure of the organization, founded by Joseph Smith and continued by James J. Strang, to gain prominence is often looked upon

as proof of their deception. The scriptures prophesied that the "gentiles" would reject the gospel, and history has confirmed this with the murder of these prophets and the rejection of their message.

James J. Strang was the only one to claim to be a Prophet following the death of Joseph Smith. . . .[42]

Brigham Young

In 1847, seeing the need for a full quorum of apostles to take the responsibility for the missionary work of the church, Young determined to reorganize the First Presidency, with himself as president. Wilford Woodruff tells us:

> I had a question put to me by President Young what my opinion was concerning one of the Twelve Apostles being appointed as the President of the Church with his two Councellors. I Answered the A quorum like the Twelve who had been appointed by revelation & confirmed by revelation from time to time I thought it would require A revelation to change the order of that quorum. What ever the Lord inspires you to do in this matter I am with you.[43]

And so on 5 December 1847, the Twelve under Brigham Young met, having deliberated on the issue for several days. Orson Hyde, one of the apostles, moved that Brigham Young be president of the church, and that he be allowed to nominate his two counselors. Wilford Woodruff seconded, and the motion carried unanimously. The twenty-seventh of the same month, at a conference at which about one thousand people were gathered at Winter Quarters, this action was approved.[44] Was this conference legal? Yes, according to the prevailing laws of the church. Did this conference include broad representation of all who had belonged to the original church? No.

The water gets muddier. When the first company of pioneers arrived in Utah in July of 1847, they began to establish a permanent settlement. Within about one week, on 6 August 1847, Brigham Young required all to be baptized for a remission of their sins. Brigham Young performed the ceremony and then confirmed them members of the church. Brigham Young was baptized and confirmed afterward by Heber C. Kimball. The rest of the camp was rebaptized and reconfirmed two days later.[45] Some would say that this action separated the church in Utah from the original church. As if this was not enough, such a rebaptism and reconfirmation was conducted once again, this time in 1856. Priesthood members were reordained to their priesthood offices as well.[46]

Brigham Young and those who followed him maintained a belief that someday the sons of the Prophet would come to Utah, and when they did, they would be given the right to take their father's place at the head of the church. In a sermon preached in Salt Lake City on 29 June 1856, Heber C. Kimball stated, "At present the Prophet Joseph's boys lay apparently in a state of slumber, every thing seems to be perfectly calm with them, but by and bye God will wake them up, and they will roar like the thunders of mount Sinai."[47] He was not alone; Brigham Young continually reassured those who followed him that Joseph Smith III and his brothers would receive the special blessings of leadership.[48] In October 1863, after the RLDS Church formalized its organization with Joseph Smith III as prophet and president, Brigham Young still maintained that "If one of Joseph's children takes the Lead of the church he will come and place himself at the head of this church, and I will receive him as willing as any one here."[49]

One historian maintains:

> Because the sons of Joseph Smith refused to affiliate with the church the apostles had maintained in continuity since 1844, the LDS Church continued the caretaker presidency of the Quorum of Twelve. From 1844 to the present, the president of the LDS Church has automatically been the senior surviving member of the Quorum of the Twelve Apostles, whether or not he organized a separate First Presidency of three men. We can be sure that Brigham Young was sincere in his willingness to confer the fulfillment of succession right upon the sons of Joseph Smith if they would accept the LDS Church in Utah as it was, not as they wanted it to be.[50]

This position seems to be borne out in the propensity of the Utah church to place the burden of doctrinal responsibility at the feet of Joseph Smith, rather than a current prophet.[51] This may explain why, even though the president of the church is referred to as a prophet, there have been very few revelations added to the canon of scripture. One prominent LDS theologian attempted to explain the reason for this. He stated this was "because all we are as yet capable and worthy to receive has already been written."[52] The Utah church considers members of its First Presidency to be apostles, the president generally (but not always) coming from among the members of the Twelve. When a president dies, his counselors (if they were previously members of the Twelve) revert to their positions of seniority, even though there are more than twelve members of the quorum during the period between the president's death and the organization of a new First Presidency.[53]

Most Utah Mormons are unaware of Brigham Young's feelings on the matter of succession. Even current historical research skirts the issue. One historian claims that the 8 August 1844 conference was a vote to sustain the Twelve to act in the office of the First Presidency, and that "this sustaining action was repeated dozens of times as local conferences convened in quarterly sessions throughout the Church." They offer no documentary evidence to support their claim of quarterly conferences sustaining the Twelve, although the official church periodical of the day, *Times and Seasons,* does contain the minutes of many conferences that were assembled in various parts of the United States. But the minutes that were published in the church paper do not even begin to cover the entire membership of the church at that time nor do they indicate that conferences were consistently on a quarterly basis.[54]

The Utah LDS view of Joseph Smith's work is possibly the most radical of any Latter Day Saint church:

> But neither must there be any misunderstanding as to the position of Joseph Smith in the eternal scheme of things. He is the restorer of the knowledge of Jesus Christ and of salvation for our day. He is the one to whom Christ revealed anew the pure and perfect plan of salvation. He is the legal administrator to whom the keys of the kingdom of God were given in modern times so that once again men would have power to bind on earth and have their acts sealed eternally in the heavens. He is the head of the dispensation of the fulness of times in which the Lord will yet gather together all things in Christ. He is the chief apostle of the latter days, the one whose witness of the Lord Jesus must be accepted by all who will save themselves in the presence of that blessed Lord.[55]

Alpheus Cutler

Alpheus Cutler was baptized in the original church in 1833, and moved with the church through its various hardships, finally settling in Nauvoo. In 1839, Cutler was called to serve as a member of the high council of the Nauvoo Stake[56] and served honorably in that capacity for many years. When the church left Nauvoo, Cutler was appointed captain of one of the companies of pioneers, but elected to remain in Iowa rather than proceed west under Brigham Young.

Cutler claimed that he had been ordained as one of seven special men who were given power, by seniority of their ordination, to reorganize the church if it became rejected. Cutler maintained that he was the seventh member, in seniority, of this special council and that the church became rejected when the saints were forced from Nauvoo before the temple had been completed and with the death of Joseph Smith.

On 19 September 1853 at Manti, Iowa, Cutler effected the reorganization of the church by requiring the members of his settlement to be rebaptized. Cutler viewed this as necessary because he maintained that a reorganization was not a continuation of the rejected church. Only Cutler himself was not rebaptized as he felt it would sever the tie of authority between himself and Joseph Smith. When the RLDS Church became firmly established in 1860, many of Cutler's followers united with it, decimating the membership of Cutler's organization. Cutler died in 1864, but his church continued, moving first to Minnesota, and then to Independence, Missouri. This church continued a practice of the endowment, which was publicly conducted in Nauvoo after Joseph Smith's death by Brigham Young, but details of the ceremony are not known. Its meetinghouses in Minnesota and Independence are considered to be temples, with the top floor reserved for the special ceremonies.[57]

The view of Cutler's followers is:

> When God gave the commandment in 1841 that a temple was to be built, he also granted a sufficient length of time for the accomplishment of the work. The Saints were admonished to labor with all diligence toward the goals and warned that failure to do so would result in the rejection of the church organization. . . . But as a church, the counsel was not heeded so that when the "appointed time" expired the Temple still lacked much of being a finished edifice. . . .

> When the Prophet sealed his testimony by giving his own life, the "rejection" which had been spoken of became fact. The meaning of rejection was so far-reaching that very few comprehended or understood what had taken place. The right to confer priesthood authority in any degree had been revoked as far as the church organization was concerned. No baptisms, confirmations, or ordinations performed would be valid. . . .

> With the restoration of the authority, in 1829, came the promise that it would never again be taken from the earth, so provision had been made for its continuance; but it could not be preserved in the rejected church. . . .[58]

RLDS Church

The movement that culminated in the ordination of the martyred Prophet's son, Joseph Smith III, as president in 1860, began in the early

1850s, under the leadership of Jason W. Briggs, Zenos H. Gurley, Sr., and others. These men had been members of the original church and led branches of the church after the Prophet's death. In their search for the prophetic successor of Joseph Smith, these men and those associated with them found they could not follow Brigham Young due to the doctrinal claims he promoted. In his search for the "true" church, Briggs was driven to seek the will of God, and in November 1851 received a revelation in which he believed the word of the Lord told him that Joseph Smith III should be the successor in the prophetic office.[59]

Briggs began sharing his experience, and shortly many felt a conference should be called. Initially titled the "New Organization of the Church of Jesus Christ of Latter Day Saints," this group made several attempts to convince Joseph Smith III that his role in his father's work should be with them. Finally, at a conference at Amboy, Illinois, on 6 April 1860, the young Joseph was accepted and ordained prophet and president of the church. Joseph stated that he was doing so in response to "a power not my own."[60]

The RLDS Church has maintained that the successor to a prophet must be designated prior to the current prophet's demise or resignation. This, they maintain, is in accordance with the word revealed to Joseph Smith, Jr. as published in the *Doctrine and Covenants*, which states, ". . . None else shall be appointed unto this gift [that of receiving revelations to guide the church] except it be through him [Joseph Smith, Jr.] for if it be taken from him, he shall not have power except to appoint another in his stead."[61] Although tradition has retained a descendant of Joseph Smith as prophet and president of the church, the key in succession is the law of prior designation.[62]

By the time the Reorganization got rolling in 1860 under Joseph III's leadership, Brigham Young was already well entrenched in Utah. Joseph's role has been summarized from a decidedly Utah Mormon orientation:

> Smith was faced with a difficult challenge. To prosper, the Reorganiza-
> tion had to forge for itself an identity based on something more than
> feelings of anti-Brighamism and antipolygamy. Its response was a con-
> servative one. Eventually, Reorganized officials rejected virtually the
> entire Nauvoo experience. Its branch of Mormonism was redefined
> within the safer limits of [Joseph] Smith [Jr.]'s earlier years. Polygamy,
> plurality of gods, baptism for the dead, temple ordinances, the literal
> gathering of the Saints, the establishment of an earthly kingdom—
> these and other subsequent additions by the founding Prophet to
> Mormon theology were progressively expunged from the faith.[63]

This viewpoint further confirms the Utah Mormon concept of placing the burden of doctrinal responsibility on Joseph Smith, Jr. The RLDS Church is decidedly different theologically from the Utah church. The RLDS Church believes that prophets may suggest or preach an idea, but such an idea does not become doctrine unless it is presented as a revelatory document and submitted to the various quorums and conferences of the church for acceptance. Its views of Joseph Smith, Jr. and those who have succeeded him as prophet of the church are such that the burden of doctrinal responsibility lies with the saints themselves as they determine their responses to what the prophet promotes as God's will. The RLDS edition of the *Doctrine and Covenants* is continually being added to as new revelations are presented to the church by its prophets. The church believes and practices the Latter Day Saint concept of continuing revelation, and would take exception to the LDS theologian's viewpoint, quoted previously, that everything has been revealed that the church is worthy to receive.[64]

An interesting comparison between the two largest of the Latter Day Saint churches provides a worthwhile summary of this segment of the discussion:

> Brigham Young and Joseph Smith III were each loyal to Joseph Smith as they understood him, but from irreconcilable points of view. Brigham Young saw Joseph first and foremost as the divine restorer, and dedicated his life from 1844 to 1877 as an "apostle of Jesus Christ and of Joseph Smith" to give the fullest expression possible to everything Joseph taught, revealed, practiced, and hoped for in the secret councils and public meetings of Nauvoo, where Brigham had his first continuous association with the prophet. Continuity was the key of apostolic succession Brigham Young led and implemented in the LDS Church of Salt Lake City. Joseph Smith III saw the prophet first and foremost as a father whom he loved and respected and who he believed had been called by God to bring forth a work and message of good. . . . Joseph Smith III could see nothing good or uplifting in polygamy, secret endowment rituals, overt and covert theocracy, or quasi-scriptural attacks on fundamental Christian theologies of God and humanity. Joseph Smith III forced himself to suspend judgment, despite overwhelming evidence, on the question of whether his father actively promoted these radicalisms, and he adopted the more neutral position that to whatever extent these things may have existed at Nauvoo, they did not do credit to his idealized view of Joseph Smith as father, restorer of righteousness, teacher of truth, and exponent of virtue. Therefore, Joseph Smith III and the Reorganization sought to honor the memory and prophetic calling of Joseph Smith, Jr., through discontinuity with what had occurred at Nauvoo.[65]

William Bickerton

Short-lived though it may have been, Sidney Rigdon's church provided the means for William Bickerton to become a Latter Day Saint.
He joined Rigdon's church in 1845 and was ordained to the priesthood.
After Rigdon's church disintegrated, Bickerton affiliated with the
Mormon Church at West Elizabeth, Pennsylvania, but upon hearing the
public announcements of polygamy and other various doctrines in
1852, Bickerton felt he had been deceived and left his affiliation.
Bickerton remained active as a minister preaching the gospel according
to his understanding. His personal testimony recounts baptisms that
he performed and visions that he received in which it was made known
to him that his work was accepted by God. Bickerton and others
organized branches and conducted conferences.[66]
    At a July 1861 conference several men were called to be apostles.
Just as Joseph Smith had received revelation without benefit of formal
ordination or church structure, so the first apostles in this movement
were also called and ordained. Several different persons have been
recorded as having received revelations that were accepted as genuine
by this church. A single-person prophet is not accepted in this tradition. Bickerton was appointed president by the apostles by October
1861, and the church was formally organized at Green Oak, Pennsylvania, during a conference beginning 5 July 1862. The twelve apostles
were ordained at this conference, and the work of the church formally
began.[67]
    Bickerton's church rejects most of the revelations that Joseph Smith
presented, according him only the calling of translating the Book of
Mormon. The organization of the church began with a presidency of
three and a separate body of twelve apostles, but more recently they
have formally adopted a presidency among the twelve apostles, re-
nouncing the idea of a separate "First Presidency."[68]
    Joseph Smith having set the precedent, there was no reason that
Bickerton could not have received heavenly manifestations and been
called to organize a church. The position of the church is as follows:

> If the Gospel of Jesus Christ had continued in its purity, as
> established by the Lord and executed by the apostles, there would have
> been no need for another angel to fly from heaven, bringing the
> everlasting Gospel to be preached on earth again. . . . This work
> the Lord fulfilled from 1823 to 1830, commencing with the first visita-
> tion of Moroni to Joseph Smith (1823), the giving of the hidden records
> to Joseph Smith (1827), the translation of the records (1829), the
> bestowal of the priesthood (1829), and the organization of the church
> (1830).

However, it is also the belief of The Church of Jesus Christ that this restoration experienced some difficulties. After it was organized in 1830, the Church adopted doctrines that cannot be substantiated by either the Bible or Book of Mormon. Consequently, in process of time, God used a man named William Bickerton to again establish the Church in its restored purity in 1862. . . .[69]

Granville Hedrick

At Joseph Smith's death, several branches of the church in southern Illinois found themselves united by geography and a belief that neither Brigham Young, nor any others, were the correct leader of the church. At a conference held 17 May 1863, John E. Page, who had been an apostle under Joseph Smith, ordained four others as apostles, forming the nucleus for a new Quorum of Twelve. The following July, at a succeeding conference, the members gathered took action to reorganize the First Presidency. Granville Hedrick, one of the newly ordained apostles, was selected and ordained to the office of President, "to preside over the high priesthood, and to be a prophet, seer, revelator, and translator to the Church of Christ." The ordination was effected by John E. Page, and others of the priesthood of the church.[70] In essence, by the same means employed by Brigham Young, Hedrick succeeded to the presidency of the church through apostolic succession. In 1864 Hedrick proclaimed a revelation that called his small band of believers to return to Independence, Missouri, and redeem the property that had been dedicated in 1831 for the construction of a temple. By 1867 this group had established itself in that city, and two years later purchased part of the property known as the Temple Lot.

Over the years this church has digressed in its manifestation of the original church. The offices of high priest and president of the church were dropped, opting first for a presiding elder, and then investing leadership in the Quorum of Twelve Apostles; the *Doctrine and Covenants* was rejected with the earlier version of Smith's revelations, *The Book of Commandments*, being preferred. The name of the church was returned to that of 1830, "The Church of Christ."[71] This church sees itself not "a faction, but a remnant of the church of 1830, bearing the same name, teaching the same doctrine, believing the same truths, practicing the same virtues, holding the revelations as originally given and enjoying the same spirit."[72]

Hedrick's followers contend that the many changes that took place in the church during the time of Joseph Smith's leadership were the cause for the divisiveness at his death. One church leader wrote,

Had there been no First Presidency over the Twelve, there would have been no vacancy in that office at the death of Joseph Smith. In other words, had he remained in the apostolic quorum, to which we have evidence proving his ordination, his death would have merely created a vacancy in the quorum; whereas, when he became an exalted leader above all others, his death would naturally produce a clamor for supremacy among his associates. And so it was that it also provided grounds for factionalism, as each claiming to being Joseph Smith's successor would obviously have a following.[73]

Summary and Conclusions

Each of the six separate church organizations we have considered came about due to the need of the faithful members of the original church to have leadership after Joseph Smith's death. Three, the movements of Strang, Cutler, and the RLDS church, claim appointment by Smith for succession. Strang received his "letter of appointment" and also claimed that an angel ordained him to the prophetic office at the very moment of Smith's death. Alpheus Cutler claimed to have been designated by Smith as a member of a secret and special council of seven high priest apostles—ordained to maintain continuity in the priesthood authority in the event that the church or its leaders went astray. The RLDS Church accepts the leadership of Joseph Smith III as the one having been designated in blessing by his father as the next prophet-president of the church.

Brigham Young's claim to the presidency seems to have developed between 1844 and 1847 when he finally determined to reorganize the church. Granville Hedrick's church bases its claims to authority on a similar principle, in this case, that the church branches that comprised the foundations of his church had been duly appointed, ordained, and organized, along with their priesthood leaders; that Hedrick's ordination as an apostle by John E. Page was valid, and that ultimately the reorganization of the presidency of the church was based on apostolic succession. William Bickerton organized his church in 1862 after praying about the fragmented situation of the Latter Day Saints, and being called in a heavenly vision not unlike the experience of Joseph Smith's in the early 1820s.

Historical objectivity, then, states that all of these various churches are representative of the original church that was established by Joseph Smith, Jr. Yet no one church is representative of the church that existed publicly at the precise time of Joseph Smith's death. Over the years each different church has responded to its understanding of what it perceived

God was saying. This has meant changes in policy and sometimes belief. Change has been necessary as the churches have each attempted to respond to the needs of its members and the changing society and culture in which the church has attempted to minister. Only one's personal faith says they can't all be "true." And truth, as the annals of history have shown, is highly subjective.

Did the Latter Day Saint movement really survive Joseph Smith's death? Absolutely! And it has been extremely successful. When Joseph died, the church he left evolved into a movement; many faithful interpreted the basic concepts of Joseph's work as they understood them and applied them in their own situations. In what format did the "original" church survive, and does it continue today? The definition of just what the "original" church was is an emotionally charged issue of faith. At the very least, the "original" church would have to be defined as that organization headed by Joseph Smith, Jr., from 1830 until his death in 1844. However, the issue becomes complicated when the parameters are established to define the doctrine of the "original" church. When Smith died, is the "original" church that organization that carried on the public ordinances and beliefs that were canonized in those books of scripture accepted by the church as they were constituted at that time? Or, does the "original" church include those practices, beliefs, and teachings that were then being conducted in private among only a select few individuals? The only possible and most objective answer is that the "original" church survived and continues today in its many colorful expressions and manifestations—through the six original fragments of the church, and through the other various churches that have evolved from their parent organizations and continue to function as independent organizations today.

The Latter Day Saint movement survived its founder's death because of the deep faith his teachings had instilled in the hearts of his believers. Those followers of Smith who remained faithful to his cause did not merely *believe* what they were doing was right; they *knew* it. The existing branches of the Latter Day Saint movement today are a powerful testimony to the tenacious faith of those original church members who honestly believed they had found the only true path of life and eternity.

5

They Found A Formula: 450 Years of Hutterite Communitarianism

Timothy Miller

In communal hisory, where group survival for more than about a generation is notably rare,[1] the Hutterites stand out as perhaps the most distinguished success story. For over 450 years the Hutterites have held fast to their way of life in the face of persecution, dislocation, and finally, prosperity. Today the movement flourishes. Although a period of toleration and prosperity in sixteenth-century Moravia is known to historians as the Golden Age of the Hutterites,[2] things have never been better for these veteran communitarians than they are today.

Other religious communes—the Catholic orders, the Buddhist sanga—have lasted longer, but none with such distinctive independence. The world-avoiding Hutterites have kept a low profile—as recently as the 1920s, when a group of German Christians began to read old Anabaptist documents and felt drawn to emulate the early Hutterites, it was several years before they learned that the Hutterites were still in existence![3]—but they have endured for well over 450 years.

The lengthy survival of the Hutterites certainly provides support for Gordon Melton's argument that new religious movements tend to survive longer than has heretofore been generally supposed. Because the Hutterites have lasted so long, the question that poses the topic of this volume—what happens to a new religion when its charismatic founder/leader dies?—needs modification for this essay. Most of the

papers in this volume deal with religious groups that have experienced
major leadership transitions only a few times—sometimes only once—
in their history. Thus the Hutterite story is quite different than that of
Siddha Yoga or ISKCON, in which the one major transition pertinent
to this volume involves the death of the person who brought the movement to the United States; or that of Theosophy or the Latter Day Saints,
in which the original movement has split into many fragments; or that
of the Shakers, who had a few decades of prosperity but then entered
a long, steady decline. The Hutterites did have charismatic leadership
under Jacob Hutter and others in their early history, and successful transitions did take place in those days. However, the Hutterite story has
run for more than four and a half centuries since that era, and much
of the time the Hutterites have been divided into many separate colonies, each with its own leadership structure. Thus thousands of leadership transitions have taken place, and transition has long since been
routinized. So the revised question to be addressed here is this: How
have the Hutterites been able to survive for so long as a coherent movement through repeated episodes of persecution and repeated migrations,
in several different countries, in poverty and prosperity, without central
charismatic leaders or a strong central bureaucracy?

The Early Years of the Hutterites

The Hutterites are Anabaptists, cousins of the Amish and Mennonites.[4] All of the Anabaptists trace their roots to the Radical Reformation, the phase of the Protestant upheaval that criticized the main
leaders of the Reformation (Luther, Calvin, Zwingli) for not going far
enough in reforming the Catholic Church. The early Anabaptist revolts
occurred in several locations in Europe; traditional Anabaptist history
has focused most heavily on the Swiss radicals, who began conducting
believers' baptisms in Zurich in 1525. The name Anabaptist, or rebap-
tizer, was soon applied to the dissenters by their opponents, although
believers' baptism was actually only one of several important points
of disagreement with other Reformation Protestantism. The Anabaptists also advocated simplicity in worship, pacifism and nonresistance,
freewill church membership, disciplined living, and strict separation
from the state and the secular world, among other things.

Many Anabaptists, fleeing persecution, settled in Moravia. Several
groups of pre-Reformation religious dissenters had flourished there for

a century, and religious toleration had become widespread. The Anabaptist missionary Hans Hut arrived there in 1527, urging people to dispose of all their possessions in anticipation of the imminent Second Coming. He found a strong following among the Moravian Anabaptists, and in the following year the experiment of religious communism among those who would become known as Hutterites began when a group of pacifist Anabaptists led by Jacob Wiedemann pooled their goods in preparation for one of their many migrations. As the old Hutterite *Chronicle* recorded the key event,

> About two hundred people (not counting children) from Nikolsburg and Pergen and the surrounding area gathered outside the town of Nikolsburg. . . . They took counsel together in the Lord because of their immediate need and distress and appointed servants for temporal affairs. . . .
>
> These men then spread out a cloak in front of the people, and each one laid his possessions on it with a willing heart—without being forced—so that the needy might be supported in accordance with the teaching of the prophets and apostles. (Isa. 23:18; Acts 2:44–45; 4:34–35; 5:1–11.[5]

The Weideman group ended up settling under a friendly noble at Austerlitz; there other communal groups of Anabaptists settled as well. And here it is that Jacob Hutter enters the story. Hutter, a hatmaker by trade,[6] had been an Anabaptist pastor in the Tyrol and had introduced communal elements into church life there. In 1533 he joined the believers in Moravia, soon emerging from a series of partisan disputes as the head of the believers and shaping a thoroughly communitarian organization.

Two years of relative tranquility ended when King Ferdinand in 1535 demanded that the Moravian nobles expel the Anabaptists. Again the Hutterites were refugees; Jacob Hutter fled Moravia for the familiar Tyrol, where he thought he could hide and from seclusion continue to direct the brethren. However, he managed to evade the authorities for only a few months. In November he and his wife were captured. He was executed on 25 February 1536, and his wife suffered that fate about two years later.

The Succession

Hans Amon, who had been Hutter's chief assistant, took over the leadership of the beleaguered band. The movement prospered under him; a steady flow of converts headed for Moravia, where the true church, as the Hutterites saw themselves, was being prepared for the Second Coming.

Amon died in 1542; before his death he named Leonard Lanzenstiel as his successor. However, Peter Riedemann, a courageous missionary and writer, had become regarded as the ablest Hutterite leader, even though he was now a prisoner in Hesse. (While in prison Riedemann had written his definitive *Account of Our Religion, Doctrine and Faith,* which has ever since stood as the standard doctrinal treatise of the Hutterites.[7]) Riedemann, escaping from confinement, returned to Moravia and played an important role until his death in 1556.

Peace and Prosperity—and More Persecution

The Hutterite *Chronicle* refers to the years from 1554 to 1564 as the "Good Years" and 1565 to 1591 as the "Golden Years."[8] Between 1529 and 1621, 102 colonies were established in Moravia with an estimated population of twenty to thirty thousand.[9] A smaller Hutterite presence was established in nearby Slovakia. Hutterites used these tolerant years to develop their internal institutions, such as schools, to carry on a vigorous missionary program, and to develop prosperous business ventures. Hutterites became well known for their craft skills, and especially for their ceramics, which became an important source of income for the colonies.[10] They also developed medical skills, and eventually the services of their doctors came to be in demand among non-Hutterites.[11]

But war and persecution eventually returned. The movement became weak, abandoning communal living about 1690, only to be saved by the conversion of a group of Carinthian Lutherans who sparked a return to community after 1762. Through these hard years the Hutterites migrated to Hungary, to Transylvania, to Romania, and in 1770 to Russia. There, in 1819, communitarianism was again abandoned. However, for many Hutterites, the ideal never died. In 1859, after the Hutterites had moved into a predominantly Mennonite area, the Hutterite preacher Michael Waldner, following a series of visions, established, with the help of fellow preacher Jacob Hofer, a colony at one end of the village of Hutterdorf. The following year another preacher, Darius Walter, established a second colony at the other end of Hutterdorf.

North America

As communitarianism was being reestablished in Russia, trends in the country boded ill for the Anabaptists. The worst blow was the introduction of compulsory military service in 1871. Concluding that another migration would be necessary, Mennonite and Hutterite leaders sent a scouting party to America in 1873. They found suitable land, and although they were not promised exemption from military service, a letter from an aide to President Ulysses S. Grant assured them that America would not fight a war for at least fifty years. So in 1874 the first group of immigrants traveled from the Ukraine to Hamburg and thence to the United States, settling in southern Dakota Territory. Migration continued throughout the 1870s, the main portion ending in 1877.

In America they founded three colonies, reflecting their organization in Russia. Michael Waldner's congregation settled on the Missouri River in a colony they named Bon Homme. The group led by Darius Walter founded Wolf Creek colony. The third group had not been living communally in Russia, but instituted the common life at Elmspring colony upon arriving in Dakota. Each of these three colonies became the founding center of a group that has managed ever since to keep a distinct identity; thus Hutterism today is divided into three *leuts,* or types. The leuts differ on certain points of theology and strictness of lifestyle, although to the outsider they appear much more similar than different.

Michael Waldner was a blacksmith, or *Schmied*, and his followers became known as the *Schmiedeleut.* Darius Walter's group became the *Dariusleut.* The leader of the third group, which became communal only in its American phase, was Jacob Wipf, a teacher or *Lehrer;* his group became the *Lehrerleut.* Some Hutterites immigrated separately from the three leuts, settling on private homesteads. They became known as *Prairieleut.* Their congregations eventually merged with various Mennonites.

But more Hutterite migrations were yet to come. The U.S. government instituted conscription for military service in 1917 without providing for conscientious objectors to give alternative service. Young Hutterite men who refused military duties were incarcerated in military jails where in several cases they suffered what can only be described as torture. Two, in fact, died from severe mistreatment in the prison at Fort Leavenworth.[12] Meanwhile, harassment and even mob action and vandalism occurred at the Hutterite colonies. The Hutterites quickly prepared to move to Canada; after being assured of exemption from military service they purchased land in Alberta and Manitoba. Most of the South Dakota colonies were sold, often at ridiculously low prices. Only Bon Homme, the original colony, remained alive in the United States.

The majority of the Hutterites have lived in the prairie provinces of Canada ever since. During the Depression the government and people of South Dakota became more concerned about failing farms and a declining rural population than about reisistance to military service, and gradually some colonies began to return, often reoccupying their previous land and buildings. Since then, expansion has continued in both the United States and Canada. John Hofer published a list in 1988 showing 377 Hutterite colonies (including seven Bruderhof colonies and the Owa Colony in Japan).[13] Lawrence Anderson has listed twenty-two other colonies now extinct.[14] Several new colonies continue to be established annually.

As the statistics on the expansion of colonies suggest, the Hutterite population continues to grow rapidly. A study published in 1954 found that the 443 immigrants in the 1870s had grown to eight thousand by 1950, a rate of growth greater than that of any country in the world.[15] Robert Friedmann, reporting on a census undertaken by the Hutterites themselves in 1969, provided a count of seventeen thousand.[16] In more recent years the incredible growth rate and fertility of the Hutterites have dropped somewhat; Karl Peter found that between 1965 and 1980 the overall growth rate dropped from 4.12 percent per year to 2.91 percent, or perhaps even lower, apparently largely because Hutterites have moved toward later marriages.[17] Nevertheless, Hutterite numbers today probably approach forty thousand.

The Secrets of Success

The common assumption is that dissenting religious movements perish early, or that they modify their more unusual or extreme beliefs and thus survive by moving toward the mainstream. As Rodney Stark has put it, to succeed new religions need to "maintain a medium level of tension with their surrounding environment," to be "deviant, but not too deviant."[18] Thus the Mormons have had their greatest growth after giving up polygamy. The Hutterites have comprised their ideals and principles very little, however. To recapitulate the question that this chapter seeks to answer, how did the Hutterites not only survive the deaths of their early leaders, but also endure persecution, migration, poverty, and prosperity for the better part of five centuries thereafter—and at the end of all that be a stronger movement than they have ever been before?

Leadership is not a major component of the answer to that question. Today leadership is decentralized, both in the movement as a whole and within the various colonies. As Kenneth Rexroth has observed, colony leaders have "just sufficient charisma and practicality to insure the cohesion of the community and the efficiency of its economic life."[19] The colony preacher is the overall leader, and the business manager oversees a good-sized business operation. The colonies are democratic, within the limits of a male-only franchise; the baptised (adult) men elect an executive committee to oversee colony operations. Preachers are chosen by lot from candidates selected by the men of the community. Given Hutterite convictions about stressing community welfare over individual preferences, naturally the leaders must be responsive to the collective will. A hierarchy, however, is part of the system. John Bennett's characterization of a Hutterite colony as a "managed democracy" is an apt one.[20]

Both at the movementwide level and in local colonies, leadership transition has gone relatively smoothly. The leadership of Jacob Hutter was charismatic and unquestioned; later leaders have sometimes had charismatic qualities, but they have been elected. Hutter appointed his own successor, Hans Amon; that choice was confirmed by a vote of the brethren. Soon all candidates for leadership were elected by the community.

It is inconceivable, given the nature of human beings and their institutions, that the Hutterites have had an unbroken succession of extraordinary leaders. Thus in normal times they function without consistently strong personal leadership. That suggests that their bureaucracy serves them well. The strength of the Hutterite bureaucracy is also attested to by the business success of most of the colonies: despite having to support unusual numbers of unproductive members (the children and elderly), despite the enormous financial burden of having to fund an entire new colony every fifteen years or so, when the existing colony becomes too large and must branch out, and despite, in many cases, an adverse agricultural climate (some colonies in Canada push hard at the northern limits of cultivation), most colonies are solvent, providing perfectly adequately for the simple but ongoing needs of their members, even when times are hard for other farmers.

Since leadership does not entirely explain Hutterite success, what keeps Hutterism as a whole, and the various colonies individually, together today? The answer to that question has several elements.

Faith. Although some would minimize the importance of a faith commitment to communal survival (two scholars, for example, have recently made such a case, arguing that "the history of communal experiments is a graveyard of hundreds of failed ideologies"[21]), most observers have found it to be crucial. Early Hutterite martyrs went to their deaths singing and thanking God for their salvation, and faith runs deep today. The Hutterites see themselves as following the most perfectly Christian way of life they can, as living according to the express will of God. Each colony Hutterite is a member of the colony church; the preacher is the most important colony leader. Bedrock faith is essential to Hutterite cohesion.

Fertility. Although in some eras the Hutterites have sought converts, most of the time new Hutterites have been procreated. From the beginning, marriage and family have been the norm. Hutterites have historically refused to accept birth control or abortion,[22] and they value children highly; with the decrease in mortality brought on by prosperity and modern medicine, their rate of growth has increased over time.[23] Although growth may be slowing today, fertility certainly helps explain Hutterite proliferation.

Communal childrearing and social control. One chronic cause of failure in communal societies has been the collision of egos. Bickering, often over petty matters, becomes rife, and internal tension makes life in the community intolerable. The Hutterites tackle that problem at its roots. They presume that human nature is malign and that strenuous efforts must be made to mold children. So from infancy one's will is always pushed aside in favor of the welfare of the community. Children are taught to behave as Hutterites almost from birth (as infants they are taught to fold their hands together when prayers are being said, for example), community values are continually stressed over individual ones, and the system of parochial colony schools means that society's main social melting pot, the public school, is missing. Disobedient children are swiftly punished, either by scolding, for minor offenses, or by the use of a strap or switch. The punishment is not accompanied by a fit of temper or meanness on the part of the adult, and it is often followed by a hug or a kind word—it is the behavior, not the person, that is wrong. Positive reinforcement is also used extensively; children are praised for good behavior. The Hutterites, in short, have a clear sense of original sin, and thus for community to work, the will must be diminished. By the time the child enters adult colony society at fifteen, he or she is well versed in community discipline. Of course adults sometimes break the rules; the community wields sanctions as needed to ensure conformity to essential regulations. Informal, decentralized sanctions usually work well; the ultimate sanction, expulsion from the colony, is used very rarely.

Boundary maintenance. Most distinctive religious and ethnic groups are constantly threatened by cultural assimilation, especially in multicultural North America. The lures of modern life, especially that of material possessions, tend to break down asceticism among younger generatons. In North America it is hard to keep the young from seeing Paris, and consequently it is hard to keep them down on the farm. The Hutterites, however, have done better than most at keeping the world at bay. Three main boundaries seem to work well: first, the continued use of "Hutterisch," the Carinthian dialect the Hutterites have spoken since the eighteenth century; second, the geographic isolation of the colonies, invariably located well away from cities; and third, the determined socialization of children from infancy. Language is not an absolute boundary, since all Hutterites speak English as well as Hutterisch. Neither is isolation complete, since Hutterites travel to town to visit doctors, buy and sell goods, and the like. Socialization may be the strongest boundary-maker today; the Hutterites have become experts at ego reduction. In any event, the Hutterites are satisfied with their life. Attrition is low—as low as 2 percent, John Hostetler has concluded.[24]

Controlled acculturation and flexibilty. Joseph Eaton, who coined the term "controlled acculturation," argued that the Hutterites slowly but surely adapt to modern life, gradually accepting cultural innovations before the pressure for them becomes so great as to threaten group cohesiveness.[25] Unlike the Amish, the Hutterites have accepted modern agriculture technology. Unlike some Christian sectarians, they have accepted modern medicine. Although there is a pronounced bias in favor of doing things in traditional ways, innovations do manage to creep in. Some colonies have computers in their farm operations and a few reportedly have begun to use television as a teaching medium in their schools.

A similar flexibility operates on a personal level as well. Although Hutterites have strict rules and standards governing life on the colony, they are aware that humans can chafe under restrictions. Thus minor peccadilloes are not ruthlessly uncovered; Big Brother is not everywhere. No Hutterite colony would ever have the spy towers that some Shaker villages did in order that the elders could watch for violations of the rules. While obedience to the rules is expected, and mechanisms of social control are many and diverse, colony members are not prison inmates. Thus, for example, Hutterite children who have portable radios, which are forbidden, may get away with their disobedience for some time. All individuals are allowed to have a few relatively minor personal possessions, such as books and magazines, a pocket knife, writing materials, and various pictures and souvenirs. Each individual has a locked chest for personal items. Moreover, it has come to be fairly common for young men, particularly, to be able to leave the colony for a time and return. In the majority of cases, the young man (usually in his late teens or early twenties) returns to the colony after perhaps a year or two, and is welcomed back. The lure of the unknown outside world is great, but a thoroughly socialized Hutterite often finds the economic insecurity, materialism, and loneliness of secular life distinctly unattractive. Of course some men and women do leave permanently; most colonies allow persons who have left to return periodically to visit their families. In sum, the Hutterites have a good sense of providing just enough flexibility to allow for limited personal preferences to operate.

Providing for human needs, both material and psychological. Individuals may own virtually nothing on a Hutterite colony, but material life there is not austere. Everyone is well fed (indeed, the Hutterites tend to be big eaters), everyone is adequately if not spaciously housed, and everyone has a sense of being needed and loved. Each individual has a small cash allowance that can be used to purchase the kinds of personal items the community allows but does not provide—a wristwatch, for example, or a present for another person. The work schedule is not grueling, and Hutterites tend to retire from heavy duties young, sometimes while still in their forties. Sometimes a colony as a whole will have financial problems (especially in connection with branching out and founding a new colony), but the basic life needs of members are always met. Moreover, there is no realistic prospect that one's legitimate needs will *ever* fail to be met. Hutterism as a whole is solvent. In effect a Hutterite is enrolled in an excellent lifelong welfare system. The Hutterites are well aware of their material and spiritual security and enjoy the sense that until the Lord returns they are set up pretty well in life. At the same time, psychological needs of colony members are met as well. The Hutterites have little alienation from their work, and the esteem in which older persons are held makes later life happier among the Hutterites than it is in much of the outside world.

Colony Size. Over the years the Hutterites have apparently figured out the right size for a colony to be to work well. Most colonies have been between seventy-five and 150 persons. Given the growth rate of the Hutterites, that means that most colonies will in time—one to two decades, typically—grow to their maximum optimal size, and then will be ready to "branch out," that is, to found a daughter colony. Branching out is expensive, for the new colony will own thousands of acres of land and must be fully equipped and ready for half of the old colony members to move into. Nevertheless, the process generally boosts community morale. Among other things, it provides new job opportunities; young men who are anxious to obtain leadership positions in the colony are often blocked by a lack of available positions, with older men holding onto their slots for life, and a new colony means that those desired jobs will be created anew.

Persecution. Just as the early Christian church thrived through terrible Roman persecutions, many movements throughout history have gained strength when faith has been put to the test. That seems to have been true for the Hutterites. As John Hostetler observed of the Russian period of declension, "What is significant from a sociological perspective is that the absence of persecution by the outside world tended to maximize internal problems."[26] Full toleration has never arrived; persecution, while less severe than in earlier years, continues today. In recent years the most important pressure from the outside world has come in the form of restriction of Hutterite geographical expansion. Rapid Hutterite population growth, combined with a preference for restricting colony population to about 150, has meant that many new colonies have had to be created. Family farmers in some places have feared that the Hutterites, with their cheap labor and ability to buy the best in modern farm technology, would squeeze out traditional farmers, and to allay that possibility have engineered legislation to restrict or forbid the purchase of land by Hutterites.

Alberta has been the scene of the most prominent attempts to restrict Hutterite land purchases, beginning with the Land Sales Prohibition Act in 1942. A postwar amendment allowed Hutterites to purchase up to 6,400 acres, but only if the land were situated at least forty miles from any other Hutterite colony.[27] The law was finally repealed in 1972, but government officials have continued to be involved in land disputes between Hutterites and non-Hutterites.[28] Ironically, the Hutterites use land efficiently, supporting many more persons on a given acreage than traditional farmers do. Nevertheless, opposition to Hutterite expansion has caused dispersion of the movement into new territory.[29] Persecution may not ensure survival, but it certainly has not devastated the Hutterites.

The Longer Prospect

As I opined at the outset, the Hutterites are enjoying a Golden Age today. Expansion and prosperity are basic motifs at most colonies, and the severe persecutions that obtained as recently as World War I now seem remote. However, smoke signals on the horizon suggest that problems may yet lie ahead. If the reader will suffer another list, here are some looming situations that may pose challenges to the thriving conditions the Hutterites experience today:

The intrusion of modern life. Although the Hutterites do a good job of boundary maintenance, the modern world is not shut out entirely, especially given the acceptance of modern technology by all colonies. One colony has reportedly already had an encounter with television, when a set purchased as an instructional tool for the school somehow ended up being used for entertainment in a family's apartment. And radios, although formally forbidden, are more or less winked at in some colonies. Broadcast evangelism has already made its mark; as early as the 1960s members of one colony in Manitoba had become converted to the Radio Church of God (later Worldwide Church of God), which does extensive media outreach.[30] Four scholars writing in 1982 found evidence of increasing defection from colonies as a result of members' conversion to evangelical Protestantism and correlated the defections with individualization and privatization that were creeping into Hutterite life.[31] Edward Boldt has argued that liberalization of the traditional rules is the biggest threat to Hutterite culture, and the encroaching outside world has brought pressure for such liberalization.[32]

Prosperity. Like just about everyone else, the Hutterites enjoy the luxuries that prosperity has purchased. Some colonies have moved from wood heat to oil or propane; others have allowed members such "worldly" luxuries as commercial beer. What has happened in many other religions may well be happening here: hard work and a disinclination to spend money on frivolities lead inexorably to prosperity; and prosperity devours the movement. Community discipline, hard work, and self-denial are hard to maintain when one has the means to take life easy. Hutterites, like many others, have trouble keeping their children in line; there are in many colonies recurring problems with use of alcohol, tobacco, and sometimes marijuana by the youth.

Lowered birth rates. So far birth rates are not a major problem, but should birth control come to be widespread, they could be. Should increased defection accompany a serious drop in the birth rate, Hutterite expansion could turn into contraction. Even short of that, Hutterite success in this century has depended on rapid population growth; the well-being of the movement seems to stem in significant part from the establishment of new colonies. Great internal changes in colony life would inevitably accompany a major slowdown in expansion.

Fraying at the edges. Despite the atmosphere of cooperation that normally characterizes Hutterite life, some colonies have experienced serious divisions—serious enough, sometimes, that they have led to the splitting of a colony and resettlement of one faction elsewhere. In this case, unlike that of conventional branching out, the parent colony is usually not enthusiastic about helping the departing faction, and as a result the new colony can have serious financial problems. There were several of these stranded colonies by the middle 1980s; they have not grown, and women have been unwilling to marry into them. No resolution to this problem is yet in sight.[33]

Other problems. No short list can enumerate the potential problems the Hutterites or any other religious movement may face in the future. The Hutterites' ready acceptance of modern agricultural technology may yet turn out to haunt them, since technology inevitably produces social changes that are not entirely desirable.[34] The changing status of women in the larger society cannot escape notice among Hutterite women, and their secondary role in colony life may already be undergoing subtle alteration.[35] Growing acceptance of private property and even private income may undermine community spirit. As with any population, there is no assurance that the Hutterites will not encounter major problems.

Some observers have pointed to governmental policies, notably the land restrictions that have posed problems in Canada, as a long-term threat to the Hutterites.[36] That is one threat we probably do not need to take very seriously. If there is any lesson in Hutterite history, it is that the Hutterites have had their most courageous moments under persecution. If they were going to fold under governmental pressure, they would have done so long ago.

The problems are real, but the Hutterites are seasoned experts at survival, and in any event predicting the future over the long term is a notably hazardous occupation. Observing the present, fortunately, is easy. Today's thriving Hutterites belie the notion that dissenting religious movements and communes necessarily have short life spans. Other religions and communities seeking vigor and longevity would do well to study the Hutterite example.

6

Democracy vs. Hierarchy: The Evolution of Authority in the Theosophical Society

Catherine Wessinger

There exists in the Theosophical Society a tension between the affirmation of freedom of thought and individual responsibility, and the affirmation of the authority of an Occult Hierarchy, whose members are known as the Masters of the Wisdom (Mahatmas), and who are believed to be the real founders of the Society. This tension has been present since the founding of the Theosophical Society in New York City by a Russian, Madame Helena Petrovna Blavatsky, and an American, Col. Henry Steel Olcott, both of whom considered themselves to be *chelas* (students) of the Masters of the Wisdom. Blavatsky, the mystic, magician, and philosopher, can been seen as the founder upholding the authority of the Masters, yet she strongly affirmed the importance of freedom of thought, writing that it was the duty of the founders "to oppose in the strongest manner possible anything approaching *dogmatic faith and fanaticism*—belief in the *infallibility* of the Masters, or even in the very existence of our invisible Teachers. . . ."[1] Olcott, chief executive and organizer, can be seen as the founder upholding democracy as the basis of the Theosophical Society, yet he wrote that his paramount duty was the carrying out of the will of the Masters.[2] So the tension between democracy and hierarchy was present from the beginning of the Theosophical Society, not only between Blavatsky and Olcott, but also within their individual psyches. This tension would lead to two crises within the Theosophical Society at the death of each of its founders. While these two crises brought severe blows to the Theosophical Society (one resulting in the secession of a large portion of the American Section), the overall growth of the Theosophical Society was not impeded. Whereas the tension between democracy and hierarchy remains, the Theosophical Society has strongly affirmed the primacy of the democratic principles of individual responsibility, and freedom of thought and expression.

Helena Petrovna Blavatsky (1831–1891) was born of Russian nobility and led a romantic and mysterious life. Married at age eighteen, she very soon ran away from her forty-year-old husband and began a life of world travel. Many of these years cannot be documented, but Blavatsky reported that she spent time in Tibet studying with Masters. Blavatsky claimed that there is an Occult Hierarchy consisting of perfected men who guide the evolution of humanity. The Rajput Master, Morya (known as M), was described as being Blavatsky's special guru. Morya and the Kashmiri, Kuthumi Lal Singh (Koot Hoomi or K. H.), were said to be the Masters responsible for the founding of the Theosophical Society.

Col. Henry Steel Olcott (1832–1907) was the more prosaic and staid of the two founders. During the Civil War, he served in the Union Army and became Special Commissioner of the War Department and Special Investigator for the Navy. Olcott was noted for his honesty and investigative skills, so he was called to serve on the three-man commission that investigated the Lincoln assassination. After the war, he built a very successful law practice in New York City. Olcott had a keen interest in spiritualism, and in those circles met Helena Blavatsky. Impressed by her apparently great psychic abilities, he was among the seventeen persons present at Blavatsky's apartment on 7 September 1875, when the organization of the Theosophical Society was first proposed. Later that year he was elected president of the new Society; Blavatsky became corresponding secretary; and William Q. Judge, an attorney, was named counsel.

The preamble of the bylaws of the new Theosophical Society shows that, even in its infancy, the Society affirmed key principles of democracy, that is, freedom of thought and the equality of all persons. At that time, the object of the Theosophical Society was "to collect and diffuse a knowledge of the laws which govern the universe." To do this, it was asserted that "whatever may be the private opinions of its members, the society has no dogmas to enforce, no creed to disseminate." In considering applicants for membership, the society knew "neither race, sex, color, country nor creed. . . ."[3]

The objects of the Theosophical Society continued to evolve through the subsequent years, with the concern for unity among all humans, or "brotherhood," becoming the first object, and the concern to investigate the laws that govern the universe becoming the third object. The objects were refined until 1896,[4] when they were finalized in the following form:

1. To form a nucleus of the Universal Brotherhood of Humanity, without distinction of race, creed, sex, caste, or color.

2. To encourage the study of Comparative Religion, Philosophy, and Science.

3. To investigate unexplained laws of Nature and the powers latent in man.

Soon after the founding of the Theosophical Society, Olcott found himself assisting Blavatsky in her composition of the first Theosophical text, the huge two-volume *Isis Unveiled* (1877). Olcott reported that during the writing of *Isis*, Blavatsky's body would be inhabited successively by a number of different Masters as evidenced by changes in her mannerisms and handwriting. He reported several miraculous events that convinced him that the Masters were inhabiting Blavatsky's body.[5]

Isis Unveiled proved to be enormously popular with the wider public, and it became the first of the primary Theosophical texts. Blavatsky's second magnum opus, *The Secret Doctrine*, was published in 1888. Blavatsky claimed that the Masters directed the writing of this work as well, and projected texts before her vision in the "Astral Light" for her reference.[6] In 1889, Blavatsky produced a very small book that has become the third of her Theosophical classics, *The Voice of the Silence,* as well as a clearer exposition of Theosophy, *The Key to Theosophy.*

Despite the insistence that the Theosophical Society has no dogmas, it does teach certain doctrines that are drawn from Blavatsky's works. Theosophy is a monistic worldview in which all things are seen as part of a divine whole. Within the whole, all beings are treading the path of progressive evolution back to the origin. The cosmos is described as being subject to laws of periodicity. "The day and night of Brahma" are the successive periods of manifestation and return to the unmanifest. Within the cosmic cycles, humans are caught up in the cycle of rebirth, which is governed by the law of *karma*. Humans ascend the path to full consciousness of the universal oneness through meditation, study, and service to others untainted by a sense of self. Theosophy is seen as the Ancient Wisdom known to the Masters of the Occult Hierarchy, which has been given out in the various world religions. So Theosophy is seen as the basis of all the religions.

Although *Isis Unveiled* was based primarily on Neoplatonism, Hermeticism, and the western occult traditions, it looked to the East as the source of the Ancient Wisdom and the home of the Masters. Since most of the founding members of the Theosophical Society had lost interest in the organization, Blavatsky and Olcott began turning their attention to India. Olcott was at first reluctant to go, but he was convinced after Morya appeared to him one night and left his turban as evidence of his visit.[7]

Blavatsky and Olcott arrived in India in 1879, and the Theosophical Society began its growth into an international organization. The two founders were well received by the Indian public, which after years of British imperial rule and missionary propaganda, was gratified that these westerners valued their Indian civilization, religion, and philosophy so highly. Olcott traveled widely in India and Asia lecturing on Theosophy. Blavatsky caught the attention of the British in India, which helped to increase the number of European Theosophists. While W. Q. Judge continued working to build up the Theosophical Society in America, Blavatsky and Olcott started *The Theosophist* in 1879 to be the official journal for the Society, and an estate was purchased on the Adyar River, Madras, to be the international headquarters of the Theosophical Society.

The early years of the Theosophical Society were exciting due to appearances of the Masters, not only to Blavatsky and Olcott, but to other Theosophists as well. Beginning in 1880, the Masters began a four-year correspondence with A. P. Sinnett, editor of *The Pioneer*, the leading newspaper in India, and sometimes with A. O.Hume. The letters to Sinnett, Hume, and others were "precipitated"[8] or made to materialize in unexpected places.

By 1888, Olcott reported that the Theosophical Society had become so large and spread out over the world that it was necessary to begin the dividing of the Society into autonomous Sections within the international organization. There were 173 active branches, with 116 in India, 10 in Ceylon, 25 in the United States, and the others scattered around the world.[9] The preface to the Revised Rules indicated a keen awareness of the tension between democratic authority and the authority of the Occult Hierarchy.[10]

1888 - The Separation of Esoteric and Exoteric Authority

The return of Blavatsky to Europe in 1885 marked the beginning of increased tension between Blavatsky and Olcott, and the esoteric and exoteric dimensions of the Theosophical Society. Blavatsky had left India in the midst of extreme controversy caused by what became known as the "Coulomb affair." Two disgruntled servants, Emma and Alexis Coulomb, had made accusations that Blavatsky had contrived false appearances of the Masters at Adyar and had produced Mahatma letters in a cabinet or "shrine" by means of trap doors. To bolster their charges, the Coulombs produced letters from Blavatsky in which she conspired with them to produce false phenomena. Theosophists countered by saying that these letters were forgeries and that the trap doors in the cabinet had been constructed by Alexis Coulomb without Blavatsky's knowledge or permission while she was traveling in Europe. Richard Hodgson's report for the Society of Psychical Research (SPR) concluded that Blavatsky was guilty of fraud.[11] As a result of the Coulomb contoversy and the report of the SPR, Olcott pursued a policy of downplaying occult phenomena.

A leadership controversy among Olcott, Blavatsky, and Judge ensued. Finally, in 1888, Blavatsky pursued the formation of the Esoteric Section ("E.S."), for the teaching of "practical occultism." She would be its Outer Head, and one of the Masters was considered the Inner Head.[12] Olcott initially objected to the creation of the Esoteric Section, but while he was traveling by ship to Paris, a letter from K. H. was precipitated in his cabin. The letter assigned to Olcott "external and administrative" affairs, and affirmed that Blavatsky should deal with "internal and psychical" matters as she was the direct agent of the Masters.[13]

At the 1888 Convention, it was acknowledged that a restructuring of the Theosophical Society was necessary since it had truly become an international organization. The Rules of the Theosophical Society were altered to form autonomous and self-governing Sections within the larger unit of the international Theosophical Society.

It was felt that the exoteric organization of the Theosophical Society was now free to make these changes due to the separation of the Esoteric Section.

> . . . it was recognized that the distinction now made between the esoteric and exoteric aspects of the Society, left the Convention free to adopt in the Revised Rules, if necessary, any of the lawful expedients usually resorted to by Societies on the material plane, for

strengthening their organization and securing their position in the world. So long as the authority of the President was liable to be questioned or disputed in purely secular matters, in the name of any still higher authority, it was impossible for any Rule to enable that officer to adequately maintain his authority against the encroachment of self-authorized meddlers and agitators, who fancied it to be their mission to direct or revolutionize the Society; but, once it became acknowledged, as it did when the esoteric division was formed, that the President derives from the General Council the authority which centres in his office, not only did it appear permissible for him to defend the dignity and prerogatives of his office, but it became evident that to prevent the constitutional authority entrusted to him from being encroached upon, or falling into abeyance, is no more than his duty to those who elected him, or confirmed his tenure of office.[14]

The Revised Rules of 1888 declared that the President's authority derived from elected members of the General Council, not an Occult Hierarchy.[15] Those rules also strengthened the presidency, confirming Olcott as President for Life, and setting the term of future presidents at seven years.

Thus it was hoped that the creation of the Esoteric Section and the revision of the government of the Theosophical Society had resolved the two "incongruous" principles: "the autocratic element" associated with the authority of the Occult Hierarchy, and "the self-government guaranteed to the Fellows by the Society's Constitution and Rules; and, indeed, with the profession of equality and brotherhood made by the Society itself." It was acknowledged that the existence of the Theosophical Society depended on the activities and guidance of the Masters of the Wisdom, yet it was also seen as impossible to govern the Theosophical Society democratically as long as it was subject to the "orders" of the Masters.[16] Yet the esoteric sphere continued to encroach on the exoteric, resulting in the secession of the greater portion of the American Section a few years after Blavatsky's death in 1891.

Aftermath of Blavatsky's Death—Secession

Blavatsky had long been ill, and she knew that she had to make preparations for her death. She pushed herself to complete the large two volumes of *The Secret Doctrine*. In 1889, she published *The Key to Theosophy*, as well as *The Voice of the Silence*. In London, Blavatsky drew around her a small group of students for intensive study. One of these was a recent convert to the Theosophy, Annie Besant.

Prior to becoming a Theosophist, Annie Besant was notorious as an atheist, Freethinker, and Fabian Socialist, and she was noted for her great talent as an orator, writer, editor, and executive. Besant joined the Theosophical Society after reading *The Secret Doctrine*, and, increasingly, Blavatsky began to look to Besant as her successor. This tended to displace William Q. Judge, who as the general secretary of the American Section, vice president of the international Theosophical Society, and one of the founding members of the Theosophical Society in New York, seemed to be the logical person to succeed Blavatsky and Olcott. Prior to her death in 1891, Blavatsky orally appointed Besant to be the Outer Head of the Esoteric Section, gave Besant her ring, and left her papers in Besant's care. Blavatsky and Besant had been coeditors of the London Theosophical journal, *Lucifer*, and after Blavatsky's death, Besant became its sole editor.[17]

Immediately after Blavatsky's death, Judge and Olcott traveled to London. Judge arrived first, and in consultation with the Esoteric Section Council, Judge and Besant agreed that they should be joint Outer Heads of the Esoteric Section, with Judge in charge of America, and with Besant responsible for the rest of the world.[18] Shortly afterward, Besant dramatically announced that she had begun to receive Mahatma letters. Besant did not begin to suspect that these letters had been written by Judge until she traveled to India in 1893 and consulted with Olcott and other concerned Theosophists.

The Mahatma letters produced by Judge were an attempt to arrogate to himself Blavatsky's authority as the mouthpiece of the Masters. Little messages such as "Judge leads right. Follow him and stick," were calculated to ensure that Besant's loyalty was directed to Judge and not to Olcott. The letters even warned that if Besant visited India, Olcott would attempt to poison her. Judge even slipped up, and signed a Mahatma letter addressed to another Thesophist with his own name.[19]

Judge and Besant, for a time allied together, began to pressure Olcott to resign. Ever sensitive to the tension between his commitment to democracy and his being president for life, Olcott notified Judge, as the vice president, of his resignation. Olcott was preparing for his retirement when he received a clairaudient message from his Master directing him not to retire. After a series of letters and cables passed between Olcott and Judge, Olcott notified Judge by cable that he had decided not to resign. At the convention of the American Section in 1892, Judge withheld the information that Olcott had revoked his resignation and allowed the American Section to elect himself as Olcott's successor. Then Judge proceeded to London, where he was voted to be the next president of the Theosophical Society by the

European convention. Upon receiving news of these events, Olcott publically announced that on the orders of his Master he had revoked his resignation.[20] A number of Theosophists began to consult and question the authenticity of the Mahatma letters received after Blavatsky's death.

The Judicial Committee that convened in London in 1894 recognized that in determining whether or not Judge was guilty of forging Mahatma letters, it had to address itself to the issue of the existence of the Masters. The Committee preferred to affirm the freedom of each Theosophist to judge. The Committee ruled:

> (a) The absolute neutrality of the Theosophical Society in all matters of personal belief, and the perfect right of private judgment in religious, mystical, and other questions have been authoritatively and permanently declared by Executive affirmation, endorsement by the General Council, and confirmation by a Judicial Committee organized under the provisions of the Society's Revised Rules. . . . (b) The authoritative and dogmatic value of statements as to the existence of Mahatmas, their relations with and messages to private persons, or through them to third parties, the Society or the general public, is denied; all such statements, messages, or teachings are to be taken at their intrinsic value and the recipients left to form and declare, if they choose, their own opinions with respect to their genuineness: the Society, as a body, maintaining its constitutional neutrality in the premises.[21]

Olcott, himself, was acutely aware of the dangers inherent in the claiming of occult authority. He stated that he knew of at least seven persons in the Theosophical Society who were claiming to be in direct communication with the Masters, and who were receiving orders that conflicted with those of the other contactees.[22] Olcott stated that he preferred to be guided by the following principle:

> All professed teachings of Mahatmas must be judged by their intrinsic merit; if they are wise they become no better by reason of their alleged high source; if foolish, their worthlessness is not nullified by ascribing to them the claim of authority.[23]

Since the Judge contoversy was not resolved by the Judicial Committee, continued agitation in the Theosophical Society resulted in increased demands that Judge either give an accounting of himself or resign. Judge retaliated by issuing an order deposing Besant as joint Outer Head of the Esoteric Section. In turn, the annual Convention of the Theosophical Society passed a resolution asking Judge to resign his office as vice president. It came as no surprise when the majority of the members attending the 1895 convention of the American Section voted to secede from the Theosophical Society. This new organization was called the Theosophical Society in America, and Judge was elected its president for life.[24]

It was clear to Olcott that the secession of the greater portion of the American Section was the result of Judge's attempt to arrogate to himself not only the functions of the democratically elected president of the Theosophical Society, but also the charismatic authority of Blavatsky as spokesperson and "visible agent" of the Masters. The charismatic authority had proved dangerous, resulting in the loss of 83 branches (lodges), leaving only five remaining in the American Section.[25]

The secession of 1895 based on the charismatic authority deriving from the Masters set a precedent for other individuals in the Theosophical movement, who would form separate groups centered on themselves as agents of the Masters. Judge's successor, Katherine Tingley, based her authority on claims of mediumistic contact with Blavatsky and Judge, and of direct contact with the Masters. William A. Dower and Francia A. LaDue seceded from Tingley's organization in 1898, claiming contact with the Masters, and formed an organization known as the Temple of the People in a community near Santa Barbara. Alice Bailey, who was dismissed from her staff positions in the American Section of the Theosophical Society (Adyar) in 1920, and who founded the Arcane School in 1923, claimed that she was the amanuensis for Master Djwhal Khul, the Tibetan. In the 1930s, Guy and Edna Ballard formed the "I Am" movement as the "Accredited Messengers" of the Masters and especially Master Saint-Germain. Elizabeth Clare Prophet currently leads the Church Universal and Triumphant as the Messenger of the Ascended Masters.[26] These are just a few of the many groups and individuals within the Theosophical movement who claim to be receiving direct revelation from the Masters.

After the secession of 1895, the rebuilding of the American Section of the Theoophical Society (Adyar) began. In the parent Theosophical Society, democracy and freedom of thought had been affirmed, but the tension between it and the authority of the Occult Hierarchy remained, and would meet in a crucial confrontation at the death of the second founder, Henry Steel Olcott.

Aftermath of Olcott's Death—
"Psychic Interference" Rejected

Olcott was keenly aware of the necessity to prepare the Theosophical Society for the time "when the original and only President it has had shall be removed in the course of nature. . . .''[27] In 1891, Olcott transferred the Adyar property to the Theosophical Society. In 1905, the Theosophical Society was incorporated, and Olcott transferred the ownership of *The Theosophist* and the bookshop to the Society.[28] Rule 9 of the new Rules provided that Olcott had the right of nominating his successor, which was subject to ratification by the members of the Theosophical Society.[29] The stage seemed set for a smooth democratic transition at the president-founder's death, but a crisis occurred when the esoteric authority, again, intervened.

Olcott reported that on the evening of 5 January 1907, as he lay seriously ill, the Masters Morya and Kuthumi appeared to him and at least two other witnesses in order to appoint Annie Besant as his successor. Olcott issued a notice to that effect, stating that "the Masters assured me last evening that They would overshadow her as they have me in the work."[30]

Olcott's notice of his appointment of Annie Besant as his successor was immediately rejected by a number of members of the Theosophical Society, especially in the British and American Sections, on the grounds that he could only nominate his successor. Therefore, an official notice was issued dated 21 January 1907, in which Olcott nominated Besant for the presidency as stipulated in Rule 9. The furor continued after Olcott's death in February, with many members, including several important leaders, rejecting what was termed "psychic interference" in the affairs of the Theosophical Society.[31]

One of those leaders, Upendranath Basu, the general secretary of the Indian Section, while affirming his belief in the reality of the Masters, rejected the authenticity of the appearances at Olcott's death bed as "lacking the balance and solemnity of the utterances of an advanced disciple. . . ." He noted that Olcott was in a very depressed state at the time of the appearances, so that his testimony of their validity was weakened. He emphasized that membership in the Society was not based on belief in the existence of the Masters and that each member had "perfect liberty" in regard to all matters of faith. He pointed out "that the Great Founders of a movement like the Theosophical Society, where honest enquiry is everywhere stimulated, and every effort is made to keep the platform broad and as nearly all-embracing as is compatible with truth and purity, are not likely to stifle thought and foster credulity by seeking to impose upon its members any belief which appeals neither to their reason nor to their moral sense."[32]

Bertram Keightley, a close associate of Blavatsky and former general secretary of the Indian Section, doubted that Olcott's mind was clear at the time of the appearances, since Olcott was a strong defender of the Society's constitution. Like Basu, he stated that he believed in the existence of the Masters, but not in the reality of these particular appearances. The effect of these orders from the Masters would be "to undermine the free judgment and sense of personal responsibility of its members. Its ultimate effect, if yielded to without protest, must be to make of the Society a Popedom, and to transform the most universal movement the world has seen into a dogmatic sect." Keightley argued that esoteric authority must not be allowed to interfere with the dogmatic government of the Theosophical Society. "Of what use are a constitution and rules, if such unrecognised and unverifiable influences are to be brought to bear upon the minds of members?"[33]

G. R. S. Mead, former personal secretary to Blavatsky and former general secretary of the European Section, urged members of the Theosophical Society to vote againt Besant, since he felt that her election to the presidency would place the Society in the hands of "an irresponsible psychic tyranny."[34]

Annie Besant, from the beginning of the controversy, affirmed the individual responsibility of each member and freedom of thought.[35] But in the face of these severe criticisms, Besant felt it was also important to affirm the reality of the bedside appearances of the Masters and her own relationship to them.

> The Theosophical Society draws its being, its life, its strength, from the Masters, and like H. P. B. and Colonel Olcott, I am Their servant, and only as Their servant do I work in the Society. I ask none to believe, but I assert my own beliefs. Wrench the T. S. away from the Masters, and it dies. Those who do not wish to have a second President, holding this belief and asserting it, should vote against me.[36]

The members of the Theosophical Society voted overwhelmingly in Annie Besant's favor, with 9,572 votes in her favor, and 1,089 against.[37] Besant immediately embarked on a vigorous campaign to increase the membership of the Theosophical Society and to expand its activities. Despite the crisis at Olcott's death, the Theosophical Society began to increase its membership, growing from approximately 14,700 in 1907 to its peak membership of just over 45,000 in 1928.[38] The crisis at Olcott's death helped the Theosophical Society to affirm even more strongly the principles of self-reliance, individual responsibility, and freedom of thought. Yet the tension between democracy

and hierarchy remained in the Theosophical Society, and at times came
into conflict.

Continued Evolution of Authority
in the Theosophical Society

The tension between democracy and hierarchy continued in Annie
Besant's administration. As a former Freethinker, Besant always supported the right of each Theosophist to form her or his own opinions.
It was during Besant's tenure as president that a resolution was passed
by the General Council in 1924 officially stating "there is no doctrine,
no opinion, by whomsoever taught or held, that is in any way binding
on any member of the Society, none which any member is not free to
accept or reject. Approval of its three objects is the sole condition for
membership."[39] This resolution is currently printed near the front of
each issue of *The Theosophist*.

Besant's administration also raised occult authority to new heights.
Besant felt that she was an agent of the Masters and that all of her work
relating to the Theosophical Society, as well as education, social reform,
and self-government in India, was done at the direct order of the
Masters. Her partner in occult investigations and in occult authority
was Charles W. Leadbeater. Shortly after Besant's election to the
presidency, Leadbeater discovered a twelve-year-old Brahmin boy, J.
Krishnamurti, whom he and Besant felt would become the physical
vehicle for the World-Teacher, one of the Masters in the Occult Hierarchy. Besant traveled the world announcing the imminent appearance
of the World-Teacher, who would present a teaching that would become
the "New Religion," and create a millennial condition in the world.[40]
She built up an organization around Krishnamurti known as the Order
of the Star, which consisted of up to thirty thousand members.[41] In her
later years, Besant reported that due to her intense involvement on the
physical plane in trying to win Home Rule for India, she had lost her
occult faculties. This charismatic function was continued primarily by
C. W. Leadbeater, James Wedgwood, and George Arundale, soon to
become the third president of the Theosophical Society.

In 1925, Arundale announced that a series of initiations had taken
place, all on occult planes and verifiable only by himself, involving an
inner group of people surrounding Besant, Leadbeater, and Krishnamurti, and which involved the selection of the World-Teacher's twelve
apostles.[42] Krishnamurti, now a young man, immediately traveled from
America to Europe to see Besant and repudiate any association with

occult initiations and disciples. Shortly thereafter, Krishnamurti had a number of experiences, which continued for the rest of his life, in which he felt that he had become one with the teacher, his "Beloved."[43]

As he began to speak as the World-Teacher, Krishnamurti emphasized total individual responsibility for salvation or enlightenment. Krishnamurti noted that as long as he was seen as an authority, the World-Teacher, his listeners relied on him for their salvation rather than themselves, so he dissolved the Order of the Star in 1929. While not denying the existence of the Masters, he did deny their usefulness as a means to salvation. During the next few years, the membership of the Theosophical Society declined dramatically, bottoming out at twenty-eight thousand in 1940.[44]

After Besant's death in 1933, George Arundale and Ernest Wood ran for president, with the occult authority intervening briefly. During the election, a letter written by Annie Besant to Arundale was published stating that "Master said that you were to become President. . . ." Ransom reported that "considerable objection" was taken to the publication of this letter as "prejudicing the election," but nevertheless, Arundale was elected the third president of the Theosophical Society.[45] From this time on, there would no longer be public "psychic interference" in the government of the Theosophical Society. Occult authority might be used very privately, but in the exoteric government of the Theosophical Society, it had no place.

The tension between hierarchy and democracy remain in the Theosophical Society. The current president, Radha Burnier, was a close student of J. Krishnamurti, and she presents his message of self-effort and individual responsibility in attaining the "quiet mind" as the core of Theosophy. Radha Burnier is also the current Outer Head of the Esoteric Section.

Conclusion

The two founders of the Theosophical Society, particularly Helena Blavatsky, possessed a charisma that derived from their claimed relationship to the Masters of the Wisdom. Crises occurred at the deaths of each of the founders as the Theosophical Society struggled to deal with the problems of succession, continuity, and the routinizaton of charisma. William Q. Judge's attempt to claim for himself the charisma of Blavatsky and the elected office of the president resulted in the secession of a large portion of the American Section and the formation of a separate Theosophical organization. Within the Theosophical Society proper, the charisma of the founders was picked up primarily by Annie Besant and Charles W. Leadbeater, who claimed to be able to communicate directly with the Masters, but the members of the Theosophical Society insisted that Besant's accession to the presidency after Olcott's death could not be accomplished by autocratic appointment. The democratic principles that were present from the beginning of the Theosophical Society were too strong to allow the imposition of authority derived from occult sources. While the tension between hierarchy and democracy remains, the Theosophical Society has placed itself firmly on record as supporting the principles of freedom of thought and individual responsibility. A ritual has been devised whereby the newly elected president may share in the charisma of Blavatsky, namely by the presentation of Blavatsky's ring at the inauguration of the new president.[46]

The history of the Theosophical Society, like that of the Latter Day Saints, demonstrates that once charismatic authority deriving from occult sources is claimed, the possibility arises of any number of individuals making similar claims to bolster their own authority. Occult authority has proved to be highly contoversial, not only for those outside the Theosophical movement, but for Theosophists as well, since the authenticity of such claims can be verified only from a position of faith. From the beginning of the Theosophical Society, Theosophists have been strong individualists who have stressed the importance of freedom of thought. Freedom of thought includes the freedom to either affirm or reject any person's claims to occult authority. Even Colonel Olcott, whose own authority was supported by claims to direct contact with the Masters of the Wisdom, noted that claims to occult authority could be abused, could result in conflicting claims being made by different individuals, and ultimately does nothing to enhance the value of the teaching being given. Occult authority seems to have been relinquished in the parent Theosophical Society since no one currently is claiming to be the visible agent of the Masters.[47] This type of charismatic authority remains in the Theosophical movement, however, as the primary mode for establishing new organizations. The parent Theosophical Society has successfully routinized the transmission of charisma, and now faces the challenge of competing with diverse "New Age" groups who have attractive charismatic leaders. Those Theosophists desiring psychological certainty of continued teachings from authoritative sources (the Masters of Wisdom) have a wide range of groups with which they may seek affiliation, or there is always the option of forming one's own organization.

7

Charisma and Covenant:
The Christian Science Movement
in its Initial Postcharismatic Phase

John K. Simmons

*"Never abandon the By-laws nor the denomina-
tional government of The Mother Church. If I am not
personally with you, the Word of God, and my instructions in the By-Laws have led you hitherto and will
remain to guide you safely on."*[1]*—Mary Baker Eddy,
founder and charismatic leader of the Christian
Science movement, describing the importance of the
covenant present in* The Christian Science Church
Manual.[2]

*"The Christian Science Church Manual covenant
transcends in importance all others on earth because
it is a collective and individual agreement of obedience to the laws that govern all human life. We
cannot well estimate anything as of more importance
than a covenant which holds the issues of life and
death—not only for oneself but also for those we love
most and for the whole world, and brotherhood of
man."*[3]*—Annie C. Bill, the only departing member of
the Christian Science movement to organize a genuine
sectarian religious organization based on* The Church
Manual.

On 3 December 1910, Mary Baker Eddy, founder and charismatic leader of the Christian Science movement, passed on into the great metaphysical beyond. Having overcome seemingly insurmountable odds in carving her uniquely American religious organization out of a male-oriented cultural environment, the last fifteen years of her life had been spent transforming her church from a charismatic to a bureaucratic institution. By placing her personal charisma, the essence of her authority, in a set of bylaws entitled *Manual of the Mother Church*, Mrs. Eddy seemed to be laying down her prophetic mantle in order to provide the church with institutionalized order and security in perpetuity.

If anything is clear from the above two quotations—one by the original charismatic leader of the organization and one by the woman who was convinced the mantle was hers to don—Christian Scientists, inside and outside the established movement, regarded the *Manual of the Mother Church* as a supreme covenant that would guide the move-ment during and after the passing of their leader. Yet if the history of the postcharismatic Christian Science movement offers anything to the outside observer, it is controversy laced with paradox. For Mary Baker Eddy was an authoritarian, charismatic religious leader who distrusted the institutionalization of her cause. As Charles Braden, author of the best ostensibly "objective" study of the movement after Eddy's demise, notes, her writings are replete with exhortations to beware of cramping doctrines that stifle true spiritual growth. She championed freedom of thought and action and warned her followers against "deifying" her should she depart from their presence.[4]

Yet she created a centrally controlled religious organization without rival in the rigidity of its restraints upon branch churches and members.[5] When the congregational pattern of church polity, characteristic of her first religious organization founded in 1879, proved too democratic and a catalyst for rebellion, she not only disorganized the National Christian Science Association but also closed her lucrative Massachusetts Meta-physical College. Apparently it was Mrs. Eddy's perception of the incompatibility of religion and social organization that precipitated the disorganizational process. However, when she reorganized the Christian Science movement around the Mother Church in 1892, her unwavering motivation must have been to create a fixed and enduring institution that would never slip from her ecclesiastical grasp. So far, in life and death, she has succeeded.[6]

The *Manual of the Mother Church* articulates the bylaws that con-trol organizational dynamics in the "fixed and enduring" institution that is the Christian Science movement. At Mrs. Eddy's request, the first codification was undertaken by a committee in 1895 and would go through eighty-nine editions before revisions ceased with her death. Since, as Stephen Gottschalk notes, "Mrs. Eddy's authority lay behind every by-law in the Manual," it is to this document that we must turn in order to make some sense of the postcharismatic Christian Science movement.[7]

Before engaging the peculiarities of the *Manual* and the interesting legal permutations that emerged in the process of applying the document to a post-Eddy period in the church, it will be helpful to consider the relationship between *charisma* and *covenant*. A covenant provides a "vessel" for authority. Using the Weberian model mentioned in Gordon Melton's introduction, while developing the "covenantal vessel" metaphor, a smooth transformation from charismatic to rational/legal authority in any given organization requires the pouring of authority from the person-oriented charismatic covenantal vessel into the institution-oriented rational/legal covenantal vessel, ideally without spilling a drop.[8] In other words, if a religious organization, or any organization for that matter, is to successfully maneuver through the traumatic death of a charismatic leader, the covenant bond between leader and believers, which is unquestionably the energizing, binding force during the first generation, *must* be transformed into an equally efficacious covenant bond between the organizational structure and surviving members of the group. "Covenant" here implies the element of reciprocity present in the word. Love of leader must be transformed into love of law. Without a sense that the Leader's essence exists and lives in the rules governing the organization, the covenantal vessel becomes a sieve, incapable of containing its rarified nectar—authority, the "ambrosia of the gods." The routinization process fails and the organization soon dissolves into self-destructive factions.

The covenantal vessel for the Christian Science movement, from 3 December 1910 up to today, is *The Manual*. And there is ample evidence, chronicled by Robert Peel among others,[9] to support the conclusion that Mrs. Eddy conscientiously facilitated the process of pouring her own charismatic authority into that document over the last fifteen years of her life, with such Weberian accuracy that the transformation could be a sociological model for routinization of charisma. She clearly felt *The Manual* to be divinely inspired and taught her students that it delineated the "highest possible human sense of church government . . . divine wisdom marking the way by which the cause of Christian Science could be protected."[10] She once declared to a student that "This Church Manual is God's law, as much as the Ten Commandments and the Sermon on the Mount."[11]

Today, the uninformed visitor to the prestigious Christian Science Center in Boston, Massachusetts would simply conclude that "not a drop was spilled" in this movement's covenantal transfer process. And in fact the initial transfer of power from Mrs. Eddy to the Church's board of directors was accomplished with hardly a ripple in the organization. But the whole story, like most religious episodes, is not so serene. The wording of several key bylaws governing appointments to important posts in the organization and other vital functions clearly made these essential bylaws inoperable without Mrs. Eddy's written approval! To complicate the situation further, Sections 1 and 3 of Article XXXV made it impossible to amend the document without the consent of the Pastor Emeritus, Mary Baker Eddy. To a whole faction of Christian Scientists, the genius of *The Manual* lay in the fact that Mrs. Eddy designed it so that the Mother Church would morally cease to function under its own covenant upon her death! Christian Science, as the Christ Principle, would be freed from organizational bonds, and Christian Scientists would then be released to continue their respective metaphysical journeys unencumbered by doctrine or precept. To the Christian Science establishment, particularly the board of directors, this notion was heresy, and though logic was in favor of the "infidels," power and money won out, resulting in the organization that is known today as Christian Science. But not without an interesting battle!

What we then find in postcharismatic Christian Science are *two* stories pertinent to the covenantal transfer of authority theme: The first is the story of the "official" Christian Science movement wherein the board of directors legally overcomes the organizational dilemmas produced by *The Manual's* estoppel clauses and carries on the process of transferring Mrs. Eddy's charismatic authority into a rational/legal bond. We will refer to this account as the "Rational/legal Covenant Story." The second is the little known but equally powerful narrative of those "Christian Scientists" who perceived in *The Manual* that side of Mrs. Eddy's personality that ultimately distrusted organization and who, consequently, sought various means to reify the charismatic covenant. The focus of this story is one Annie C. Bill, the only devoted follower of Mrs. Eddy to actually start a new sectarian "Christian Science" movement in the post-Eddy era. Thus we also have the "Reification of Charisma Covenant Story."

The Rational/legal Covenant Story

The board of directors eventually inherited Mrs. Eddy's authority. In-house Christian Science histories tell of no controversy, depicting the board's rise to power as simply a playing out of Mrs. Eddy's will.[12] However, the *The Manual* doesn't make things that simple. For about seventeen years Mrs. Eddy repeatedly changed the structure of the organization, centralizing the once-democratic movement to resist schismatic tendencies that had already reared their heads. From 1892 to 1901, key authority lay with twenty "First Members" of the Mother Church whom she had selected; in 1901 Mrs. Eddy shifted that authority to a newly powerful board of directors. Editions of *The Manual* after that date place the board in charge, but with a huge loophole: Vacancies on the board must be filled with candidates approved by Mrs. Eddy. In other words, she had to approve new board members even after she had shuffled off this mortal coil![13] In fact, as is evident from the chart below (Figure 7.1), not one of the major positions in her church could be legitimately filled without her written and/or oral approval.

Figure 7.1[14]

Reference	General Content	Effect
Art. I, Sec. I.	Church officers to consist of Pastor Emeritus,* Board of Directors, President, Clerk, Treasurer, Two Readers.	Immediately upon Mrs. Eddy's death, the post of Pastor Emeritus vacant. Church incomplete.
Art. I, Sec. II.	President elected yearly subject to approval of Pastor Emeritus.	Within one year of Mrs. Eddy's death, there could be no *legitimate* President.
Art. I Sec. III.	Clerk, Treasurer, Editors, Publishing Society heads, manager of Committee on Publication in Boston, all appointed for one year, subject to approval of Paster Emeritus *"given in her own handwriting."*	Within one year of Mrs. Eddy's death there could be no Clerk, Treasurer, Editors, Publishing Society heads, or manager of Committee on Publication, *legitimately* appointed.
Art. I Sec. IV.	Readers in Mother Church elected every three years. Names to be submitted first to the Pastor Emeritus.	Within three years of Mrs. Eddy's death there could be no *legitimately* appointed readers.
Art. I, Sec. V.	Five Directors hold office subject to Mrs. Eddy's approval. Her request is sufficient to dismiss them.	As they retired or died, there could be no more *legitimately* appointed directors.

For many Christian Scientists, at the time of her death and on up to the present, these clauses are not some clumsy oversight on the part of Mrs. Eddy, nor something she would have gotten around to changing had she not passed away. They are consciously designed to be "estoppel" clauses preventing a single authoritarian body from controlling her church after her death. Why did she insert these estoppel clauses into *The Manual?* We will engage this question in more detail during our investigation of the reified charismatic covenant, but at least three possible explanations emerged.

First, from this perspective, Mrs. Eddy sought to prevent the covenant binding Christian Scientists to the movement from passing through the routinization process. In effect, she wished her church to be dissolved after her death and "wrote" its death warrant into these paradoxical clauses. This is unlikely even though it is claimed by many "scientists" outside the organization, since it is known that on 22 September 1909, shortly before her death, Mrs. Eddy remarked to one of her trusted legal advisors that Christian Scientists who go about saying we need no organization "don't know what they are talking about." In the same conversation, she "spoke with authority and precision on the absolute need for organization as a protection to the cause of Christian Science."[15]

Second, Article 23, section 6 of *The Manual* states,

> If the Pastor Emeritus, Mrs. Eddy, should relinquish her place as the head or Leader of The Mother Church of Christ, Scientist, each branch shall continue its present form of government in consonance with The Mother Church Manual.[16]

Many excommunicated Christian Scientists interpreted this bylaw to mean that Mrs. Eddy, upon her death, wished to dissolve the ecclesiastical hierarchy present in the Mother Church and return to a more democratic church polity in which the Mother Church's status would be reduced to equality with all other branch churches. All Christian Science churches would then be governed by the rules set forth in *The Manual* without the authoritarian governance of a single overriding church body.

In this scenario, which is still advocated by "renegade" Christian Scientists today, upon the death of the first of the five board members, which happened in 1912, the remaining four members should have realized that replacing a member—without Mrs. Eddy's permission—was a violation of the above *Manual* guideline. The only proper course of action would have been to relieve themselves of board member status, and, as a four-member governing body, simple carry out the duties of maintaining the church in Boston, no longer the Mother Church, the sun in the center of the entire organization empowering all other branch churches, but now, The First Church of Christ, Scientist, in Boston,

Massachusetts, one among many. In this manner, the four members would be obeying both *The Manual*—by not appointing a new member without permission of the deceased leader—and the Deed of Trust by maintaining the Boston church. When all five of the Eddy-appointed board members had gone on to join their leader, the governance of the church in Boston would revert to standard operating procedure for any branch church as delineated in *The Manual*.[17]

The third explanation for the inclusion of supposed estoppel clauses entertained by the anti-establisment faction extends from the second and will be the focus of our investigation of Annie Bill. Mrs. Eddy foresaw that a new leader would emerge from one of the branch churches to "recharge" the church covenant with new charisma and lead the movement forward in the twentieth century. The fact that Mrs. Eddy regularly sacked anyone who shined forth with the slightest glint of leadership ability would seem to undercut this scenario. But, as we shall see, to those who embrace this account, this is exactly what Mrs. Eddy had in mind.

However, from the perspective of the board of directors in 1910, these three organizational reactions to their leader's death were completely unworkable. How could it possibly make sense to disband a healthy, growing religious movement that was satisfying the spiritual needs of so many religious seekers? Disorganize the central control of the entire movement? Nonsense! By this time the Mother Church, as the power center of the movement, held extensive properties, conducted a million-dollar-a-year business of publishing and distributing literature, and ministered to loyal followers around the world who were dutifully trying to follow the spiritual directions of Mary Baker Eddy. It would amount to organizational suicide to somehow diffuse power throughout the branch-churches polity. To be sure, the directors earned a tidy salary, but it is hardly fair to think they were acting from selfish motives in their attempt to commandeer power. Someone had to run the organization, and at least the Deed of Trust seemed to confirm that Mrs. Eddy wished the board of directors to take over this function if she should depart from their presence.

Did Mrs. Eddy foresee the conundrum she left for her followers? Critical observers have claimed that she wrote the estoppal clauses so that the church could not function after her death;[18] officially approved church historians argue that she was merely setting up checks and balances for the future.[19] In any event, it was all bound for the courts (church historians speak of the "Great Litigation"), where the final decision was rendered in 1921 by the Supreme Judicial Court of Massachusetts.

It is not possible in this essay to completely recount this complex legal battle. For our purposes, it is enough to identify the issues and see the inner institutional conflict as an inevitable step in the process of covenant transformation. Mrs. Eddy could have simply given the board of directors control over the movement's lucrative publishing business. But she did not. Instead, in February 1898, she drew up a deed of trust that "established the Christian Science Publishing Society as a separate legal entity on a permanent and solid basis."[20] As was the case with the board of directors, the three appointed trustees were accountable to no one but Mrs. Eddy. The general membership, as is still the case today, had no say in their appointment or policy-making.

Call it organizational genius or administrative confusion as you choose, but Mrs. Eddy wrote into *The Manual* overlapping duties for each powerful group. Article 25, section 8 states that "only the Publishing Society of the Mother Church selects, approves, and publishes the books and literature it sends forth."[21] Yet, in Article 8, section 14, the board of directors are given the following responsibility: "and it shall be the duty of the Directors to see that these periodicals are ably edited and kept abreast of the times."[22]

To make matters more interesting, in Article 25, section 3, she gave the board of directors power to "declare vacancies in said trusteeship, for such reasons as to the Board may seem expedient."[23] Directors, then, have the power to "fire" trustees without having to account to anyone but Mrs. Eddy. Another twist: The same section, following paragraph, states, "Whenever a vacancy shall occur, the Pastor Emeritus reserves the right to fill the same by appointment; but if she does not elect to exercise this right, the remaining trustees shall fill the vacancy, subject to her approval."[24] From a trustee's perspective, since Mrs. Eddy's approval could not be obtained, it was up to them to replace any person fired by the directors.

Not surprisingly, the Great Litigation was fought out over these clauses, as each powerful group made its play for control of the church. The battle was postponed during the immediate years following Mrs. Eddy's death due to an unusual circumstance: Archibald McLellan, a trusted Eddy advisor, was both editor-in-chief at the Publishing Society and a member of the board of directors.[25] However, upon his retirement, the inevitable occurred: The directors disapproved of several pieces of literature the trustees were prepared to publish, informed them that they were expected to act only under the guidance and permission of the directors, and, when the trustees balked at this power play, swords were drawn; on 3 January 1918, the directors issued an edict demanding that the trustees submit their letters of resignation.[26]

Not until 21 November 1921 was the Great Litigation finally settled, when Justice C. J. Rugg finally ruled on behalf of the Directors, essentially supporting them on the following issues: First, Mrs. Eddy wished them to have supreme authority over the entire Christian Science movement, not just the Mother Church. In fact, the Mother Church was the central organization of which all other Christian Science organizations were but branches. Second, Mrs. Eddy never intended to separate the Publishing Society from the other activities of the church in spite of creating the society through a special deed. Third, it follows, then, that the trustees work under the authority of the Mother Church over which the directors have complete control. Fourth, the rank and file membership of the Christian Science movement had come to accept this arrangement since the death of Mrs. Eddy, and such tacit approval indicated that the will of the leader, for lack of any sound evidence to the contrary, was being adequately administered by the directors. The board of directors won. In effect, the directors had, from their perspective, successfully overseen the covenantal transfer of authority from the charismatic leadership of Mrs. Eddy to the rational/legal authority of *The Manual* as interpreted by the courts. To this day the Christian Science movement functions, postcharismatically, according to the dictates of *The Manual* as interpreted by an autocratic, self-perpetuating board of directors. However, many Christian Scientists did not agree with the court, nor with the transfer of authority from a charismatic convenantal vessel to a rational/legal one. One such person was Annie C. Bill.

The Reification of Charisma Covenant Story

The death of Mary Baker Eddy created a wave of speculation that washed over the boundaries of the Christian Science movement, out into the harbor of American religious culture. Love her or hate her, people pondered the fate of the deceased. Augusta Stetson, an ardent follower of Mrs. Eddy—even in excommunication—declared,

> The same situation exists today as when Jesus of Nazareth died and was buried. After three days he manifested himself, to prove that there is life after death. Mrs. Eddy will do the same, for she occupies in the world of today precisely the same position that Jesus occupied in his day.[27]

Not everyone was content to sit around the sepulcher waiting for the stone to roll away. In response to this rather prevalent brand of millennial enthusiasm, Billy Sunday, the fiery baseball player turned Fundamentalist revivalist, exclaimed, "If old Mother Eddy rises from the dead I'll eat polecat for breakfast and wash it down with booze!"[28]

Certainly the postcharismatic history of the Christian Science movement reflects an element of dissent against the iron-fisted rule of the board of directors. Many brilliant metaphysical thinkers and healers left the movement to start private practices, write metaphysical treatises, or launch unsuccessful assaults upon the seemingly impenetrable Boston fortress.[29] With the exception of Religious Science, most New Thought groups had already been organized during Mrs. Eddy's lifetime. Christian Scientists who found appealing the more open-ended metaphysical system which was New Thought had left the movement long before her death; that leaves Annie Bill as the only person who actually was able to create a rival religious movement in the early postcharismatic years. And, it was her visionary, prophetic embrace of *The Manual* as covenant that prompted her activity.

Soon after the "discovery" of Christian Science in America, the religion found an enthusiastic audience in Great Britain; and Annie Bill, well-read, thoughtful daughter of an Anglican rector, was a rising star in the Third Church, London. "What goes up, must come down" could well be the motto of the Christian Science movement, and, as was the case throughout the Eddy years, Mrs. Bill fell into disfavor by supporting the heretical written opinions of another bright member of the church, Frederick L. Rawson.[30]

When in November 1909 (a little more than a year before Mrs. Eddy's death), Third Church, London, issued what amounted to a "shunning" order against Rawson, forbidding its members to speak to him on the subject of Christian Science, Annie Bill had had enough. On 11 December 1909, she tendered her resignation to Third Church, London *and* the Mother Church, Boston.

The death of Mrs. Eddy a year later and the subsequent action by the board of directors staggered Annie Bill, who was still embroiled in her skirmishes with Third Church. For Bill, *The Manual* was not just a listing of bylaws for the purpose of running a religious organization but an "inviolable covenant," not only between Mrs. Eddy and Christian Scientists, but between God and all human beings. Certainly *The Manual* was vital to the spiritual heritage of the Christian Science movement. But the book held vastly greater import for all humanity; as a divinely inspired, sacred document, *The Manual* revealed the covenantal organizational dynamics put in place by the Creator—the key to existence, the law of life itself! Of *The Manual* she wrote,

We stand to-day required, and 'prepared' to prove that the absolute
scientific unity of the letter and the spirit of the CHURCH MANUAL
COVENANT is inviolable; not one jot nor title of its law shall fail: for
that covenant is eternal between man and his creator, uninterruptedly
and consciously renewed in every period of progress. . . . The Christian Science Church Manual covenant transcends in importance all
others on earth because it is a collective and individual agreement of
obedience to the laws that govern all human life.[31]

Disapproving of the routinization of charisma process under way in
the Christian Science establishment, Mrs. Bill set out to "reify" the
charismatic covenant by raising *The Manual* to the status of charismatic
leader! And, in her thinking, since *The Manual* clearly stated that no
new members of the board of directors could be appointed without
the permission of the Pastor Emeritus, Mrs. Eddy, under divine inspiration, had "obviously" designed the estoppel clauses envisioning the
emergence of a new leader who would understand and reflect the
organizational brilliance present in *The Manual*. In a flash of spiritual
chutzpah, Annie Bill realized that she was that person! And since the
Boston-based Mother Church had violated the sacred covenant by
placing the board of directors at the helm, she became absolutely
convinced that Christian Scientists the world over would recognize her
as the new leader of the movement. Buoyed by her metaphysical
euphoria, she undertook a series of startling moves that ultimately
brought the legal wrath of the Christian Science establishment in Boston
down upon her.

In a directive from the Central Assembly of her London church,
dated 7 October 1914, Annie Bill made an astounding claim. Since her
organization was the only "constitutionally sound" church since the
demise of Mrs. Eddy, she was assuming the sole right to all the authorized titles and publications that were the property of the Mother
Church, Boston! Not content to issue empty declarations, Mrs. Bill
immediately began to publish almost exact replicas of the Christian
Science *Manual*, the *Journal*, and the *Sentinel*.

If this weren't enough to arouse the ire of the directors and trustees
in Boston, she then formally insisted that she had a right to the property of the Mother Church in Boston, which was worth millions of
dollars. Apparently she fully expected all Christian Scientists who were
loyal to Mrs. Eddy to resign from the old organization and join the
"true" Mother Church. One example of the seriousness with which
she took her mission is the many letters she wrote to heads of leading
religious bodies, including the Pope, describing her intentions and
welcoming them to begin ecumenical dialogue with the authentic Christian Science organization.[32]

Not wanting to give Mrs. Bill undue publicity, the Mother Church in Boston had been content to warily watch her activities. But when she took advertisements in major American newspapers delineating her claims to be the leader of the "true" Mother Church, enough was enough! Through a representative of the Publishing Society in England, Charles W. J. Tennant, an affidavit was filed declaring that "Mrs. Bill and her followers were seeking to mislead the public into believing that her publications were actually the publications of the Mother Church, Boston, and that she was seeking to benefit herself by such misrepresentation."[33] Realizing the hopelessness of her legal position, Mrs. Bill backed down. She would discontinue use of the literary titles that were the commercial property of the directors in Boston; and, after several changes in name, refer to her church as the Christian Science Parent Center. But, in writing of the dispute, she implied victory based on her loyalty to *The Manual*:

> We have taken this decision [not to defend the charge] upon the ground that we do not wish to contest a purely commercial issue, which, however it might end, could not fail to injure the cause of Christian Science. An issue of this kind would fail to raise the fundamental Principle of Loyalty to Covenant, which is the essential difference between us.[34]

The question of who was loyal to *The Manual* covenant continued to cause consternation to the Boston establishment, especially after Mrs. Bill brought her church to America in 1924. Her eloquent and lengthy explanation of the paradigmatic nature of the *Manual*, in terms of its organizational dynamics, apparently sparked the religious imagination of all-too-numerous Christian Scientists wont to expand their metaphysical boundaries.

Mrs. Bill named the insight that she received from her spiritual understanding of *The Manual* the "Universal Design of Life." A detailed explanation of her metaphysical ruminations is beyond the scope of this essay, but to summarize them, the Universal Design of Life might be described as a systems view of life with a covenantal-dispensational twist. All of creation works through seven stages: "Covenant" becomes similar to the organizational bond that creates a larger organism out of interrelated, interdependent smaller units; the atom is the primary microcosmic model for all other self-organizing systems.

In the first stage, the covenant core is identified with a person, a leader. The leader generates the gravitational force that binds the group together, and, through Stages 2 through 4, a new "truth" is assimilated that is reflected in the growth of the group. Essentially, this is a time of self-assertion for the organization; in Annie Bill's mind, it was represented by the early years of the Christian Science movement under Mary Baker Eddy. The organizational and spiritual zenith of the group is reached.

Stages 5 and 6 are necessary evolutionary stages. Like a caterpillar entering its self-created womb, the organization senses a "higher truth, higher destiny," the leader resigns, and the movement enters an interim period, sans leader, during which a new covenantal core germinates. Stage 7 finds the "butterfly emerging from its cocoon," as a new leader comes forth to guide the group to the next evolutionary level.

For Mrs. Bill and other believers in her system, Mrs. Eddy really did not "die" but simply went into kind of systemic hibernation, knowing full well that it was a necessary step for the harmonious evolution of the Christian Science cause. Mrs. Bill represented the personified covenant core, the leader of the next dispensation.[35]

From the perspective of the routinization of charisma, Mrs. Bill's "universal design" has intriguing implications. Charisma is *never* routinized. The seven stages are cyclical, and, upon passing through the cycle one always returns to a newly reified covenant relationship between a charismatic leader and her followers. For Mrs. Bill, it was *The Manual of the Mother Church* that delineated this covenant; thus the book reverberated with biblical covenant themes present in the American civil religious consciousness.

One rather distressing covenantal interpretation of the destiny of humankind arose from Mrs. Bill's embrace of Anglo-Israelism, the theory that the modern peoples of northern and western Europe and North America were the descendents of the ten ancient lost tribes of Israel and destined to lead the world, spiritually, to the millennial dispensation. The racism inherent in this view is, perhaps, more offensive to readers sensitized by the Civil Rights movement and other late twentieth-century consciousness-raising events than to Mrs. Bill and her followers who understood it primarily as a covenantal doctrine authorizing the Parent Church as "the remnant" that would fulfill Old Testament prophecy regarding the Messianic Age.[36]

Nevertheless, the theory seemed to attract the turn-of-the-century metaphysical crowd. Apparently Mrs. Eddy was quite intrigued with the idea, especially after a devotee, one Mrs. Field-King, presented her with "proof" that Mrs. Eddy's line of descent could be traced back to King David. Fortunately, sparing the movement later embarrassment, Mrs. Eddy became "nervous" with this type of "materializing" of her mission and authority, and gave the theory no real credence, at least in verifiable written form.[37]

However, when combined with Mrs. Bill's "Universal Design of Life," Anglo-Israelism provided an ontological blast of charisma by reifying the covenantal bond by identifying the Parent as a "faithful remnant" similar to the Hebrews who returned from Babylonian captivity to rebuild the temple in Jerusalem, and by providing a world mission for the church as human history entered the final stage, or dispensation, before a new, spiritualized consciousness emerged. As befitting a charismatic leader, Mrs. Bill interpreted all biblical messianic prophecy as referring to her and Christian Science, as represented, faithfully, now by the Parent Church:

> In this period of Christian Science the fact is being demonstrably illustrated that the remnant forms the head and the corner-stone which links each successive period in spiritual evolution. This unmistakably identifies the people of Israel with the Christian Science movement and its advanced unfoldment of the system of logical spiritual discovery and harmonious world evolution. . . .[38]

Through a reified covenant, a covenant present in *The Manual of the Mother Church*, Annie Bill would bring charismatic leadership back to the Christian Science movement and guide that noble cause toward "harmonious world evolution."

Conclusion

Two stories: one, the establishment tale, offers a schematic model for the routinization of charisma. Some spillage occurred, but, overall, in the Christian Science movement, the "pouring of authority" from the charismatic covenantal vessel to the rational/legal was, comparatively speaking, neatly done. Today, *The Manual* remains a viable routinized covenant that, as interpreted by the self-perpetuating Board of Directors, continues to guide the Christian Science organization.[39]

And what of Annie Bill and the Parent Church? Today no remnant remains. Her organization met with solid but brief success. Having acquired an important convert, A. A. Beauchamp, who turned the services of his publishing house, including his magazine, *Watchman of Israel*, over to the movement, the new church grew steadily. The *Census of Religious Bodies* reports that in 1926 the Parent Church consisted of twenty-nine congregations with 582 members in the United States. In 1928 the numbers had expanded to forty-four branch churches, including churches in Great Britain, Australia, and Canada, and by 1930, eighty branch churches existed servicing twelve hundred members.[40] While these numbers may not appear to indicate overwhelming success in relation to other religious organizations, they are substantial in comparison to movements within the metaphysical camp.

During the later years of the 1920s, Mrs. Bill came to believe that many of the rumors surrounding Mary Baker Eddy, were, in fact, true; particularly, she had plagiarized large portions of the central textbook, *Science and Health with Key to the Scriptures*. Accordingly, she eschewed the use of Eddy's writings, created her own textbook, *The Science of Reality*, and reorganized the Parent Church into the Church of the Universal Design.[41]

After Annie Bill died in 1937, Francis J. Mott, who had been with the movement since 1922 but had resigned in 1934, followed Mrs. Bill's "design" by convincing the interim leaders of the organization that he was the new, seventh-stage "seed" leader who, when planted in their fertile pasture, would grow to guide the church on its next evolutionary step. He must have been quite convincing because the majority of the members of the Church of Universal Design voted to dissolve the church and reorganize as The Society of Life in 1937. After some years of "perfecting their standpoint and their new message," the group transformed The Society of Life into the Church of Integration, of which, today, there is no institutional trace.[42]

What do these two Christian Science stories teach us about religious movements when prophets die? First, the routinization process can never be fully understood apart from the cultural matrix out of which the religious movement arises. Mrs. Eddy's church succeeded; Mrs. Bill's failed. But before we simply jump to the conclusion that charismatic movements are inevitably ephemeral, doomed to a single generation, we need to recognize what type of person so meekly responded to the board of directors' ascension to power following Mrs. Eddy's death. In 1910, and, for that matter, 1990, the rank and file member of the Christian Science movement can accurately be characterized as a white, middle class, socially conservative American concerned with security and stability in the culture.

In his book on popular religion in America, Peter Williams points out that "religious expression usually correlates with and derives its imagery from the experience of everyday life."[43] Here we have an unspoken, unwritten "covenant" between the empowering ethos of society and the way human beings in that society wish to describe and engage "ultimate concerns." To a student of American culture, it should not come as a surprise that metaphysical religions born in America, such

as Christian Science and New Thought groups, are popular because the
cluster of concepts present in these religious expressions mirror key
elements in the American culture core.[44] For a Christian Scientist,
health, wealth, and happiness are qualities of God that are "scientif-
ically" demonstrable for human beings to *know* that they reflect the
Divine Mind. This metaphysical ideal finds social expression in that
concept loosely described as the "Protestant work ethic"—simply put,
"Think positively, work hard, maintain the status quo, and all things
shall be added unto you."

To be sure, Christian Science would not have been as successful
as it has in American society if it did not genuinely satisfy very real
theological/ontological needs harbored by its adherents. But the clear
fundamentalist metaphysical answers to life's problems presented in Mrs.
Eddy's writings and organizationally supported by *The Manual* provide
for middle-class Americans a spiritual "mazeway" that works in their
cultural experience. The American religious imagination, for the most
part, enjoys and survives an occasional blast of charisma; but when
it gets in the way of commerce, it's time to bind charismatic religious
expression with rational/legal constraints. Annie Bill's charisma-
reification cycle never had a chance in this country.

A second observation: This "When Prophets Die" volume initiates
an important comparative investigation of the routinization of charisma
process. Could the "two-story model" present in the history of Christian Science be applicable to other new religious movements? Specifically, upon the death of the prophet, does a successful routinization
process demand that a sectarian group emerge that attracts those more
emotive, innovative, energetic members away from the mainstream
adherents? Occupying the "firebrands" of the movement with their
own organizational process might facilitate the institutionalization of
a rational/legal covenant in the dominant group.

A final point: In American studies, more study needs to be undertaken on the relationship between charisma and covenant. The United
States is really an "Old Testament" nation in the sense that the culture
core reflects covenantal values present in the grand biblical drama: a
chosen people with a manifest destiny to be God's people or to build
God's kingdom on Earth are convenantally bound to obey God-ordained
moral precepts, and by so doing they will insure their prosperity; to
disobey is to violate the covenant and invite punishment.[45]

Other covenantal concepts from the Hebrew Bible resonate with
the American religious imagination and the American political system:
a charismatic leader, a Moses, a Thomas Jefferson brings "The Law."
The law, then, becomes a covenant code, is routinized, and applied to

every facet of social life. Periodically, "prophets" must emerge from the religiopolitical matrix—a Hosea, an Abraham Lincoln, a Martin Luther King—who admonish laxity in application of the covenant code and reignite the fires of convenantal enthusiasm. This interaction between charisma and covenant, as we have seen in the postcharismatic history of the Christian Science movement, may, in fact, be at the very heart of the American religious experience.

8

When Prophets Die:
The Case of the Spirit Fruit Society

H. Roger Grant

A durable American religious utopia, one of the few to appear at the dawn of the twentieth century, carried an unusual name: the Spirit Fruit Society. As in the majority of religious sects, both past and present, a single individual initially led and molded this group. He was Jacob Beilhart (1867–1908), a man with drive, integrity, and considerable charisma.

Although Jacob (he preferred to use only his Christian name) did not seem destined to have a rendezvous with utopia, some early signs pointed in that direction. Jacob could not recall a time when he had not thought about religious matters. Raised in a strict German Lutheran household on a prosperous farm in northeastern Ohio, when only a teenager he fell under the spell of a kindly family of Seventh-day Adventists. Soon Jacob converted to this vigorous faith, which was shaped by the determined millennialist, Ellen Gould White. His excitement for Mrs. White's sect led him to attend her struggling college in Healdsburg, California, for the winter term of 1887–1888. Then Jacob took up full-time preaching, first in Ohio, and subsequently in Kansas and Colorado. After two productive years, however, he resigned. "I decided that I would preach no more until I could do something besides talk." So he moved with his wife, Olive Louema "Lou," an ardent Adventist, whom he married shortly before they entered Healdsburg College, to Battle Creek, Michigan, the mecca for American Adventism. Here was located the church's popular Battle Creek Sanitarium, headed by

Dr. John Harvey Kellogg, a leading health propagandist, physician, and son of a White confidant. Jacob entered the Sanitarium's nursing program, and excelled in his studies. More important, he became intrigued with faith healing. But this fascination—perhaps obsession—troubled Dr. Kellogg and the powerful Adventist community; Jacob soon had no choice but to break his ties with both.[1]

The Beilharts remained in Battle Creek. While at the Sanitarium, Jacob nursed C. W. Post, the future cereal magnate, and the two became close friends. Shortly Jacob joined Post at the latter's newly opened health spa, the La Vita Inn, where they treated guests with "mental suggestion." But Jacob and Post separated after about a year, likely because of the former's preoccupation with religion. Jacob craved a meaningful faith. He studied with students of Mary Baker Eddy and other New Thought sects: he considered Christian Science, Divine Science, Spiritualism, and Theosophy. Yet nothing satisfied him. "I soon settled down to this:— All of these theories are very nice, but it is hard to run the universe when you know as little about it as any of these folks seem to know who claimed to be teachers. So I said to myself, I will submit myself to the life, of God, or whatever it is that creates and sustains things."[2]

In a short time Jacob's life changed dramatically. Odd jobs sustained his growing household, which soon consisted of Lou, two babies, and Jacob's brother and sister, while Jacob at last moved toward formulating an acceptable religious outlook. "I let love work in me. I was unoccupied." The process succeeded. "Faith, Love and Trust took the place in the heart once wrecked by jealousy, fear, and doubt . . . and Love began to create, Spirit Fruit was born, and sent out." The Beilhart clan left Michigan for Ohio in the late 1890s, and Jacob launched a modest publishing venture, a four-page monthly periodical, *Spirit Fruit*, to share his views. He subsequently acquired a small acreage, which included a roomy brick house, near the north edge of Lisbon, a bustling county-seat community, and his religious settlement took shape rapidly.[3]

By 1900, Jacob's thoughts about religion and life generally had gelled. Not surprisingly, they contained ideas that mirrored tenets of popular metaphysical faiths. Essentially Jacob sought a oneness with all humankind. Any type of selfishness, anger, or the like, he believed, caused strife, pain, and personal unhappiness. Thus "Spirit Fruit" emerged when an individual achieved union with the universe. He contended that "the way of self must be entirely avoided; and we must learn to hear, understand and obey the true Voice, which to us is the

Voice of the Spirit Universal [God] revealing to us the principles of Life, if obeyed, will never fail."[4]

Jacob's message of gentleness attracted about a dozen committed adults into his immediate fold. "Spirit Fruit was born for those who became part of the Farm." With an economy based on agriculture (dairying and poultry) together with income generated from odd jobs and freewill contributions, the Society flourished. But during the spring of 1904, an ugly and exaggerated exposé of "free-love" activities disrupted the tranquil life of Jacob and his coreligionists. When Mary Beilhart, Jacob's younger sister and an original Spirit Fruiter, gave birth to her second illegitimate child, local (and then national) "yellow" journalists attacked the "cult." Members of the Fourth Estate and others, too, saw Jacob's experiment in goodness as a threat to traditional and cherished "village virtues."[5]

Although Jacob successfully disarmed his local critics with a well-attended "open house" and lecture, still the sect left Lisbon for Chicago by late 1904. In many ways life in the Windy City was more difficult than it had been in Ohio, largely because colonists lived in seedy residential hotels and could not garden or farm. Less than a year after their arrival in Chicago, Spirit Fruiters launched a sizable dairy operation off the shores of placid Wooster Lake near Ingleside, Illinois, forty-five miles northwest of Chicago. Their religious commune thrived, and colonists seemed exceedingly pleased with their lifestyle. "We have created a blissful state," remarked Kate Waters, a former teacher, college professor, and physician. Moreover, Spirit Fruiters returned to their former inconspicuous position in the public's eye. Their practices did not openly affront their neighbors. Colonists were intelligent, industrious, and honest and there was no nudity or raucous behavior.[6]

Disaster struck the Spirit Fruit Society in 1908. Jacob was stricken with appendicitis on 19 November and medical treatment failed. He died early on the morning of 24 November after "intense suffering." Although the shock was considerable—"Jacob had been a vigorous man of 41 years of age up until the time of his attack"—Spirit Fruiters considered their late leader to be still a vital part of their lives. "There is no sorrow existing at the colony today," remarked I. E. Rockwell, a well-to-do businessman and early follower of Jacob, to a local reporter. "We did not weep because of his earthly death but we all want to believe that he will still lead on his hosts from his higher position which he now holds."[7]

And Jacob did. The colonists, probably without exception, believed in spiritualism, although after the 1890s Jacob himself never espoused any bonafide spiritualist doctrines. Virginia Moore, Jacob's lover (Lou, Jacob's wife, strongly attached to the Adventist faith, could not accept communal life and so had returned with their two children to her parents' home in Kansas about 1901), became president. (The colony, incorporated as a religious society in Ohio, had officers, but merely for legal reasons.) Virginia and her mother, Charlena "Ma" Lewis Moore Young, entered into regular contact with the dead Jacob. Remembered Robert Knowdell, one of the children born into the Society:

> [I]t seemed that the survivors instinctively looked to Virginia to assume the burden of titular head, along with her mother "Ma," because of her unique clairvoyant endowment. There is no question in my mind that they all believed that the spirit never dies, and Ma's daily writings, as she sat in a trance, . . . were accepted as their link between the present and the hereafter. . . . [A]ll sat in silence around the dining table after the noon meal until Ma concluded the "Message of the Day," which would then be read aloud by Virginia.[8]

These "Messages of the Day" surely strengthened communal bonds. Conceivably they institutionalized Jacob's charisma in the presence of Virginia. These messages likewise expressed a religious belief. Perhaps in more understandable terms, Spirit Fruiters revealed that even though their beloved Jacob was beyond their physical reach, he was surely not beyond their love.

Specifically, these daily messages served several useful functions and they likely contributed to the Society's leisurely rather than rapid decline following Jacob's sudden death. Most of all, these communications became the religious "event," the first form of structured service. When Jacob was alive, he talked ("lectured") to outside audiences, and he commonly conducted weekend or Sunday seminars in the colony house, both in Lisbon and Ingleside. These presentations attracted friends and those curious about Spirit Fruit. Yet Jacob never insisted upon any fixed format for these discussions: he simply set a time. When strangers were absent, talk among his closest followers on religious matters was casual. Seemingly, there was no good reason for organization. "We lived there [Ingleside] as part of our experience in Universal Life," observed Kate Waters. "We sought to grow in love. It was our expression of *continual* [sic] worship, if you will." With Jacob's passing, however, the lectures and seminars ended. Communal life, though, continued, and it allowed Spirit Fruiters to share and enjoy universal love. "We still give freely of ourselves," remarked Virginia in 1911, "and we are always attempting to prevent the evil of selfishness from entering our lives." Yet these daily messages undoubtedly reminded everyone of Jacob's teachings and the way of life each had chosen. "I think these messages," argued Robert Knowdell, "became the focal point of their religious being."[9]

Another value of these messages included their comforting qualities. Apparently Virginia and Ma received additional contacts from Jacob when there was a crisis or individual distress. "These messages always had a settling effect," recalled Evelyn Beilhart Hastings, the older of the "love" children. "Jacob's words that Virginia would read seemed sort of meaningless to me, but I suppose that they brought solace and guidance to the folks."[10]

Still another aspect of Jacob's spiritual contact involved its impact upon the decision to maintain the society. "Virginia once said," reflected Evelyn Beilhart Hastings, "that the Daily Messages kept her going, that she had purpose in her life." Since Virginia was the leader, her determination to "keep going" was not insignificant. Others, too, seemingly felt this way. Indeed, several outside followers of Jacob from Massachusetts came to live in the colony following his death. They wanted to be an intimate part of "Jacob's family."[11]

The Spirit Fruit Society, however, unmistakably slipped after 1908. While commitment to Jacob's teachings did not flag, the colonists at Ingleside abandoned the Society's outreach activities. Virginia, the official leader, did not embark upon any program of lectures or seminars. Her passive-type personality was likely a contributing factor. (This docility was a common trait of the other communards.) And the colony's presses stopped; there would never be another issue of the sect's publications after Jacob's death. "The folks remained together, I guess content to be self-contained without bringing more people into the group for those seminars," related Evelyn Beilhart Hastings. Clearly, Jacob, while seeking to share his religious insights, never sought to create a large commune. Small to him and undoubtedly to his core followers meant better; individuals in utopia should be limited to those who wholly grasped the meaning of Spirit Fruit. "I think large community life is not a success," Jacob once concluded, adding, "there are very few ready for true freedom."[12]

Even though the Spirit Fruit Society ended its outreach efforts after Jacob's death, his followers continued to labor hard to make their unique religious experiment work. This involved more than successfully handling the daily and annual cycle of domestic and farm chores: they decided in 1913 to move to California. Several factors conceivably prompted this decision. For one thing, midwesterners knew about the Golden State's positive image, except perhaps for earthquakes. Although no one had direct California ties, Virginia or some other Spirit Fruiters may have recalled that Jacob had talked glowingly about the state. Surely, too, they knew of the thriving Theosophical colony at Point Loma. Then, also, the simple desire to start afresh, with a site that was more manageable and in a more temperate climate, likely had strong appeal.[13]

By 1915, Spirit Fruiters had launched their third farming operation, "Hilltop Ranch," where they would stay for the next thirteen years. This eighty-acre parcel, located near the Santa Cruz County village of Soquel, offered a potentially amenable environment in a much appreciated Mediterranean-like climate. But unfortunately the land lacked fertility and there were no improvements of any type. Still, Jacob's followers persisted, and in time they created a diverse agricultural base and erected a comfortable, albeit cheaply built house.

While at Hilltop, several of the core members drifted away. Two who left were Ralph Galbreath, then forty-seven, and Emily Leonhardt, seventeen years his senior. They departed together and in an amicable fashion. Perhaps they left to become independent property holders, yet they, in some ways more than the remaining communards, wanted to promote Jacob's teachings. Soon, living on an acreage in Newhall, California, near the San Fernando Valley, Ralph and Emily, who never married, became closely tied with an eccentric local philosopher, LeRoy "Freedom Hill" Henry. During the mid-1920s the Freedom Hill Pressery, located in Burbank, California, reprinted a large portion of Jacob's writings, a publishing venture that continued with Henry and others until the mid-1940s.[14]

Although never part of the core group of Spirit Fruiters, Freedom Hill Henry showed great enthusiasm for Jacob and his religious notions. In a letter to the librarian at the University of California at Berkeley, he explained that "[M]y chief object in reprinting the Beilhart papers is to have them preserved for future generations." He added: "I believe they will be read a thousand years from now as we now read the letters of Paul. . . ." Remembered Robert Knowdell, "Freedom Hill Henry became sort of the publishing arm of the Society after its move to California." But Freedom Hill Henry was not much of an organizer. "He was a nice old village philosopher who thought that my uncle's writings would sell themselves. . . . I guess that it was what Jacob would have wanted anyway." Indeed, the founder of Universal Life never sought to create a church militant. The anarchist ideal—not the Church of Rome—was his model. The Spirit Fruit Society always glorified voluntary action.[15]

Ralph and Emily, though, apparently contemplated a more organized effort to "save" the Society. Again, as Robert Knowdell recalled, "I think that Ralph and Emily desired to make my uncle's beliefs the basis for some on-going and expanded kind of church." He made this insightful statement: "The folks at Hilltop were getting too old and too tired to break out of their routine. . . . [T]he ranch took up too much of their time . . . [and] they couldn't see themselves carrying on with any type of outreach activities." Surely Ralph and Emily knew this.[16]

Likely the zeal of Ralph and Emily and the publications of the Freedom Hill Pressery brought the sect to the attention of several individuals who would subsequently exercise a pronounced impact on the colonists. About 1920, the Society gained two new residents. The backgrounds of "Dr." William Wilsdon, a stocky, bearded Englishman, and Charles Ritchie are obscure. Wilsdon, or "Uncle Billy" as he insisted on being called, was in his midseventies and a bachelor. He knew about Jacob's writings and claimed to be a "convert." Ritchie, who came because of Wilsdon, was in his early sixties, a widower, and a recent immigrant from Canada. A quiet fellow, he was apparently "slow in the head."[17]

The Spirit Fruiters, who by this time included Virginia and seven others, accepted the presence of Wilsdon and Ritchie. Uncle Billy claimed that he *alone* understood the writings of Jacob and thereafter demanded that everyone accept his authority. These trusting, gentle souls acquiesced, and "he moved into Virginia's position."[18]

Life became hellish. After declaring Ma's messages from Jacob to be "pure rubbish," Uncle Billy ordered these sessions stopped and then used that after-meal time to harangue and embarrass members. The trauma created by Wilsdon's antics prompted several members to leave, and this severely injured the commune's financial base.[19]

That colonists would not inititally resist Wilsdon was predictable. The Society's strongly held core philosophy of life glorified passive, nonviolent behavior and human connectedness, even though Uncle Billy thoroughly disrupted their daily harmony. Conceivably, though, their dead leader's spirit would guide them. What would Jacob do? Of course, he would turn the other cheek and hope for the best. Maybe their collective love could transform the dreaded Billy.[20]

Just as Jacob and his followers believed that good could come unexpectedly, a savior of sorts appeared at Hilltop after a year or so. The newcomer was William Large, a powerfully built six-foot-two Irishman, about fifty-five years old "with a likable personality and a tremendous sense of humor." Like Uncle Billy, the second "Billy" claimed to know Jacob's teachings, although his background is a mystery.[21]

As might be expected, Wilsdon showed utter contempt for the newcomer. He tried to embarrass and ridicule Large before the group. The younger Billy, however, did not allow himself to be browbeaten.

Rather, he first laughed in Wilsdon's face and then ignored him completely. Shortly, though, Large had had enough of Wilsdon and his dim-witted friend. At an evening meal he told Uncle Billy to leave. "Virginia and I have decided you are to be given a choice: either you vacate this premise within twenty-four hours, or I will personally throw you down the hill and your belongings after you!" Wilsdon and Ritchie left the next day.[22]

The forced exodus of Uncle Billy Wilsdon ushered in a period of relaxation and readjustment. The nearly forgotten spirit of companionship and good will returned, and the noontime group ritual—spiritual communications—resumed. Although the ranks had dwindled, the five remaining individuals, joined by Billy Large, carried on with their strenuous life. This aging sect tenaciously clung to its communal ways. Membership appeared to possess sacred qualities, and the emotional interaction between these communards remained great. Yet no one suggested expansion, not even Large. "The folks had withdrawn from the world really . . . they just wanted to live out their lives in peace and enjoy the goodness that Jacob had created within them."[23]

Unfortunately, the twilight years of the Spirit Fruit Society were marred by great sadness—Virginia's declining health. In 1924, she developed carcinoma of the uterus; she was then forty-four, and her overall health slowly worsened. In time she abandoned her participation in Ma's Message of the Day, and thus ended a vital and meaningful religious ritual begun in 1908. By the latter part of 1928 members decided to leave Hilltop. They sold most of their possessions at a public auction and moved into a rented house in Soquel. When Virginia died in June 1930, the Society dissolved. No one, not even Billy Large, sought to maintain it.[24]

It seems doubtful that anyone could have energized the Spirit Fruit Society internally during the 1920s. Billy Large perhaps was in a position to do so, but he lacked the zest and probably the skills to do so. He seemed content to work on the ranch and be Virginia's lover. Members, as already noted, were satisfied to live out their days in tranquility. They lacked any discernible desire to preserve Jacob's blueprint for human happiness.

The sect unmistakably experienced an organic life cycle. The gestation and youth periods at Lisbon were lively as were the years of maturity at Ingleside. Then old age characterized the Society at Hilltop, and death overtook it in Soquel. Observed Robert Knowdell: "Without Jacob around the group developed like any human does—it grew old and perished with Virginia's death." Thus the Spirit Fruit sect died with the prophet's consort.[25]

The better chance for the Spirit Fruit Society to have maintained itself and thus to have avoided what became its fate in 1930 lay in the activities of Ralph, Emily, and Freedom Hill Henry. But for whatever reasons, they could do little to sustain Universal Life. If anything, they hurt the group by conceivably prompting arrival of the wicked Uncle Billy Wilsdon. Still, Freedom Hill Henry preserved the writings of Jacob; most issues of his newspapers and pamphlets would probably have been lost or difficult to obtain if his pressary had not reprinted them. Admittedly, these works had some minor impact. The most notable comments came from a resident of Delhi, India, in 1929, a Dr. R. Narayan. "[R]eading of Jacob Beilhart's 'Spirit Fruit and Voice' made a remarkable change in my viewpoint." Narayan, moreover, included Jacob's volumes (ones reprinted by Freedom Hill Henry in the 1920s) in his *Descriptive Catalogue of Dr. R. Narayan's Lending Library of Books for Seekers after Truth*, and perhaps exposed Jacob's ideas to a larger audience.[26]

One wonders what would have happened to the Spirit Fruit Society if Jacob had lived a normal lifespan. Maybe the communal sect would have been longer lasting, like the two others that thrived contemporaneously within the Chicago area: the Christian Catholic Apostolic Church in Zion of John Alexander Dowie, and Koreshan Unity of Cyrus Read Teed. Nevertheless, the death of Jacob, this particular "prophet," did not kill off his sect immediately. His core of followers developed strong bonds of commitment: they liked each other; they found solace in a gentle, loving household; and they thought daily of Jacob and his message of Universal Life.

The saga of the Spirit Fruit Society suggests one scenario for the direction of religious utopias after a prophet's death. Obviously, Jacob's passing in November 1908 failed to trigger the Society's total collapse. Rather, this tiny religious utopia moved into a moribund-like stage, which lasted for more than a score of years. Then when the sect's second head, Virginia Moore, died, it did so as well. Jacob's death, however, was unmistakably a watershed event in the Society's history. Its vitality ended with the physical loss of its founder-leader, but an inertia of sorts developed and sustained hard-core followers for various lengths of time. The Spirit Fruit Society represents superbly what might be considered an intermediate type of phenomenon of what happens when prophets die. It differs from the "conventional wisdom" that says that when a leader departs so does his handiwork, and also from those utopias that experience a longtime, albeit perhaps splintered continuation.

9

The Rastafari of Jamaica

Barry Chevannes

Introduction

The Rastafari of Jamaica owe their religion not to any single founder, but to several prophetic voices all preaching around the same time, between 1930 and 1933, and independently of one another. Some sixty years later, the Rastafari has remained an acephalous religious movement. Charismatic personalities have come and gone, many of them passing into obscurity along with the groups they led, yet the movement grew, even up the social ladder and across the seas. This chapter examines and explains this phenomenon. As in the chapter on the Hutterites elsewhere in this volume, the central issue is not what has happened to the Rastafari after the death of its founder, but what has accounted for its vigorous growth and flourishing despite its lack of centralised leadership. In this respect the reader is provided with another sharp contrast to the other religious movements presented in this book, the better to arrive at more general conclusions. In what now follows, the main phases of growth in the history of the Rastafari movement are identified and their main features described, but the focus rests upon the issue of leadership.

Rastafari Beliefs

Two tenets are central to the beliefs of the Rastafari: the divinity of the late Emperor Haile Selassie I of Ethiopia, and the repatriation of the Africans exiled in the Americas. From these two are derived others: God is black, and by virtue of this all black men have within them the divine attribute. Also, the presence of black people in Jamaica is not just analogous to the captivity of the children of Israel in Babylon, but is the Babylonian exile itself, foreshadowed in the Bible. Blacks are true Israel and Jamaica is Babylon.[1]

In later developments associated with the rise of the Dreadlocks in the 1950s several beliefs and practices have come to characterise the Rastafari. First is the use of *cannabis sativa*, or ganja as it is known in Jamaica, as a sacrament, which they smoke in their sacred communal "reasoning" (discussion). Second is the wearing of matted hair, known as "dreadlocks." It is this practice that most people associate with the Rastafari. They themselves regard growing dreadlocks as a necessity on the part of anyone who has acquired the consciousness of himself as a black man and refer to the practice as "to dread up," or "nat up." Such locks are sacred. Rastafari cite the Nazarite vow[2] as Biblical precedence, but at the same time regard the practice as permanent rather than temporary.

Third, the Rastafari have evolved a strong male bias to their religion. Women are not considered capable of achieving Rastafari consciousness except through the guidance of their male Rastafari spouses;[3] they are, regardless of age, known by the title of "daughter;"[4] they do not as a rule participate in rituals; and they must observe the menstrual taboo.[5]

Fourth is the development of a new argot, centralised mainly on "I," the personal pronoun,[6] and expressing underlying philosophical concepts about man and nature.[7] Many Rastafari words are now common to everyday creole speech among young people.

Fifth, from the 1960s, Rastafari and Jamaican reggae music have come to share a close identity. Reggae, as a protest music, became the medium of expression for Rastafari, by far the most articulate protest movement in Jamaica.[8]

Origins

Before presenting the events and personalities responsible for actually bringing the Rastafari into being, I first examine two structural factors, namely class and race.

At the time of the founding of Rastafari in the 1930s, Jamaica's social structure looked roughly like a broad-based pyramid, at the very top a small ruling elite, comprised of colonial administrators, merchants, and wealthy landowners; below them the coloured, mulatto professional, and business people;[9] and at the bottom the working masses: peasants, workers, and artisans.

The peasantry owed its formation to the exodus from the estates immediately following emancipation from slavery in 1938. It grew not only in numbers in the ensuing decades but in its own internal social differentiation as well. The more impoverished section at first sought refuge in migration to the banana plantations of Central America, to the Panama canal, to the United States, and finally to Cuba, and when these avenues became closed early in the 1920s and what Marshall calls a "period of saturation and decline" set in,[10] they flocked to the major towns and cities, looking for a better life. Out of this demographic movement came the founding members of the Rastafari.

This social pyramid was at the same time a racial one, white at the top, black at the bottom, and coloured in between, a distribution inherited from slave society and reinforced during the colonial period. Speaking of the period up to 1865, Philip Curtin remarked that whereas in the American South, economic and social issues hid behind the race question, in Jamaica the reverse was true.[11] In the Morant Bay Rebellion of 1865 (which most scholars attribute to hunger for land, to injustice, or to poor administration: to anything but race, that is), "colour for colour" was the rallying cry of many of the rebels. Race and colour figured also in the agitation of the Revival[12] prophet Alexander Bedward, who was arrested in 1895 for sedition.[13]

So powerful is the role of race and colour within the system of social stratification that M. G. Smith, in an attempt to come to grips with it, adapted Furnivall's economic model of pluralism to argue that Caribbean societies on a whole were divided by socio-cultural pluralism.[14] The three racial segments belonged to the same society, the same polity, but they each had their own distinct and separate cultural practices and norms.

While few Caribbeanists still hold to the plural society model, none can dismiss race and colour as of no consequence. A vital consideration is the fact that there still operates within the social structure of Jamaica, as also of other Caribbean countries, an ideology of race and colour, with white colour and European culture valued as good and positive, and black colour and African culture despised as bad and negative. Nothing has escaped this ideology, not even mating patterns and other social institutions.

Inevitably, racialist ideology bred its own opposition, which took both religious and political forms. First was the rise of Myal religion that replaced tribal with pan-African identity in the eighteenth century.[16] Myal incorporated many Christian beliefs and from 1860 adopted the name Revival. What is significant in this development is that Revival or Myal became a folk religion, in much the same way that Vodun ("voodoo") became a folk religion of the Haitian people. It had a belief system that functioned throughout the country independently of any organized structure. Such structures as did exist functioned independently of each other. In other words, Revival was an acephalous movement that gave the Jamaican peasant masses a worldview.

But it was a warped worldview, in the sense that it incorporated elements from the prevailing racial ideology. For example, the millennial dream of Prophet Bedward, the greatest of the Revival prophets, pictured a heaven in which the saved would become white.[17]

The rejection of this worldview is what the Rastafari movement is all about. How this became possible depended on two other developments in popular consciousness: the rise of Ethiopianism among the people, and the teachings of Marcus Garvey.

Garveyism

A second source of opposition to racist beliefs was Garveyism.[18] Realising that blacks were themselves handicapped by their own feelings of inadequacy and inferiority, Garvey refashioned the views of blacks about themselves, attacking the ideological underpinnings of racism, upholding black racial dignity, but at the same time being hard on those blacks whose beliefs and actions, he thought, contributed to their being treated as inferior.

In Jamaica, although Garvey formed a political party, ran for public office, and served as an elected representative, his most lasting impact lay in the opportunity his teachings provided for correcting the ideological defects in the Revival worldview, an opportunity seized by many Jamaicans, including those who became the founders of Rastafari and many of those who became its earliest members. However, for the bold step to be taken to identify the Emperor of Ethiopia as God, there was need for a particular focus. This was provided by Ethiopianism.

Ethiopianism

The term *Ethiopianism* has been used to refer to the tendency among certain black nationalist movements to identify Ethiopia as a symbol for all Africa, present, past, and future.[19] The basis for this lies in the ancient use of "Ethiopian" to refer to any black person, as well as in the antiquity of the country that adopted the name. Ethiopia is mentioned in the Bible. Many of the prophetic and nationalist churches in South Africa were "Ethiopian."

Prior to the emergence of the Rastafari, Ethiopianism in Jamaica had three sources: the Bible itself, on whose strength alone some of the earliest Rastafari declared that they were Ethiopians; the influence of the African Methodist Episcopal Church, "with almost half a century behind it of links with Ethiopianism and the independent church movement in South Africa";[20] and Garvey, whose repeated use of Ethiopia or Abyssinia to symbolise all of Africa was all too familiar to his followers and supporters.

Later, after the Rastafari appeared, there were several other factors that intensified Ethiopianism, such as the activity of certain individuals, some of whom claimed to have actually been to Ethiopia; the circulation of texts such as the *Ethiopic Bible of St. Sosimas*[21] and of the *National Geographic* pictorial of the emperor's coronation; the invasion of Ethiopia by Fascist Italy and the war of liberation that followed, including the use of the "Holy Ark of the Covenant, the most sacred relic of the Christian Church of Ethiopia, which it is firmly believed came from Solomon's temple in Jerusalem" to lift the morale of the soldiers;[22] and the international campaign of support waged by the Imperial Government itself, including the establishment of the Ethiopian World Federation.

The Coronation

At the time the only independent nation in all of Africa, Ethiopia quite suddenly got worldwide attention with the coronation of Ras Tafari as Emperor Haile Selassie I, in November 1930. He took as his imperial title "King of Kings, Lord of Lords, Conquering Lion of the Tribe of Judah." The last part was based upon the claim of the Ethiopian Royal House to be in direct line of descent from Menelik I, son of the Queen of Sheba, or ancient Ethiopia, and King Solomon of ancient Israel.

That the governments of white countries could pay such homage to a black nation was not lost on some Garveyites. A play put on by Garvey the year before, entitled *Coronation of the African King*, would have been still fresh in their minds and thought of now as prophetic. More importantly, Tafari's imperial titles received the greatest interest.

The Messiah prophesied by the Hebrew prophets was to come from the tribe of Judah, to which King David, Solomon's father, belonged. Isaiah not only made mention of this, but referred to him as the Lion of Judah. And in the Book of Revelation, "he had on his vesture and on his thigh a name written, King of Kings and Lord of Lords." Was this not a case of Ethiopia stretching forth her hands unto God? And if this was so, did it not make sense now that the kings and princes of the world paid him homage?

With such exegesis as this, at least three men came to the conclusion independently of each other, and began to preach, that Ras Tafari, the newly crowned Black Emperor of Ethiopia, was God, the returned Messiah.[23] Leonard Howell is generally thought to have been the very first to begin preaching this doctrine, but Joseph Hibbert and Archibald Dunkley were also early on the scene. At first an associate of Howell, Robert Hinds also had his own independent organisation. Together these four men are regarded as founders of the Rastafari movement in Jamaica, though there were clearly others.[24]

Except for a brief spell by Howell in the rural parish of St. Thomas, the early preachers directed their message to the urban poor, who, as I have already said, were mainly rural migrants. They quickly made their impact felt. By 1934 Howell and Hinds were indicted together for sedition. By 1936–37, with Howell still the main preacher from his base in St. Thomas, there were calls being made by prominent persons in the society for the suppression of the movement.[25]

Leadership

Due to an insufficient understanding of the religion, earlier scholars mistakenly filled the space of charismatic leader with Marcus Garvey.[26] They based their view on the fact that the Rastafari attributed to Garvey the prophecy of a new king in Africa whose coronation would signal the hour of redemption of the black race, and on Garvey's back-to-Africa movement, which seemed the same as the Rastafari doctrine of Repatriation. This is quite wrong. Marcus Garvey was critical not only of the emperor but of the group of people who believed him to be God.[27] Moreover, the Rastafari themselves do not regard Marcus Garvey as their founder, though they revere him as a great prophet.

Could Haile Selassie be considered the charismatic leader, a human being endowed by his followers with divinity? When the emperor visited Jamaica in 1966 he was met by an enthusiasm knowing no parallel among state visits to the island. But Selassie himself at no time acknowledged being the leader of the Rastafari, either on this or on any other occasion, and remained an Ethiopian Orthodox.[28] Charismatic leadership requires an organic relationship between leader and followers, which has never existed between the emperor and the Rastafari.

The fact is the Rastafari is an acephalous black nationalist religious movement, more akin to the Zionist and Ethiopianist movements in South Africa than, say, to the Black Muslims in the United States. Groups there are (and while all groups share in the core beliefs, they nevertheless remain separate and independent) organized around charismatic and noncharismatic leaders. One consequence of this is that the Rastafari movement itself outlasts the ups and downs of its leaders and groups. Development of this argument will be the burden of the remainder of this chapter.

The Founding Phase

I consider this phase to have lasted for roughly twenty years, ending with the breakup or supersession by 1954 of the organizations of the four founding leaders: Howell, Hinds, Hibbert, and Dunkley. Following are the main features of this period.

Any new movement, be it religion or political party, must seek to win a following on the basis of its new ideas. The "King of Kings" people, as the Rastafari called themselves, were no different. Although the millennial dream was present from the beginning and Howell had on one occasion fixed a date for repatriation, 1 August 1934, the main thrust of the new faith was spreading the message that Ras Tafari, a black man, was God, King of Kings and Lord of Lords. Instrumental in convincing many people were the picture of the Black Christ, which they would unfold and pass around at high points in their street meetings, and the Bible, the revealed word of God. The book of the Bible most used by millenarian movements within the Christian tradition is The Book of Revelation, in which is set down the vision of the new Jerusalem, won after the triumph of the forces of good over evil. Written during or shortly after the first century, the Book has for a long time been known to be powerfully symbolic, the lamb representing the returned messiah and the beast with whom he does apocalyptic battle representing imperial Rome. The coronation events, taken as prophetic; Tafari's regal claims and titles; the invasion of Ethiopia by the Italian ruler, Mussolini; the picture of the emperor seated upon a white horse; and of him standing with an unexploded Italian bomb beneath his

foot—all would have conspired to prove the fulfillment of the prophecies in the Book of Revelation and other sections of the Bible. And
they prove not only that Ras Tafari is God, but that God is black. The
life histories of the earliest converts confirm that during the 1930s, at
least, the main focus of the Rastafari preachers was on these points of
doctrine.[29]

A second feature was their confrontation with the state police. As
far as I am aware, Hibbert was the only one of the four leaders who
was not at some point sentenced to imprisonment or interned in the
mental asylum. All had their meetings broken up or their missions
raided by the police. Howell, considered the most dangerous, was
routed three times.

According to Post, action against the Rastafari was inevitable, given
their preaching of an end to the colonial system.[30] However, the fact
that other anticolonial groups were not similarly treated suggests that
there was more to it. Post himself provides a clue when he draws
attention to the remarkable similarity of Howell to Bedward. Bedward's
arrest had been prompted by the fears that an antiwhite outbreak was
a distinct possibility given his charismatic agitation.[31] Then, too, following his deportation from the United States in 1926, Marcus Garvey was
carefully watched by the government. However, while Garvey's black
nationalism remained within the legal-political framework, that of the
Rastafari went outside it. They preached withdrawal of allegiance to
the king of England, but, even more dangerously, their doctrine explicitly devalued the ideological standing of whites. In my view, the
Rastafari were a dangerous group to the society because they threatened
the principles of white overlordship on which whites had based their
hegemony. They remained a source of great concern to the government
up to the first decade of independence in 1962.

A third feature was the charismatic leadership of the four founders.
Each was not just a talented preacher, but a man seemingly possessing
gifts from God. Hinds and Dunkley were regarded as prophets, and
Hibbert was thought to possess powers to see into the past and future.

The main charismatic figure was Leonard Howell. Not only did
he attract the largest street crowds, but he regarded himself and was
regarded by his followers as divine. By 1934 songs were already being
sung in his honour.[32] His authority was supreme. He was believed to
be a member of the Trinity, along with Garvey and Selassie. Like Hibbert,
he too maintained a healing practice, so much so that the police raiding
party of 1954, not finding him at Pinnacle, swooped down on Number
60B East Queen Street, "occupied by self-styled Dr. Leonard Howell,
former 'King' of Pinnacle."[33]

Fourth, none of the vibrant organizations built up by these original preachers outlasted them. Indeed, all except one of these preachers died in obscurity. The exception is Dunkley, who as of writing is still alive but without a following. Hinds was the first to pass away. When he died, not a single person was on hand to attend his funeral. He was buried in a pauper's grave.

On being dispersed, the Howellites settled in various places as best they could, some in Kingston, others in lower Clarendon, and still others in a community adjacent to Pinnacle, where the "Gong" (short for Gangunju) also lived after his release from the mental asylum and until his death in 1981. But as was the case with the Bedwardites, all that remained to link them with their historic past were memories.

The question we must ask ourselves is why such obscure ends for once indisputably charismatic figures? In the case of Hinds, former followers attribute his downfall to corruption and sinfulness.[34] But an examination of the process of disintegration of Hinds's King of Kings Mission provides us with an experience that does seem to run parallel to others within the Jamaican historical tradition.

At first a colleague of Howell, Hinds launched out to form his own King of Kings Mission, which grew into the largest Kingston-based Rastafari organization of the late 1930s and early 1940s; so large, according to informants, that he was forced to devolve authority onto a "Cabinet" made up of some of his most senior and talented followers, some of whom could themselves go out on the streets and preach. What this immediately led to was greater independence from Hinds, so that by early in the forties a few of these senior elders had already broken off to form their own small groups. One of these was Morris, from whose group Downer later broke to form his own. At the time of my interview with him in 1975, Downer had long since ceased being the leader of a Rastafari group.

Here then is a process of fission and growth, similar to that noted by Sundkler among blacks in South Africa,[35] where the general ideas of black consciousness are not the result of any one personality but of wider structural causes. As Post observes, "The cult has always been above all a *system of beliefs and a state of consciousness, lacking homogeneity even in this respect.*"[36]

This process of fission and growth is remarkably similar to that which saw the spread of the Revival religion, which, as I have said, unified the Jamaican black population with a worldview that fused African and European belief systems.

The Later Phase

The next phase in the growth of Rastafari, from the late 1940s to 1960, was one dominated by a group I have elsewhere called reformers.[37] This is the group through whose militancy the later additions to the beliefs and practices of the Rastafari to which I drew attention at the beginning of the chapter were made. Thus we might say that reformism was the first characteristic of this particular phase, as they set about purging Rastafari of the remnants of Revival religion, such as the ritual use of candles, the use of books of magic and mysticism, baptism, and the like.

The second feature in this phase was the increase in agitation for Repatriation, a demand already shown to have been made as early as 1934. The call for Repatriation was made more strongly and more consistently during the decade of the 1950s, culminating in classic expressions of the millennial dream. It should be seen against the background of wider social discontent, expressed in a general strike known as the 1938 uprising, and a resurgence of back-to-Africa agitation. The expectations on the part of many people that 1938 and the several years after it had generated were not met either by the land and other reforms initiated by the colonial government or by either of the two political parties that were born out of 1938 and its aftermath, namely the People's National Party (PNP) and the Jamaica Labour Party (JLP). And so, as early as 1945, or one year after the first general elections, thousands of people marched in Kingston under the slogan "Give us work or send us back to Africa."[38] The march was followed in the next five years by other demonstrations and actual emigration to Liberia.

Understandably, therefore, Rastafari expectation of Repatriation grew. In 1958 an all-Rasta Convention called by Prince Emmanuel at his headquarters in the Back-O-Wall slum was expected by many to end in Repatriation. It was well supported, and many were said to have sold or given away their belongings in anticipation of their departure.

The following year, the Reverend Claudius Henry announced 25 October 1959 to be "Decision Day, when all God's scattered people will be returning to Africa," in promotion of which blue cards were sold to be used in place of passports.[39]

The failure of both these prophecies did little to damage the personal charisma of each of these two leaders, though they lost standing in the eyes of other Rastafari, who saw them as "false prophets."

In 1960 Henry was imprisoned for sedition for inviting Fidel Castro to take over Jamaica on their departure for Africa and possesion of a number of illegal weapons. The desire for Cuban intervention, however, reflected a belief still current among the Rastafari that Fidel represents the Amerindians, and in the Rastafari concept of justice the return of Africans to Africa is to be accompanied by the repossession by the original inhabitants of the Americas of lands stolen from them.

The Henry episode took a more complicated turn when a guerrilla group operating under cover of Henry's church killed two British soldiers in a clash. The wave of hostility toward all Rastas that ensued prompted a study by the University of the movement in Kingston. This marked the start of a new phase in the development of the movement.

The New Phase

Beginning in 1960 the Rastafari movement and the rest of the society have been engaged in what Nettleford has called a "mutual accommodation"[40] and Barrett "routinization."[41] Nettleford examines the relationship from the point of view of two significant events in the 1960s. The first was the government-sponsored mission to Africa recommended by the *University Report*. Nothing practical came of it, but the study, the mission itself, and the majority and minority (Rastafari) reports by the delegates stimulated considerable debate throughout the society. The second event was the state visit of Haile Selassie in April 1966, which served to legitimise the Rastafari further.

The second feature was the adoption of Rastafari by the urban youth throughout the 1960s and 1970s, in answer to unemployment and poverty.[42] The capture of the minds of the urban youth introduced a new quality into the Rastafari movement, for they brought with them their social characteristics as well. In this way, for example, the emerging popular music, reggae, came to be associated with Rastafari. Under the artistry of talented youths, these two forms of protest, music and religion, were fused. The political establishment was not slow in realising the importance of and exploiting this development.[43]

Third, beginning late in the 1960s, the Rastafari began to make headway among the middle class. The basis on which this took place was the development of black power radicalism among the intelligentsia from 1968 on. The group that has hosted most middle-class Rastas is the Twelve Tribes of Israel.[44]

Fourth, mention must be made of the internationalisation of the Rastafari. As I suggested at the outset, this is in part linked to the influence of reggae. But the effects of migration cannot be ignored. In Britain, in particular, the British-born children of West Indian immigrants adopted the Rastafari religion and lifestyle in what some saw as a search for identity,[45] or a response to anomie[46] and to British racism. Today there are Rastafari in most of the countries of the Caribbean,[47] including Cuba, where I have met some; in Brazil, Suriname, and Guyana; in some Central American countries; and in all the major cities of North America, Europe, Japan, Australia, and, of course, in the motherland itself, Africa.[48]

The group exploiting this new dimension the most is the influential House of Nyabinggi. As I have already said, the movement is acephalous, in the sense that there is no single head or authority, whether a person or a committee. But at the same time most Rastafari have a common identity as believers that allows for ritual unity. The facilitator of this is the House of Nyabinggi. All Rastafari who do not proclaim a head— the Bobo, whose head is Prince Emmanuel; the Twelve Tribes, whose head is Prophet Gad; and the Henryites, whose head until he died in 1986 was Claudius Henry—identify themselves as belonging to the House. The "House" concept allows for membership solely on the principle of being a Dread. It thus links the international diaspora together.

Organizationally, it operates a simple structure based on eldership, which allows for Rastafari to exercise leadership roles based on religious commitment and personal talent rather than acquired status.[49] Any Dread therefore could become an elder. A council of "seventy-two" elders (in reality any number that assemble), all men, operating democratically and allowing free expression, oversees the business of the House, such as planning and executing the celebrations and, now, the international delegations and contacts. Delegations over the past decade have been to the United Kingdom, Canada, the United States, and several Caribbean countries, and three International Conferences have taken place.

Given this open sort of structure, it is difficult for personalised leadership of the Howell, Henry, or Prince Emmanuel type to emerge. Many dynamic and influential personalities have emerged throughout the history of the House, but the pattern is for their influence to decline after a few years.

The Future

The emergence of an intellectual stratum within the movement has already led to philosophising[50] and self-examination[51] of a kind that could well bring about shifts in the teachings of Rasta. What happens to the movement, however, depends equally on the status of the racial and colour questions, which incontestably lie at the foundation of this religion. Research carried out in 1983 found that existing class differences between the racial groups in Jamaica were due to racial and not solely to class origins.[52]

But there is still no clear consensus as to how racism operates in Jamaica. Gordon speaks of "racial forces" operating directly "in terms of economic power," and indirectly "through the medium of culture and ideology"[53] while Professor Stone sees the ethnic minorities as having to practice racism "because they have not really been challenged by a sustained effort by Blacks to break into corporate power."[54] In this regard, Stone identifies weak ethnic bonding of blacks as a debilitating flaw that puts them at a disadvantage in relation to the ethnic minorities.

It seems reasonable to conclude, therefore, that Rastafari will continue to attract and hold a following to the extent that race and colour remain fundamentally unresolved questions. To the extent, however, that the social structure is able relatively quickly in the current period to absorb blacks, Rastafari will have to adjust its ideas in order to remain an influential movement. Should it fail to make such an adjustment, it still will have made an inestimable contribution to shaping a more positive worldview.

10

The Call of the Lotus-Eyed Lord: The Fate of Krishna Consciousness in the West

Steven J. Gelberg

While it would be premature to write its epitaph, the Hare Krishna movement, one of the most visible of the new religious movements that rose to prominence in America in the last quarter century, has lately been in a state of deteriorating health.[1] For a time it appeared that the International Society for Krishna Consciousness (ISKCON) was undergoing a relatively smooth and successful transition to new leadership following the passing of its charismatic founder and leader, A.C. Bhaktivedanta Swami Prabhupada, in 1977, but eventually an unexpected series of dramatic internal events broke that calm and plunged the members of the movement into protracted, contentious disagreement over fundamental institutional issues.

ISKCON is now a movement in transition. Recruitment and institutional cohesion are down; many centers are experiencing financial crisis, and some have closed. Lowered standards and weakened commitment have led to confusion about concepts of, and policies concerning, membership. Large numbers of the elder and more experienced members have left the movement over the last several years, re-entering a secular world formerly rejected as bleak and brutalizing, in pursuit of education, skills, credentials, and job security. All these factors have contributed to a general lowering of morale among members, for indeed, as Kenneth Westhues suggests, "The waning of the strength of a religious community is to the members the waning of themselves."[2]

I will here explore the problem of transmission of authority in ISKCON mainly by exploring the implications for the movement of this fundamental question: What happens when a religious tradition or movement historically and culturally rooted in one part of the world is picked up and transplanted onto foreign soil and appropriated by foreigners? A number of subsidary questions follow on the heels of this one: During transplantation, when is the integrity of the tradition preserved and when has it become fundamentally transmuted? At what point does healthy and necessary adaptation become degenerative assimilation? Is there some spiritual "essence" of a tradition that can survive cultural transplantation? Can those in the new location who embrace the transplanted tradition truly embrace it—that is, experience a true and profound encounter with it and become genuinely transformed by it—or is their act of appropriation merely one of "make believe," imitation, exotic role-playing, however sincere the attempt at immersion and self-transformation may be? How, ultimately, does one define and measure the genuineness of any cross-cultural religious transplantation?

Such questions have been raised as long as missionaries have taken their faith to foreigners. In our own time, these questions have been revived with the proliferation of Hindu and Buddhist movements in the West that have attracted a predominantly Western clientele. But the questions have been buried under a mountain of polemics, propaganda, litigation, and public censure. Even scholars, although often interested in matters of authenticity and orthodoxy ("Has such-and-such group altered the teachings of the parent tradition? Do they perform the right rituals?"), rarely confront the more subtle psychological issues involved, especially those concerning the question of a genuine, interior, psychological encounter with and appropriation of a "foreign" path, with all that implies for radical self-transformation. To get at the heart of the matter requires, at the least, a genuine encounter with followers of Eastern traditions on a personal level. My own prolonged participation in the Hare Krishna movement has, I believe, yielded some useful perspectives and insights into the issues I will be addressing below vis-à-vis ISKCON.

In all the essentials, doctrine and practice in the Hare Krishna movement conform to those of the parent tradition, Chaitanya Vaishnavism, itself an important and authentic movement within the broader Indian tradition of Vaishnava *bhakti*.[3] It appears, then, that the tradition has been transmitted to the West—but has it been fully received? The genuine seed has been planted, but has it germinated in foreign soil, broken through foreign weeds, and begun to grow toward maturity?

It should be noted at the outset that the Chaitanya tradition has long defined itself as a universal faith, eminently worthy of exportation. Vaishnava devotional traditions have almost always been willing to embrace the low-caste and the foreigner.[4] Chaitanya himself is said to have predicted that Krishna's holy names would one day be sung "in every town and village of the world." The Chaitanyaite Bhaktisiddhanta Saraswati (1874–1937) tried, unsuccessfully, to initiate a mission in London; it was his disciple, A.C. Bhaktivedanta Swami, who sailed to the United States in 1965 and founded ISKCON there. Bhaktivedanta, later known by the honorific "Prabhupada," had doubts about his mission; Americans seemed too hopelessly mired in the pursuit of hedonistic materialism to be capable of embracing the simple, ascetical life of devout Vaishnavas. He later recalled that prior to his journey to America he "never imagined that even one person would accept" the strict and ascetic lifestyle he wished to propagate.[5] Yet if Krishna wanted his glories to be chanted in every town and village, who could stop it?

It was with this sense of paradox—of Americans' impiety and profligacy, and Krishna's power to effect an auspicious dispensation—that Bhaktivedanta initiated his mission in a tiny storefront in New York's Lower East Side. The first followers, mostly hippies, had few strictures placed on them; for now, chanting the Hare Krishna mantra was sufficient for initial "purification." The movement was informal; the devotees' attention was fixed on Bhaktivedanta himself, not on a mysterious, highly elaborated religion from India. Gradually, however, the community began to mature. Thomas Hopkins, an early academic observer of the movement, found that between 1967 and 1969 the movement had changed and developed significantly. Many devotees were now studying the Vaishnavite scriptures, observing a full range of Indian rituals, and adopting Indian food and dress.[6] A decade later Hopkins underscored the significance of Bhaktivedanta's having installed a traditional Hindu ritual structure into a Hindu movement in America ("That's something that no other movement has succeeded in doing, not even really tried to do"), and noted, more generally, the contrast between ISKCON and other Hindu movements in America which, he suggests, generally repackage Hindu traditions in Western language and symbols in order to make them more intelligible and palatable to the American spiritual consumer.[7] And in the years following Hopkin's observations, Bhaktivedanta continued to Hinduize the movement even more in its ritual, social, intellectual, and behavioral life.

But Prabhupada's weighty vessel of Chaitanya Vaishnavism ran upon shoals soon after it arrived in Western waters. A bit of history is in order here.

Finding his rapidly growing movement increasingly difficult to administer personally, in 1970 Prabhupada appointed twelve of his most senior disciples to a semi-autonomous Governing Body Commission to oversee ISKCON, with each member assigned to a particular region of the world. From 1970 until Prabhupada's death in 1977, the GBC met annually in India as a planning and administrative board under Prabhupada's supervision. But displays of poor judgment, self-aggrandizement, and infighting among GBC members soon appeared. Prabhupada worried for the future of his young movement: "What will happen when I am not here, shall everything be spoiled by the GBC?"[8] For Prabhupada, it was not enough that his young leaders be competent administrators; he wanted them to be spiritual and moral exemplars as well. He felt emphatically that ISKCON would succeed only if its leaders were true role models: "The example and kindly guidance of our elder members . . . is the most profound force for motivating our students both new and old towards advanced Krsna consciousness. . . . Our personal example must set a guide for them."[9]

Even higher standards were expected of those who later, after Prabhupada's death, would become initiating gurus in ISKCON. In ISKCON's parent tradition, Chaitanya Vaishnavism, the guru is defined not merely as a transmitter of sacred knowledge, but as a representative of God and channel for divine grace. Prabhupada warned that the absolute power attendant on the position of guru, to whom disciples must surrender absolutely, might well corrupt a spiritually immature person.[10] And there is no greater spiritual tragedy than a guru gone bad.

In 1978, at its first meeting following Prabhupada's death, the GBC asserted that Prabhupada had named eleven senior disciples to the position of guru. Within a few years each of them had initiated hundreds of new disciples and had come to be regarded as a "pure devotee," infallible, spiritually advanced, and worthy of the kind of veneration previously reserved for Prabhupada. Between 1980 and 1986, however, five of those eleven were exposed for sex- and drug-related improprieties and other ungurulike behavior. Because all five possessed very substantial regional power and international influence, these incidents sent deep shock waves through the movement, disrupting the organization and severely disquieting devotees.

In reaction to these scandals, a storm of protest arose among many of Prabhupada's disciples. A reform movement gradually took shape, and from it emerged a blizzard of position papers and manifestos seeking corrective measures.

In an incisive essay that became a rallying point for the reformers, Ravindra Svarupa dasa (who holds a doctorate in philosophical theology) argued convincingly that the way the concept of guru had been institutionalized in ISKCON after Prabhupada's death "lies at the crux of ISKCON's most grave and intractable problems."[11] He maintained that Prabhupada's limited authorization for the eleven senior disciples to officiate at initiations on his behalf during his last days (with the acknowledgment that after his death these eleven—but not necessarily only these eleven—might go on to initiate disciples on their own behalf), had been inflated into a magic-wand appointment, conferring semi-divine status on the eleven gurus. The essay points out that guru is not a post attainable through ecclesiastical fiat, but an exalted preceptorial function for which one becomes qualified only by virtue of full submission to one's own guru and by the blessings of Krishna. Thus Prabhupada "did not *appoint* them guru . . . for how can one be appointed to status of full surrender?"[12] Many reformers contended that this misconception had bred inflated self-image, pride, and arrogance among most of the gurus, which led them to backslide in their own observance of ISKCON's spiritual practices, accept excessive adoration and appropriate an opulent style of living, and assume a condescending and authoritarian posture toward their fellow Prabhupada disciples. "Our foolish mistake," admitted one guru later, "was one of imitation. . . . Thus the prayers, titles, big vyasasanas [elevated seats], lavish guru-pujas [worship], Vyasapujas [birthday fetes], lavish living quarters, the personal comforts."[13]

Another source of heated criticism and debate concerned the superimposition of guru authority upon the GBC system of zones of administration. That is, the gurus came to exercise more or less exclusive rights to initiate in the geographical regions already assigned to them as GBC representatives and, further, quickly extended their domains into the administrative territories of nonguru members of the GBC where initiators were needed. This, according to critics, "in effect created many separate ISKCONs or rather, Zonal Societies for Krishna consciousness."[14] As one devotee wrote,

> The creation of eleven gurus in ISKCON has proven to be the most divisive and destructive event in the history of ISKCON. It has caused a polarization of ISKCON into areas of influence: "This is so and so's temple. He's the guru here. If you don't like it, get out!" Thus Srila Prabhupada's disciples were made to feel like foreigners in their own temples. No wonder the majority of them have left![15]

The GBC (comprised largely of gurus) lost the confidence and loyalty of many devotees, who came to view it variously as indecisive, self-interested, and inept. Most seriously, the GBC was perceived to have been co-opted by reactionary gurus and to be in complicity with the corrupt and corrupting guru system. The North American Temple Presidents Association, for example, in 1980 charged the GBC with having "fully supported unqualified men as acaryas [gurus], even in the face of great evidence of their unworthiness. It has misled and misguided thousands of innocent men and women by directing them to surrender to those who have not surrendered to Krishna. . . ."[16]

As the reform movement within ISKCON gained momentum in the early 1980s, it met dogged resistance from most GBC members and gurus. When, however, in 1985–86 three gurus, all powerful apologists for the status quo, were exposed for gross moral impropriety and corruption, most of the resistance to reform collapsed. A humbled GBC approved virtually all reformist demands at its March 1987 meeting. The membership of the GBC itself was reconstituted by removing errant gurus, expelling from ISKCON Kirtanananda Swami, controversial guru of the New Vrindaban community in West Virginia, and adding fifteen devotees widely respected for their integrity. New gurus were named and checks and balances were established to regulate them. The zonal-guru system was abolished, and a judicial system was established for the adjudication of disputes.

Although these reforms have been widely applauded within the movement, it could take ISKCON years to heal the wounds inflicted by years of turmoil and deterioration. Many who might have contributed to a rebuilding, including shunned and disillusioned early reformers, are gone. Many others remain, hopeful about ISKCON's future and committed to working toward reconstruction.

Some sobering and humbling lessons have been learned, albeit the hard way: the corrupting influence of power, especially absolute power, the dangers of mixing political power and spiritual authority, the sometimes deceptive nature of charisma, the rarity of true saintliness. Having had its self-confidence badly shaken, it is likely that the movement will relinquish some of its youthful arrogance and missionary triumphalism, although the invigorating idealism and enthusiasm of its earlier days will be missed.

Although ISKCON is clearly not the vigorous, unified movement it once was, it shows a sometimes surprising resilience. Despite the high rate of defection, the loss over the years of many of the movement's most gifted leaders and administrators, the laicization of many of its married members, and the generally destabilizing effects of years of internal confict, a small but deeply committed inner core of full-time members continues to follow the demanding regimens of Krishna consciousness in more than two hundred temple communities world-wide. These devotees still rise at 4 A.M. for contemplation and worship, to study and discuss the scriptures; they organize large, public festivals, chant and dance in the streets, disseminate literature, and recruit new members. In many cities, every Sunday evening the temple fills to capacity with young, inquisitive seekers, pious Hindus, and others, to chant, hear a sermon, and feast. Somehow life in ISKCON dances on, if not quite as spritely as before.

The political chronology explained, let us now pick up the threads of our initial enquiry concerning authenticity. Returning to circa 1969, when the movement was rapidly becoming more ascetic and more overtly Indian, it is relevant to point out how all this reenculturation and resocialization looked to those submitting to it. From an external perspective it might have appeared simply that a small group of westerners were—especially as the movement developed—consciously embracing a "Hindu" tradition and becoming self-consciously Indian-ized, replacing their natal culture with another more exotic and appealing one, and perhaps exulting in such religious and cultural expatriation. However, the view from "inside" was quite different. For participants in the movement, "Krishna consciousness" was not Indian but "transcendental" (a potent, legitimizing word attached to anything constituent of that sacred culture). As we saw it, we had not affiliated ourselves with a cumulative tradition formed and shaped by particular historical, ideological, and social contingencies, but rather were partaking in an enlightened, transcendent culture—beginningless in time, cosmic in scope, archetypal and paradigmatic for all true human civilization. Our food was not "Indian," but that favored by Krishna, God. Our dress was not that of Indians but that which liberated beings in the spiritual world (Vaikuntha) had always worn—the natural dress of the soul. Puja was not a "Hindu" ritual, but a natural ceremonial expression of the soul's worshipful attitude toward the Deity. Our texts were not Hindu scriptures, but the utterances of enlightened sages speaking out of the fullness of their wisdom and their compassion for all suffering beings throughout the myriad universes of creation. Our chant was intoned to the God of gods and Lord of the universe—the divine author of the Eternal Religion of which the historical religions of the world are but dim and imperfect reflections. To our way of thinking, then, we had not moved from one culture into another but had transcended culture altogether. The cross-cultural transplantation of Krishna consciousness was, for us, not a horizontal movement from East to West, but a vertical movement, as it were, from transcendence to terra firma.

Whatever the truth behind our convictions about the transcendent and universal character of Krishna consciousness, the tradition, once established in the West, exercised a strong appeal to many of those cultural dissidents of the late 1960s who sought meaning, truth, community, and ecstasy. For some, the appeal of Krishna consciousness lay in its strongly theistic and devotional character. For others, the appeal was aesthetic, a response to the movement's shimmering artworks and profound, beautiful tales and myths.[17] In sum, Krishna consciousness was, for some seekers, able to transcend cultural relativity and speak compellingly to deep psychological, social, aesthetic, and spiritual needs.

That Krishna consciousness appealed to some young westerners is clear enough, but the basic question remains: Can an Eastern tradition take root in the West and engage sustained participation of westerners over the long haul? One who asked that question perceptively was the poet and perpetual spiritual seeker Allen Ginsberg, who met Bhaktivedanta in the movement's early days in New York and, though he never became a devotee, kept in close touch with the movement and actively promoted the chanting of the Hare Krishna mantra. In 1969 Ginsberg asked whether the sheer exoticness of Krishna consciousness might reduce its capacity for attracting wide participation in the West.[18] What will be the fate, Ginsberg wondered, of a religious movement "as technical as this, so complicated, requiring so much sophistication in terms of diet, daily ritual . . .? Just how far can this spread by its very complexity?" Prabhupada replied that rigorous practices were necessary to effect a real change in consiousness. Ginsberg then asked, "How many people can that encompass in a place like America? Or are you intending to get only a few devotees . . . who would be solid and permanent?" Bhaktivedanta answered that indeed, "Krishna consciousness is not possible for everyone. . . . Understanding Krishna is not a very easy thing." Although not everyone could be expected to be totally committed to Krishna, the task of a relatively small Krishna movement would be to enlighten the wider public to the knowledge that "sense gratification is not the aim of life."

Ginsberg persisted: "There is a thirst by many, many people for an alternative." At this point in the conversation Prabhupada shifted from an elitist to a more egalitarian stance concerning the accessibility of Krishna consciousness: "If they're actually thirsty, they can adopt this Krishna consciousness. What's the difficulty?" Even a child, he maintained, could chant Hare Krishna. Moreover, Indian dress and diet were not necessary to Krishna consciousness, as long as one kept a vegetarian diet.

A bit later Ginsberg returned to his original theme: "The need is for a large, single, unifying religious movement in America." Replied the Swami, "So, here is Krishna, the All-Attractive. . . . Everything you want will be found in Krishna." The essence of Krishna consciousness, after all, is easy: "Simply chant Hare Krishna. . . . If somebody does not want our rituals, that is not an important thing. We simply recommend that you please chant, that's all."

Ginsberg then wondered: Might it be possible for Americans to find a spiritually efficacious mantra in their own language? Although Prabhupada at first had some problems thinking of any acceptable alternative, he eventually concluded, citing Chaitanya, that God has innumerable names. "We simply say you should chant God's Holy Name. And then you will become purified. . . . If you have an all-attractive Name in your scripture—not manufactured but authorized—then chant that."

The conclusion I draw from the Ginsberg—Prabhupada dialogue is that while the Swami viewed Krishna consciousness—Chaitanya Vaishnavism—as, if not the only, the paramount and most expedient path to spiritual liberation, he acknowledged that few were prepared to embrace it. The fault lay not in the path, but in people's reduced capacity for spiritual commitment and discipline. The path may be difficult (we are, after all, in the dark age of Kali), but those who are sincere about spiritual attainment can surmount the difficulty. In any case, if westerners cannot accept the path of Krishna consciousness, it is not due to any inherent exoticism in the practice itself, but in their simple unwillingness to make the effort.

Let our enquiry now proceed from the theoretical to the concrete: Does ISKCON represent a true and successful transplanting of a non-native religious tradition to Western soil? The question has individual and corporate dimensions: To what extent have individual Westerners, through ISKCON, had a true encounter with the Chaitanya tradition? And does ISKCON itself represent the beginnings of a viable, ongoing community of Western Vaishnavas?

Let us first address the question as it relates to individuals. Prabhupada was determined to create an environment within the ashrams of the Society in which his disciples could radically detach themselves from the material world and absorb their attention in the sacred and transcendent world of Krishna: "If the members of [ISKCON], putting faith in Krsna as the center, live in harmony according to the order and principles of *Bhagavad-gita*, they are living in

Vaikuntha, not in the material world."[19] Daily life is structured in
ISKCON communities to effect spiritual advancement. Devotees rise
by 4 A.M., attend an early service with much chanting, engage in two
hours of individual chanting, attend another service, attend a study
session, and only then have a communal breakfast. Afterward members
engage in a full day of community-centered service of missionary
outreach activities.[20] Such a regimen does not guarantee spiritual
development, but it certainly encourages and facilitates it. As one who
lived the life for many years, I can attest with conviction to the transformative effects of such an intensely lived religious life. Almost anyone
entering into dialogue with Western Krishna devotees will sense that
the devotees have been successfully absorbed into a vital and deeply
felt form of Hindu spirituality.

Yet the progressive institutionalization of ISKCON itself is a prime
mitigating factor *against* the spiritual development ISKCON seeks to
promote. Religion, paradoxically, both needs and is debilitated by institutionalization; without institutions, religious experience can remain
ephemeral and elusive, but the creation of institutions necessarily leads
to a loss of spontaneity and creativity.[21] Religious movements that
explicitly ideologize/theologize—and thus legitimate—institutionalization may inadvertently accelerate the debilitating effects of the process.
In ISKCON's theology the movement itself is explicitly sacrilized. In
Prabhupada's words, "Krsna has descended in the form of the Krsna
consciousness movement." The practical effect of this sacrilization has
been a tendency to define spiritual success more in institutional than
in personal terms. The individual devotee tends to exist for the institution, rather than vice versa. Formal and informal teaching sessions have
generally tended to deemphasize individual contemplative practice and
spirituality in favor of stressing the role of the devotee in the contextual
missionary enterprise. It is, in fact, from the proper execution of that
role that true "spiritual advancement" flows, according to the norma-
tive rhetoric. Thus too much attention on the part of an individual
devotee toward individual spiritual practice might be viewed as inap-
propriately self-indulgent. When stress is given to the importance of
devotional/contemplative practices, it is often voiced in the name of
the missionary imperative—the need to prepare for the hard, practical
work of spreading the word.

This activist ethic might be explained in part as a function of the
devotees' own western-influenced psyches. But Prabhupada himself was
a decided activist whose aphoristic mandate "work now, samadhi later"
has for years been part of the folk ideology of the movement. In
ISKCON inward spirituality had tended to be gauged in terms of out-

ward achievement in an institutionally defined sense. There are in
ISKCON men and women who might be judged saints by the most
rigorous Vaishnava standards, but who often recede into near invisibility
in the movement because they have not distinguished themselves as
successful institutional actors and doers. Sad to say, the Vaishnava
principle of self-surrender to Krishna has often been trivialized as
obedience to a sacrilized hierarchical corporate system.

Other factors than institutionalization have helped keep Western
practitioners from deep spiritual engagement with the Vaishnava tradition. One is a kind of anti-intellectualism stemming from the venerable
religious critique of the limits of human reason; in ISKCON, the devotee
is encouraged to study scripture not for the sake of religious scholarship itself, but for the practical end of shoring up commitment to the
ISKCON worldview and becoming a more effective agent of the movement. Thus, although study of the sacred texts is part of ISKCON daily
life, few devotees become serious students of the tradition in all its
richness. The majority are taught to be content with a rather slim
working knowledge of the very texts the movement has so diligently
and profusely distributed since the late 1960s.

Individual immersion in ISKCON's parent tradition is also limited
by ISKCON's self-imposed quarantine against other contemporary forms
of Chaitanya Vaishnavism in India. Competition among Vaishnavite
gurus in India for disciples has played a role, as has Prabhupada's abhor-
rence of perceived heresies on the part of other teachers and sects. Thus
Prabhupada deliberately isolated his inexperienced Western disciples
from Indian Vaishnavas in general to keep them from potential contamination. A certain kind of orthodoxy may have been preserved, but
potentially nourishing contact with exemplary persons within the living tradition in India was enjoined. Such insularity has caused
psychological and cultural inbreeding within ISKCON that has weakened its spiritual fabric and engendered an unhealthy elitism with regard
to other forms of Chaitanya Vaishnavism. ISKCON's virtual isolation
from the contemporary wellsprings of its Indian roots has deprived
devotees of an important potential source of spiritual inspiration and
invigoration.

Finally, spiritual weakness among Western devotees has derived
from a lack of close and intensive guidance by gurus for their disciples.
Prabhupada had several thousand disciples by the time of his death,
relatively few of whom had had close, sustained contact with him. Most
of his American successor gurus have similarly initiated large numbers
of disciples. Although the guru-disciple relationship does not depend
entirely on physical proximity, important spiritual support *does* emerge

from face-to-face encounters. In ISKCON, discipleship has arguably become something of an abstraction. In India, the more common pattern has been for a guru to minister personally to a smaller group of disciples in an ongoing relationship. The relative lack of this kind of close bonding has hindered spiritual development among some of the Western followers of Krishna.

Let us now turn to an examination of the corporate dimension of the authenticity question—that is, whether or not ISKCON has, as a movement, been successful in establishing itself as a viable Vaishnava community in the West. My answer to this question is, on the whole, rather negative. Several factors have prevented the movement from setting deep roots in Western soil.

The first obstacle is ISKCON's rather stark ideological rejection of the world, and the social isolation that results from that posture. The scriptures undergirding ISKCON are uncompromising in rejecting materialistic society; they see the spiritual quest as requiring radical detachment from worldly attitudes and desires. Thus the ISKCON devotee's essential attitude toward nondevotees has generally been one of mild disdain. Those who seek only to satisfy the animal needs for food, sex, sleep, and self-preservation are essentially no better than animals. These elitist and judgmental elements in the tradition have dominated those encouraging compassion, tolerance, and spiritual empathy with all created beings. Thus devotees generally interrelate with outsiders only in carefully circumscribed, ritualized forms motivated by the missionary imperative. Such insularity does not make for good public relations, much less for productive dialogue with the rest of the world.

ISKCON's theological exclusivism has also impeded a true trans-planting of Krishna consciousness to the West. Viewing itself as an island of truth in a sea of illusion, ISKCON has rarely sought intellectual or theological common ground with its host society. Religions and philosophies not rooted in the "Vedic" revelation have tended to be dismissed out of hand. The insistent and unthinking scriptural literalism with which many devotees preach Krishna consciousness does little justice to the richness and subtlety of Vaishnava texts and commentaries. Theodore Roszak once complained that ISKCON devotees "wield the Bhagavad Gita with all the small-minded literalism and parochial arrogance of any hard shell Baptist preacher quoting scripture."[22] Although some openness has emerged since Roszak wrote those words, much of the arrogant exclusivism remains. Thus there is little possibility that ISKCON will make any real impact on anyone save those willing to venture the long and arduous swim out from the American ideological mainland to the fortified ideological island of ISKCON.

A prime factor in making ISKCON less than attractive to most Western seekers is its uncompromising asceticism. Prabhupada preached a thoroughgoing antimaterialism that included not only the traditional ascetical bans on such items as meat-eating, intoxication, and sex, but also on such pastimes as movies, plays, concerts, sporting events, popular music, and the reading of literature—in short, any indulgence of the mind or senses that does not contribute directly toward the one goal of spiritual purification, enlightenment, and liberation. While those prohibitions are well founded in the Vaishnava tradition, no Indian group in the West has taken these rules and pursued behavioral purity as doggedly as has ISKCON. While ascetic behavior may well lead to spiritual elevation, very few westerners are really capable of it in such extreme terms. In the movement, many (most?) devotees feel the tension between the ideal and the real, expectation and performance—a tension that can create inner turmoil as well as hypocrites galore. My own perception is that an inability or unwillingness to continue a strictly ascetic life plays in most cases a major role in apostasy. It would be impressive if ISKCON were to leave even a small handful of committed ascetical Vaishnavas in the West, but it is doubtful that we could speak, then, of Krishna consciousness as a foreign religious tradition that has actually taken root and grown as a viable and vital alternative to materialistic American culture.

If numbers are a proper criterion for missionary success, Krishna consciousness has not been terribly successful, to date, in indigenizing itself. While Prabhupada often emphasized quality over quantity of disciples, one could hope that a more humane and patient attitude— one that takes a more compassionate view of human weakness—might come to prevail, allowing people more ready access to the tradition at lower levels of asceticism and commitment, as well as acknowledging the legitimacy of the gradual path toward enlightenment. Many efforts in that regard have been made at the local temple level in recent years, but the movement is still far from formulating a clear understanding of the role of lay members versus that of the more highly committed members. Historically, of course, most high-intensity religious movements do, eventually, become more instrumentally oriented and seek to broaden their base of appeal through liberalization and compromise, but often at the cost of the movement's spiritual integrity and vitality. Thus one can sympathize with those who seek to retain "purity" and remain small even while wishing that the tradition could also become, somehow, more authentically "available" to more people, and thus be able to genuinely contribute to the religious life of the West.

Let us also note that an ascetical regimen is not as foreboding when there are exemplars of the path, those who through asceticism and spiritual practice have come to taste the spiritual fruits of their efforts. ISKCON, unhappily, has over the past several years witnessed the humiliation and subsequent apostasy of many "advanced" devotees: thus general confidence in the attainability of the experiential goals of Krishna consciousness has waned. The majority of the appointed successors to Prabhupada have been exposed for corruption and/or immorality (e.g., embezzlement of funds, sex scandals). Thus has come a lowering of expectations for the practical attainment of lofty states of Krishna consciousness; the willingness of members to make substantial sacrifices to attain that experience has similarly decreased. Diminished expectations within the movement will make it harder for devotees to convince others that Krishna consciousness is a practical path to high spiritual attainment.

The failure of most devotees to sustain high ascetical behavior has dampened devotees' convictions not only about the practicability of Krishna consciousness, but about its very truth as well. The example of committed ascetics has been held as proof of the truth of Krishna consciousness itself. Krishna consciousness was "true" because it "worked." It did free its practitioners from sense gratification and desire. But that assumption has been badly shaken. ISKCON's self-image as a bastion against concupiscence and vanity has been tarnished, and this tarnishing has colored the mood of many members.

Perhaps the failure of the ascetic ideal stems from devotees' lack of deep immersion in Vaishnava spirituality. Without an ongoing experience of the higher taste of spiritual satisfaction and bliss, say devotees, the lower attraction of the material world beckons and eventually becomes compelling. As ISKCON has attempted to gain the world through markedly instrumentalist means, it may have lost its own soul—with little missionary success to show for its efforts.

Another obstacle to the successful transplantation of Krishna *bhakti* to the West is the extreme social conservatism of ISKCON, particularly in its attitudes toward women. A movement that preaches a traditional Indian ethic of females as intellectually and spiritually less developed and as corrupters of men to be controlled or "protected" is not likely to be appealing to many women—or empathetic men, for that matter— in the modern West. ISKCON would have to be judged as blatantly sexist by any contemporary standard, and although some women seekers are indeed attracted to the security of a celibate ashram with its promise of redemption from the world of sexual politics and exploitation, most are simply not willing to pay the price of second-class status and subordination to the dominion of males who themselves are demonstrably far from spiritual enlightenment.

Finally, to the extent that the rooting of a tradition is dependent on an institutional base of operations, transplanting will be hampered by ISKCON's recent institutional decline. Internal political destabilization, economic crisis, scandal, and the spiritual disillusionment of many members has certainly taken its toll on institutional cohesion. Many former core members have left. Since minority worldviews tend to be fragile, the gradual wearing away of ISKCON as a strong and cohesive society might lead to a weakening of commitment to a Krishna conscious worldview among devotees. Such a weakening can hardly enhance the dissemination of Krishna consciousness in the larger society.

Although a valiant attempt is being made by the recently reconstituted leadership of ISKCON to rescue the movement from disintegration, it seems likely to me, as a longtime participant/observer, that ISKCON's days of glory are long gone, that the heroic efforts have come too late. The best hope for the survival of Krishna consciousness in the West may lie not in attempts to prop up institutional structures, but in the continuing experience of Krishna consciousness in the hearts and minds of devotees, be they within or without the institutional boundaries of ISKCON. ISKCON in diaspora already is spawning informal grassroots fellowships of institutionally disenfranchised devotees, and it is in these kinds of informal communities that Krishna consciousness in the West may live on, rather than within the artificial and tenuous insularity of ISKCON.

This may require, however, a fundamental change in the way Krishna consciousness "looks" in its Western setting. In the course of the development of a religious tradition in a new cultural environment, the external forms of that community usually change and adapt to local cultural and psychic conditions. Although such mutations may represent a corruption of a tradition, they may also indicate that the tradition is becoming truly indigenized—made truly "available" to those in the new environment. External forms may be merely props that must eventually fall away as the spirituality being practiced and promulgated takes root. As Jacob Needleman has suggested, many historians of religion may take "the props for . . . more than they are," when "what they are really witnessing is often the falling away of the props as the spirit of the religion matures in the inner life of its followers."[23]

I may be wrong about this. Perhaps Prabhupada's rigorous version of Chaitanya Vaishnavism cannot with integrity be adapted to a secular environment. Perhaps Krishna consciousness in the West—in contradistinction to India, where the culture is more congenial to it—can survive only as a monastic institution.

However, the inherent universality of Krishna consciousness, along with the imperative to spread it "to every town and village" in the world, seems to suggest the need to create a greater and more diffuse vehicle to render it more truly accessible—even at the risk of contamination. A Krishna consciousness grown and nurtured in the supposedly germ-free environment of a culturally and ideologically insular institution is not a Krishna consciousness that has really entered the bloodstream of the larger social body of the West. The transportability and viability of Krishna consciousness as a religious culture will not be truly tested, it seems to me, until it is allowed to become diffused within its host culture through religiously committed world-dwelling Western devotees. It remains to be seen, however, whether or not sufficient numbers of western devotees of Krishna have experienced a deep enough immersion in the Chaitanya tradition to allow for spiritual survival away from the intense social milieu of ISKCON. It is, I must suggest, still too early to say for sure whether or not westerners have truly heard the call of the Lotus-Eyed Lord.

11

Siddha Yoga: Swami Muktananda and the Seat of Power

Gene R. Thursby

The bond between the teacher of religious or philosophical wisdom and his disciple is uncommonly strong and is regulated in an authoritarian fashion, particularly in the sacred laws of Asia. Everywhere the master-disciple relationship is classified among those involving reverence.

—Max Weber[1]

Swami Muktananda Paramahamsa (1908–82) established the Siddha Yoga movement in the United States and guided its development here during the three world tours that he undertook in the last dozen years of his life—the first tour in 1970, the second in 1974–76, and the third in 1979–81. He was already a widely known spiritual master in his home country when he arrived here to establish a branch of the movement that had grown up around him in India. His own teacher (guru) had instructed him to extend the movement to the West, and a few American friends and followers gave strong support to the initial endeavor. To understand what Muktananda established and its subsequent history here, we can begin by considering its background in India.[2]

Siddha Yoga in India

In India, Siddha Yoga is an instance of a traditional type of religious movement, the *sampradāya* or the *panth*. According to Joachim Wach's classic study *Sociology of Religion*:

Sampradaya is not translatable by the term 'sect' or 'denomination' because that implies secession from a larger body (church). The Indian term does not have so much a negative as a positive connotation, implying a group with special concepts, forms of worship, and adherence to exclusive leadership exercised by an outstanding religious personality or by his physical or spiritual descendant.[3]

And W. H. McLeod describes the meaning of *panth*:

> Etymologically it derives directly from the notion of a 'path' or 'way' and it can still assume this literal meaning. . . . In its actual usage the word covers the kind of group or community which Dumont characterizes as a 'sect' and does so without invoking the problems associated with the European term.[4]

The core feature of Siddha Yoga as a Hindu movement in India and as a nonconventional religion in Euro-American cultures is the relationship between "an outstanding religious personality" (a guru who is a charismatic spiritual master) and any number of devotees or followers who seek a "path" or "way" of spiritual formation. To the outsider, and the newcomer to Siddha Yoga, the guru is a person who is accorded special deference and respect. But in the philosophy of the movement, there is another level of meaning of the term 'guru,' too. At that level, the guru is a respository of spiritual power (*śakti*) that flows through the person of the Siddha Guru to create an intense and transformative bond for the spiritual benefit of devotees.[5]

This assumption about the spiritual power of a higher and esoteric reality, the Guru-Principle (*guru-tattva*), also connects the movement to ancient forms of Shaiva and Shakta Hinduism that are "tantric" in their theory and practice. "What distinguishes tantric . . . teaching," according to Agehananda Bharati, "is its systematic emphasis on the identity of the absolute (*paramārtha*) and the phenomenal (*vyavahāra*) world when filtered through the experience of *sādhanā*."[6] The movement locates itself within a legendary lineage of perfected masters known as the Siddha Parampara, and it envisions the aim of spiritual formation or *sādhana* as the experience of "recognition" that at once enhances and effaces the distinction between the relative and the absolute. This universal goal of unitive mysticism is said to be the specific state of the realized master, and so all of the procedures and practices that devout followers undertake in response to expressed or implied promptings from the Siddha Guru may be considered part of their *sādhana*.[7]

The formal beginning of the *sādhana* process is the act of *dīkṣā* or initiation. What is determining in Siddha Yoga initiation is not a particular ritual form but rather *śaktipāt* or the "descent of divine energy." The theory of what should occur is derived principally from the Kashmir school of Shaivism. Like most traditional Hindu philosophies, its image of time is cyclical and devolutionary. It pictures the present age as dark and divided; yet it holds that spiritual realization—and with it emancipation from the otherwise endless round of suffering, death, and reincarnation—remains possible. This nondual ontology defines the soteriological problem as one of ignorance and, in consequence of it, seeming powerlessness. But the apparent individual, asleep to his or her inherent and higher nature, may be awakened by the grace of a true guru.[8]

This philosophy also assumes that the phenomenal individual is composed of a hierarchy of many levels or "bodies," among which the physical body is the most obvious but the least real. More real is the "subtle" body in which an elaborate network of channels allows circulation of conscious energy, except where blocked. Prior to *śaktipāt*, dormant *śakti* lies slumbering at the base of the spine in the "subtle" body. In this mode it is termed *kuṇḍalinī*, and initiation by guru's grace generates an "awakening" that attracts it to move upward as *śakti* and to open channels of awareness that eventually will enable the realization of all of the levels inherent in the initiate's full being. Experiential reports by Siddha Yoga initiates tend to correspond generally to this theory. There is no emphasis on secrecy, and accounts of initiatory experiences—at the beginning and in the course of *sādhana*—freely circulate within the movement.[9]

The Exemplars: Nityananda of Ganeshpuri and Swami Muktananda

Throughout his later years Swami Muktananda repeatedly stated that he himself had achieved nothing and that every apparent accomplishment was but another gift from his guru, Nityananda of Ganeshpuri. According to the Siddha Yoga account, in his youth Nityananda had been initiated as a disciple of a guru named Ishwara Iyer and later was a renunciate and monk of the Nandapadma order. All reports agree that a few years before the second World War he settled in the village of Ganeshpuri, about fifty miles northeast of the coastal city of Bombay, in a valley in the Thane district of the state of Maharashtra. By that time Nityananda was an *avadhūt*, an instance of the "enstatic" type characterized by Mircea Eliade in his study of Yoga, one who is not bound by ordinary social conventions nor by monastic rules. He tended to speak only briefly and infrequently; but he was popularly believed to be able to manifest extraordinary powers, and so he attracted many people who willingly came a considerable distance to Ganeshpuri in order to see him. They wanted to enjoy his *darśan* or presence, and to obtain remedies for their particular needs. Proceeds from their offerings were used to build a religious center, to improve the local hot springs and temple, and to fund a school and a hospital.

The effect of Nityananda's presence on many of his devotees was so deep and powerful that they regarded him to be natural form of divinity and they referred to him as "Bhagawan" (Divine Lord). Some also identified him with Ganesha, son of Shiva, who is honored annually in the great civic festivals of Maharashtra as the divinity who overcomes even the greatest obstacles. And many assumed there could be no human successor nor an institutional line of succession from such a being because he was too great. Neither could death have any real power over him, so in 1961 when he relinquished bodily form his devotees interpreted it in a way prescribed by yogic tradition. He was understood to have entered the permanent enstatic state called *mahāsamādhi* in which the undying consciousness returns to its true, nonintentional, and independent condition within itself. Therefore, the body of Nityananda was arranged in an upright meditative posture and was enclosed in ritually prepared, salted ground. Above it an image was installed to mark the place as a shrine where the divine consciousness was expected to continue to manifest the same spiritual power for devotees and pilgrims that previously had been mediated by the life of the saint.

Even so, toward the end of his life a few of his devotees began to accord to one of his close disciples, Swami Muktananda, a degree of respect and honor second only to what they offered to Nityananda. During that period, Muktananda took up permanent residence at his own Gavdevi Ashram (now Shree Gurudev Siddha Peeth), about a twenty-minute walk away from his guru's religious center. Later, after Nityananda left the body, those who regarded Muktananda as an extension of the same power were doubly drawn to Ganeshpuri—to the shrine of Bhagawan Nityananda and to Muktananda as a living master.[10]

Although there is a more adequate historical record of the life of Muktananda than of that of Nityananda, we must assume that much of the received version has been given its shape by piety, too. Partly that is due to the fact that Muktananda left home at age fifteen and became a monk of the Saraswati order. This status, and his transformation from seeker to saint in his later years, resulted in great reticence on the part of his followers to record personal details of his life history. The accounts we have of his life typically divide it into four periods.

The first period encompassed the fifteen years following the easy birth to his mother during the full moon of the Indian month of Vaishak (April-May) in 1908. The birth had been preceded by her ardent prayers for a son, pilgrimage to a local sacred center, and recitation of the mantra "Om Namah Shivaya." The child was named Krishna, his mother tongue was to be Kannada, and he was brought up in a well-off land-owning family near Mangalore in what is now Karnataka State. At fifteen he briefy encountered Nityanada, who was living as a wandering holy man, and this was the experience with which he associated his own decision to leave home.

The second period of Muktananda's life extended from his departure from home up to his reunion with Nityananda. He went to Hubli and entered the ashram of Siddharudha Swami. There he undertook the renunciation ritual to become a monk of the Saraswati order, and he was given the new name 'Muktananda' ("The Bliss of Spiritual Liberation"). While there he studied the traditional nondual metaphysics of Advaita Vedanta. In 1929, following the death of Siddharudha, he went to study for a short time under Mupinariya Swami at Dharwar. Then he began a period of travel, and is said to have gone the length of India three times. Afterwards he settled at Yeola (Nasik) in Maharashtra, where he alternated between periods of solitude and of interaction with devotees who began to gather around him there. He also became acquainted with two unconventional saints, Zipruanna and Harigiri Baba, both of whom encouraged him to travel to Ganeshpuri in order to see Nityananda.

The third period of his life began with his renewed contact with Nityananda, probably in 1946, and intensified in what Muktananda understood to be his initiatory experience on the day of India's independence, 15 August 1947. On that day as he sat outside Nityananda's room, the master emerged wearing wooden sandals (*pādukā*) that he left before Muktananda. He also spoke the mantra "Om Namah Shivaya," placed a blue shawl over Muktananda's shoulders, and gave a deep, penetrating gaze that sent Muktananda into a meditative state that he later described as the experience of an inextricable tie to Bhagawan

Nityananda as his guru and as the source and true nature of his own consciousness. Muktananda then left Ganeshpuri and spent the next nine years undergoing a process of inner transformation, which he described in his spiritual autobiography *Play of Consciousness*. By 1956 that retreat phase of intense internal work was completed, and he returned to Ganeshpuri and to renewed direct contact with Nityananda. The Siddha Yoga understanding of the subsequent resolution phase, from 1956 to 1961, is that Muktananda had completed his spiritual transformation and that Nityananda could acknowledge him as a living realized being—a Jivan Mukta or a Paramahamsa—like himself. So he invited Muktananda to settle at Ganeshpuri, where the two shared a common mission as the senior and the junior "Baba" (father) to the devotees. During those years, at least some of the devotees regarded the two as only apparently separate expressions of an essentially unified consciousness. Stories circulated to the effect that Muktananda possessed special powers (precognition, multilocation, etc.), which attested to his spiritual realization and deep connection with Nityananda.

The fourth and last period of Muktananda's life is dated from Nityananda's *mahāsamādhi* on 8 August 1961, to his own on 2 October 1982. Siddha Yoga claims a succession from Bhagawan Nityananda to Muktananda in an unbroken transmission of spiritual authority, marked principally by two events. The first was public and symbolic. Some months before Nityananda's passing, his devotees constructed a small temple meant to serve as his *samādhi* shrine. When it was completed, Nityananda instructed them to install the living Muktananda in it instead. The second event that Siddha Yoga interprets as marking a succession was intimate and private. Muktananda's own account is that two days prior to the *mahāsamādhi* and while they were alone, Nityananda passed him the position of guru by means of mantra, mudra (symbolic gesture), and other acts that ritualized the succession.

After Muktananda assumed the position of guru or senior Baba, he continued to enact and to provide a model for the behavior proper to a devotee as well as adding to it the modes appropriate to a master. However, unlike Nityananda who lived in utter simplicity, the guru Muktananda adopted the regal or Maharaja style, and so the spiritual seat or *gaddi* to which he ascended seemed nearly as much a royal throne as a religious seat of power. Nevertheless, throughout the remainder of his life he regarded that power as due entirely to Bhagawan Nityananda's grace. Although not all of Nityananda's devotees actually transferred their allegiance to Muktananda, that is the usual way of things in the process of Hindu guru-disciple succession in India. Muktananda had established a separate institution, in any case, about a mile from Nityananda's shrine. There he attracted many new devotees and soon had his own large following. By the end of the 1960s, he had consolidated his position as guru, enlarged the ashram, and was drawing a number of his devotees from foreign countries. In the summer of 1969, he went on retreat to Mahabaleshwar where he wrote his spiritual autobiography. In May 1970, he announced that he would act on his guru's command that he carry Siddha Yoga to the Western world.[11]

Swami Muktananda and Siddha Yoga in the United States

During the late summer through early winter of 1970, Swami Muktananda came to the United States on his first world tour. He was accompanied by Ram Dass, but his principal sponsor was an American devotee, New York art dealer Rudi (Albert Rudolph, 1928–73). Rudi had been importing oriental art from India for several years and went there two or three times a year to consult with his suppliers. A friend in Bombay whose hobby was "collecting saints" took him to Ganeshpuri to meet Bhagawan Nityananda in 1960. Although neither India nor spiritual practices were new to Rudi (he had participated in the first Subud group in Manhattan, had been in a Gurdjieff group for several years, and was teaching his own students), the single brief meeting with Nityananda redirected his life and work. But by his next visit to India, Nityananda was gone, and in 1962 Rudi took Swami Muktananda as his guru. In 1966, Muktananda playfully dubbed him "Swami Rudrananda" but did not have him initiated in the traditional way as a Hindu monk. Muktananda also repeatedly tested him, and during the 1970 American tour this caused Rudi considerable distress.

Rudi withdrew from the guru-disciple relationship with Swami Muktananda early in the next year when they met again in India. However, he continued to derive strength from what he experienced as a profound inner connection with Bhagawan Nityananda and to teach American students independently of Muktananda right up to his death in 1973. Rudi's most accomplished students also made their own pilgrimages to Ganeshpuri to honor Nityananda and to seek Muktananda's blessing for their teaching work. One of them was Franklin Albert Jones (b. 1939) who subsequently attracted followers as Bubba Free John and then as Da Free John. Now he lives in Fiji as a renunciate guru and is known as Heart-Master Da Love-Ananda. Another was Michael Shoemaker who became the principal but not sole successor to Rudi in the Rudrananda movement. In 1978, under Muktananda's sponsor-

ship, he was made a monk in India and was given the name Swami
Chetanananda Saraswati. Currently he presides over the Nityananda
Institute in Cambridge, Massachusetts. Although Rudi and his successors
were inspired by Muktananda, wished to have his authorization for their
work, and at various times reported they had received it, there is no
conclusive evidence that he gave them significantly more than the
universal blessing that he bestowed on all who approached him.[12]

When Swami Muktananda returned to the United States on his
second tour in 1974, he established his movement as a legal entity by
incorporation of the Siddha Yoga Dham of America [SYDA] Foundation. Until 1980 the corporate headquarters was in Oakland, California; then it was shifted to its current location in South Fallsburg, New
York. The SYDA Foundation acts on behalf of the movement's home
institution and premier center—the Shree Gurudev Siddha Peeth in
Ganeshpuri, India—and supports the work of its presiding guru in
several ways: by holding real estate; by providing basic maintenance
for a corps of renunciate religious workers and nonrenunciate staff
members; by meeting routine expenses for travel, publicity, and public
programs; by arranging for publication of books and periodicals; and
by creating an archival record of the public activities of the guru.[13]

While in Aspen, Colorado, Muktananda regularized the basic form
of the ceremony that introduces newcomers to Siddha Yoga. Called the
"intensive" program and typically extending over two highly structured
eight-hour days, it is designed to accomplish basic socialization into
spiritual practices and initiation into the guru-devotee relationship. During the intensive, participants hear lectures by the guru on an announced
theme and inspirational talks by monks or highly articulate lay devotees,
learn traditional Hindu chants, gain experience in repeating the "Om
Namah Shivaya" mantra and in meditation practice, and receive
śaktipāt—the core act of transmission of spiritual energy for which
the intensive program provides the formal context. Making *śaktipāt*
available to numbers of people drawn from the population at large was
Muktananda's innovation. As Charles S.J. White has noted, "what is
unusual about Muktananda's 'way' is that, for the first time, the secret
initiations and experiences of the Śakti Pāt, the yoga of the goddess,
of the primordial energy of Śiva, is presented openly in a manner
suitable to universal acceptance."[14] Following the *śaktipāt*, participants
are invited to talk about their experiences in the assembly of newcomers
and old followers. During the intensive they also may become familiar
with the daily routine and rules of the Siddha Yoga ashram (in cases
in which the intensive is in that kind of setting rather than held in a
hotel or other secular locale).[15]

The ashram is a traditional institution transferred from India, and during the 1970s about a dozen were established in many large cities (e.g., New York, Boston, Houston, Atlanta) and university towns (e.g., Ann Arbor). As a residential center for communal living and spiritual practice, each ashram had a Siddha Yoga monk in residence to provide guidance. The ashram manager was likely to be a lay follower, as were the other designated functionaries for finance, maintenance, food and cooking, and publicity and programs. The rest of the ashram residents were also expected to be involved in the ongoing work in some lesser capacity, although most of them also held outside employment. All Siddha Yoga ashrams followed the same daily schedule of activities, rest, and ritual, as prescribed for them by Swami Muktananda. This set a pattern in which there was relatively little individual free time and instead an emphasis on a common life that was explicitly oriented toward the guru and lived as service, principally expressed in routinely shared work and formal devotions. The number of ashrams increased during the third tour, but then in the early 1980s the guru began to restrict monks to no more than a six-month term in a particular ashram, and the Foundation discontinued its financial subsidies for the ashrams, except the major ones in Oakland and South Fallsburg.[16]

Another Siddha Yoga institution, also transferred from India, is the "center." It is a functional unit, usually set up in a devotee's home, where regularly scheduled meetings are held to introduce new people to the practice of meditation and other Siddha Yoga activities that support spiritual development. Their number tends to fluctuate, but averages about two hundred in the United States. The Foundation supports a central office that continues to coordinate the recruitment, training, and maintenance of a network of volunteers who serve as center leaders. In addition, a correspondence course complements the work of the centers and extends participation to a more widely dispersed population.[17]

Swami Muktananda's third tour, from 1979 to 1981, saw the completion of major additions to a new ashram in South Fallsburg that became the site of the movement's corporate headquarters. He wrote more books, met new devotees, and accepted invitations to stay in places not previously visited. His devotees renovated an abandoned hotel on Miami Beach, for example, for use as an ashram during his stay in Florida for the winter and spring of 1979–80. He also introduced additional practices from Hindu devotional and ritual tradition into the Siddha Yoga daily routine and the round of the religious year.[18]

The intended purpose of these practices and institutions, and of the Foundation that is responsible for their organization and support, was to be extensions of the guru. And their combined effect has been to foster a centripetal pattern. Although there is no formal membership as such, the more highly motivated devotees study and meditate in their own residences, attend programs at a center, perhaps live for a time in an ashram, and at least once a year will participate in the programs, intensives, and training courses offered at the Oakland or South Fallsburg ashram—and by these means are drawn toward the physical presence of the guru. A smaller number have gone on pilgrimage to Ganeshpuri, or have sought the more rigorous disciplines of the preliminary stage of a celibate religious life and eventually the fully renunciate monastic life. A total of about six dozen men and women of various nationalities were initiated as monks of the Saraswati order under the sponsorship of Swami Muktananda. By the time of his *mahāsamādhi*, about a dozen of them were senior monks who had been serving the organization for nearly a decade. And the newest of them were the twenty-six who received preliminary initiation in 1980 in Los Angeles and then the traditionally prescribed final rites, along with nineteen other candidates, in 1982 in Ganeshpuri under supervision of Swami Brahmananda Giri, Mahamandaleshwar of Sringeri Math.[19]

Siddha Yoga After Swami Muktananda

Swami Muktananda was a remarkable institution-builder. His passing was a loss to the Siddha Yoga organization and, because he was a charismatic type, many followers felt a deep personal loss that made the transition imposed by his death more difficult. Yet in the months prior to his *mahāsamādhi* in October 1982, Muktananda prepared his followers by making provision for orderly continuation of organizational leadership and transfer of spiritual authority. He sought to guarantee an easier and surer transition than he himself experienced twenty-one years earlier when he had assumed the *gaddi* or guru's seat.

Muktananda was very busy in his last year in India, following the third tour. The Gurudev Siddha Peeth to which he returned in the late autumn of 1981 had been enlarged and improved in his absence, and he returned in time to preside at Diwali, a major festival of the Hindu year that is celebrated during the new moon of October-November. Through the remaining cool months, he received visitors, was interviewed by the press, gave public lectures, and addressed the Seventh International Transpersonal Conference, which met in Bombay. But his main responsibility was to organize a series of formal ceremonial occasions, to be observed from 29 April through his lunar birthday on 8 May, which were to conclude with a public ritual of "passing the lineage" to his two successors-designate.[20]

The two were siblings, an elder sister and her younger brother. They were two of four children in a family that had been devoted to Muktananda for decades, and both of them had been placed under his care from an early age. She was the former Malti Shetty (b. 1955), who had served as English-language translator for Muktananda from the beginning of the second tour until the end of his life. Her brother, Subash Shetty (b. 1962), had been prepared for a leadership role during the third tour. His preliminary induction into monastic life took place in Los Angeles in 1980, while the initial rites for her opened the series of April-May 1982 ceremonies at Ganeshpuri. Upon taking the final monastic vows on 3 May, with forty-three other candidates, Subash was given the name Swami Nityananda and Malti became Swami Chidvilasananda.

Two complementary ceremonies, held on 5 and 8 May, concluded the series of public rituals. On the fifth there was a *rājābhiṣeka* to honor Swami Muktananda as Siddha Guru. The main symbolic acts included a ritual shower-bath of the sort given a Hindu image of a divine being or a traditional Indian king at his coronation. On the eighth there was a corresponding *paṭṭābhiṣeka* that was to consecrate his designated successors. The ceremonies were performed by Hindu ritual specialists acording to the traditional canons of correct procedure. What was unusual was that there were two designated successors to the *gaddi* rather than one, and this exceptional feature was explained as a practical necessity due to the amount of work and travel required in order to serve an international movement effectively.

From the conclusion of the cycle of rituals in May until early October, there was an interim period marked by the rainy season. Toward the end of it, from 13 to 26 September, Muktananda took his successors on a pilgrimage to Kashmir. Then, just a week following their return to Ganeshpuri, his *mahāsamādhi* on the night of 2 October all at once created the conditions for another ritual cycle and for a complete shift in leadership. During the next three days the deceased elder guru was honored, at last by ritually placing his body in the *samādhi* pit that he had ordered to be excavated in the foundations of the original Gavdevi Ashram structure, beneath the place where he had lived for nearly twelve years. On the seventeenth, in a ceremony that partly recapitulated their 8 May consecration, Chidvilasananda and Nityananda were formally installed as the presiding gurus of Siddha Yoga. They began to share the seat of power, and a few months later their devotees honored them with the titles Gurumayi and Gurudev.[21]

The two continued to guide the movement through the period of adjustment brought upon them and their followers by the full-scale succession. Although they differed from one another considerably in manner and style, for three years they shared the leadership. Then, in Ganeshpuri at the end of the month-long third anniversary commemoration of Swami Muktananda's *mahāsamādhi*, Gurudev Nityananda gave up his position. He announced his retirement on 3 November 1985, explaining that Swami Muktananda had instructed him privately that he would be on the seat only for a limited term and as a form of service in support of Gurumayi. On 10 November, Gurumayi Chidvilasananda was formally installed on the *gaddi* as the sole guru of Siddha Yoga.[22]

At the time, this turn of events in the transfer of leadership was presented as a cooperative endeavor that had been undertaken by the mutual decision of the joint successors. And Nityananda's resignation was actually two-fold. First, he relinquished his role as guru. Second, he insisted that he must give up his standing as a monk, and that was the more irregular part of the resignation because the authoritative texts that determine traditional Hindu rules of correct order do not provide any routine ritual provision for this course of action. However, the Mahamandaleshwar devised and authorized a series of rituals of reversal for the purpose of creating a new identity for him as a nonrenunciate householder. With it came a new name: Venkateshwar Rao. But the new identity of Venkateshwar proved to be a volatile one. Early in 1986, *The Illustrated Weekly of India* published two cover stories that reported that he was beginning to claim that he had not voluntarily resigned but had been forcibly "dethroned." The *Weekly* eventually printed a retraction and an apology, but in the meantime the two reports, and the questions they raised about behavior within the movement and about the circumstances surrounding the succession to Siddha Yoga leadership, damaged the reputations of the blameworthy and the blameless alike.[23]

Even though eventually withdrawn as groundless, for a time the stories reported in the *Weekly* had the effect of creating confusion among those who read them. Soon after the second article was published, Gurumayi Chidvilasananda determined to distribute a rejoinder to the charges in order the clarify the situation more quickly than could be accomplished by recourse to a judicial resolution making its way slowly through the legal proceedings required by the courts. Because Venkateshwar reportedly claimed that he was a victim of intimidation, she had to make public that he had resigned due to the shame of having broken his monastic vows, thereby having made himself unfit to guide others. It also made him unfit to continue to serve as head of the Shree Gurudev Siddha Peeth, the home institution of the Siddha Yoga movement and a public trust in India, because lifelong celibacy was a requirement of the office.[24]

In order to protect the legitimate authority of the guru's seat and office, there was a responsibility to address the charges. But what made it crucial to address and to refute them was the charismatic function of the person of the guru. Swami Muktananda had defined the focus and the heart of the movement as "the yoga of the guru's grace." Therefore, the very foundation of Siddha Yoga is trust in the legitimacy, the power, and the special spiritual qualities of the guru. It also is the responsibility of the guru to test the devotee, as Muktananda had stated in his characteristically strong manner:

> The Guru must find out whether a particular person who has come to him is fit for self-realization. . . . . What is really to be looked for is how far the particular disciple will be able to go on the path and how much natural stability he has. And then how much love he has for the Master. At times the Guru may even behave in a manner which is shocking. He may get angry with you but you may not be at fault—he has to test you. He will keep on testing you until he breaks the back of your pride. So one can take the Guru's moods and attitudes and so on as all a part of the process of teaching.[25]

This phase in the succession from Swami Muktananda was a time of testing for Siddha Yoga and all of its devotees.

Venkateshwar went through an unsettled period following his departure from Siddha Yoga, during which he sought to make a fresh start as a spiritual teacher on his own. One transitional project that he abandoned was the attempt to develop a new style of teaching, which he called "recognition dynamics." Then he resumed use of the name of Nityananda (without the monastic discipline or garb), renewed his claim to be a true successor to Muktananda, and began to preside at spiritual gatherings held in a traditional Indian style. These activities drew both formal and informal opposition. Shortly after the *Weekly* stories and the rejoinder to them came into circulation, the SYDA Foundation instructed its general counsel to collect sworn testimony from anyone who might have direct knowledge of events or actions that had bearing on the succession. The conclusion drawn from the evidence offered by those who came forward was that Nityananda (Venkateshwar), from the time he had been selected to succeed Swami Muktananda, repeatedly broke his monastic vows and abnegated his leadership responsibilities. The testimony also provided grounds for opposing his attempts to continue to represent himself as a qualified spiritual leader. A few disgruntled devotees and disillusioned former devotees intermittently disrupted his programs, directly threatened him and his followers, and sought to prevent him from continuing to act, in their view, as a pretender to the throne. He, in turn, had to be placed under injunction by an Indian High Court in order to assure that he would not act on his threat to take possession of the Siddha Yoga ashram in Delhi. Nevertheless, in July 1987, he founded his own not-for-profit organization, calling it Shanti Mandir (Temple of Peace), with headquarters in Livingston, New Jersey. There—without the trappings of his earlier exalted position, without formal title, and wearing simple white clothing—he once again became engaged in leading chanting, giving a mantra, and offering one-day intensive programs.[26]

By resolving the leadership irregularities, Siddha Yoga became more effective in providing its traditional services and better able to develop in new directions. In order to protect the right to lawful use of basic terms, practices, and materials utilized in the movement against unexpected challenges such as posed by Venkateshwar's attempts to regain a role as spiritual leader, the SYDA Foundation registered them. Renovations and improvements were made in the buildings and grounds at South Fallsburg and at the home ashram in Ganeshpuri. Charitable work in India, which includes a mobile clinic for the rural poor, was extended. Publications by and about the presiding guru were brought into print. New forms of the intensive program were introduced and, from 1989 onward, satellite technology began to make it possible to link Ganeshpuri with people around the world by direct television transmission.

At the center of all these activities is the Siddha Guru. After so many years of extensive travel since she was placed on the *gaddi* by Swami Muktananda in 1982, Gurumayi Chidvilasananda announced that she would reside in Ganeshpuri from the autumn of 1989 through the early months of 1991. A result has been that devotees have been converging there in greater numbers, and during the 1989–90 year-end holidays the ashram was filled to more than its capacity by some two thousand foreign and Indian visitors each day. If ever there had been any doubt about the ability of a young woman to bear the full weight of the spiritual leadership of this movement, it should have been dispelled by her years of dedicated work to communicate a clear model of *sādhana* to her devotees. As one of the most articulate of them, Joseph Chilton Pearce, has put the matter:

Gurumayi was clearly the inevitable and logical inheritor of [the] lineage. For twenty-one years Baba [Muktananda] had prepared her, through a most grueling physical, spiritual, psychological and intellectual training, to receive the awesome power of his heritage. No lesser person could have held the Shakti of Baba's lineage when it came. Through Bhagawan Nityananda, Baba was himself the inheritor of a vast, cumulative spiritual energy passed from Siddha Master to disciple through the ages.[27]

Conclusion

At an intensive held in Bombay less than a month before his death, Swami Muktananda had "addressed a long, fiery tirade in Kannada to the . . . South Indian devotees who had been with him and [Bhagawan] Nityananda for 25 or 30 years, saying that even though they had been with him so long they had no interest in what he really had to give."[28] Those few old devotees looked upon him more as their sibling in the family of Bhagawan Nityananda than as their spiritual master. For them the charisma of the "original" master was an untransferable resource. Their allegiance was fixed. And there was another small part of the Siddha family, too, that Muktananda might have mentioned in similar terms. Its members were a small group of devotees of Bhagawan Nityananda who had been willing to transfer their allegiance, but who had given it to a different claimant to succession.

In contrast to this variety of spiritual kinship patterns that were generated around Bhagawan Nityananda, Swami Muktananda established a set of standards to regulate the transfer of allegiance and authority in Siddha Yoga. A basic requirement was that a Siddha Guru must have been the disciple of a true guru and commanded by his or her own guru to become a guru. An additional requirement was that a Siddha Guru must be learned in the traditional scriptures. The final requirements, subtle and difficult to assess, were that a Siddha Guru must be fully enlightened, be able to bestow grace through śaktipāt, and be able to control the awakened śakti in the disciple. People who spent time as seekers in the presence of the Siddha Guru, Muktananda believed, would soon find sufficient evidence in the appropriate inner changes in their own state of being. These standards served to support the orderly process of transfer of allegiance from Swami Muktananda to his authorized successors during the three years that they shared the Siddha Yoga seat of power. Then, at the end of the three years, because it became evident that he did not meet these requirements, Swami Nityananda quite properly resigned his position.[29]

Since he had disqualified himself, Siddha Yoga subsequently deleted him from its history in order to maintain the traditional emphasis on the unbroken continuity of lineage: "In modern times the spiritual power of the Siddha lineage was embodied in the person of the great Indian holy man Bhagawan Nityananda. His successor was Swami Muktananda, who, five months before he passed away, named Gurumayi Chidvilasananda as his spiritual heir."[30] This account reflects the key role of lineage (*parampara*) in the transmission of spiritual authority, and so it omits what proved to be ephemeral in the interval between the time when Swami Muktananda publicly designated and invested his joint successors to the time when the movement's spiritual power came to reside exclusively in the person of Gurumayi Chidvilasananda.

The departure from monastic life of about half of the SYDA corps of renunciates during that phase of the succession is further evidence of its transitional character. Among the most senior American monks, for example, one who left because of an open conflict with Swami Nityananda has since established a successful secular career in the computer software field. Another found requirements of the renunciate life too restrictive but since then has founded an independent institute to foster spiritual development. And a third gave up the charismatic orientation of Siddha Yoga in order to promote a technological approach to meditation that is based on the sound-induction methods of brain hemispheric synchronication pioneered by Robert Monroe. All three previously held secondary but prominent leadership roles within the movement. In these cases, and in others involving relatively young non-Indians who had become Hindu monks, the *mahasamadhi* of Swami Muktananda prompted them to consider a departure, either from the monastic life alone (about a quarter of the corps) or from the life and from the movement. Especially for those who left both behind, there remained a question of what kind of identity to endorse with their life. The three noted here were fairly successful in negotiating a major shift in vocation, while a few other former monks are still seeking a suitable way to resolve their effort to establish an identity that will be a viable alternative to the one they had while in the renunciate life. Venkateshwar-Nityananda seems to have completed a major transition of his own by establishing Shanti Mandir, in which he is able to maintain a leadership role—although at a more simple level and with but a small fraction of the following that he enjoyed in Siddha Yoga.[31]

During the short-lived transitional phase in the succession of authority from Swami Muktananda solely to Gurumayi Chidvilasananda, Siddha Yoga seemed for a time more typical of a general pattern that recurs in many Indian movements that have a guru at their center. Subdivisions tend to form in these "spiritual families," especially when a new generation comes to dominate the following or the leadership. The Radhasoami movement that began in north India and is now international is another example of the same pattern. A section of Radhasoami parallels Siddha Yoga in its preoccupation with succession issues and in its concern to identify the one true guru. In a recent study of Radhasoami, Lawrence Babb has noted:

> With the passing of every generation there are new disciples and splits, and the branching lines of descent show every sign of continuing to ramify as long as the movement exists.
>
> But from the inside, the history of the movement. . . . appears not as branching lines but as one line. Because there can only be one sant satguru at a time, the other lines of spiritual 'descent' are not really lines of descent at all.[32]

Those who are currently on the Siddha Yoga path are confident in the conviction that the line of descent of authority over the last three generations came down from Bhagawan Nityananda of Ganeshpuri, passed to Swami Muktananda Paramahamsa, and now empowers Gurumayi Chidvilasananda. They understand themselves to have been, and to continue to be, the spiritual beneficiaries of a great—and unbroken—lineage of teaching and transformation that continues to be active and effective today in the same way that it was in the past. They acknowledge the presiding guru of the lineage as a special manifestation of divine power, activity, and consciousness. They share the same faith that was expressed by a devotee of a decade ago who tellingly remarked while departing for an evening audience with Swami Muktananda: "Time to go see God."[33]

12

When the Prophet is Yet Living:
A Case Study of the Unification Church

Michael L. Mickler

How does one go about assessing the postcharismatic fate of a new religious movement when the leader yet lives? Is such an inquiry presumptuous, even illegitimate? Or are there insights obtainable prior to a prophet's loss? Are judgments framed in the glare of charismatic personalities inherently less valid than analysis constructed retrospectively, or are the dynamics of the yet-living prophet and his following more accessible to the immediate observer than to the later analyst? These questions may not be absolutely answerable. However, this study assumes that there are no privileged vantage points from which to survey either the successes or the wreckages of charismatically led religious movements.

If one *does* concede the possibility of assessing the postcharismatic fate of movements led by yet-living prophets, the initial question remains: How does one proceed? Commonly both movement adherents and outsiders speculate most about the succession of leadership following the founder's death. Obviously, the choice of a successor is important. Nonetheless, focusing on this issue exclusively obscures consideration of the resources (or lack of them) with which the new leadership has to work. Thus rather than simply rate the strengths and weaknesses of candidates for second-generation leadership, it makes more sense to undertake an assets/liability analysis of the movement as a whole, taking into account its various internal components and its relational pattern with the wider social milieu.

In adopting a "balance sheet" approach to the postcharismatic future of the Unification Church (UC), one must recognize that, in Laurence Iannaccone's words, "Economic models are not without precedent in the study of religion."[1] Peter Berger argued, some twenty years ago, "The pluralistic situation is, above all, a *market situation*. In it, the religious institutions become consumer commodities. And. . .a good deal of religious activity in this situation comes to be dominated by the logic of market economics."[2] More recently Rodney Stark and William Bainbridge have utilized concepts derived from exchange theory ("reward and costs, exchange and substitution, and I.O.U.'s") to explain religious commitment.[3] Nor is the employment of market terminology limited to sociologists. Dietrich Bonhoeffer, in a widely influential tract, detailed the "costs" of discipleship and distinguished between "cheap" and "expensive" grace.[4] Such usage, however, has usually functioned at the level of metaphor and analogy and has not coalesced into a widely accepted theory.

My usage of market imagery is not primarily focused on the front end of religious transactions—that is, on those appeals inducing seekers to "buy into" this or that religious commodity. The emphasis here is on what might be termed "long-term customer satisfaction." For this study I have isolated four areas of investigation: ideology; leadership and organization; recruitment and socialization; and public identity.[5] Having examined assets and liabilities in each of these areas, we will be better able to evaluate the UC's current "equity" and likely postcharismatic fate.

Ideology

Ideology, as it will be discussed here, has two important dimensions. First, it refers to the body of doctrines, myths, and symbols of a social movement, institution, class, or large group that defines that group's understanding of the world. In the case of religious groupings, worldviews normally are endowed with sacred significance and are understood to have derived from divine revelation or from a depth inaccessible to any but the founder. Second, ideology points to social, cultural, and political structures reflective of beliefs as to the rightness of certain arrangements. For mainline faiths whose values and traditions have long comprised the taken-for-granted fabric of public life, explicitly ideological preoccupations tend to fade. However, for less entrenched movements there is considerable pressure to reconcile a central core of beliefs with an uncomprehending and unappreciative social environment.

From this perspective, the UC's single most important ideological asset is its sense of being rooted in sacred authority. Like any other religion, the UC grounds its belief system in a core of nonnegotiable affirmations. The first is the affirmation of Sun Myung Moon's encounter with Jesus on Easter Sunday, 1936, and his call to carry on and indeed complete Christ's work. This type of call and encounter, a virtual prerequisite for numerous founders of religions, is essential to the UC's self-understanding as a divinely ordained institution. A second bedrock assertion is the affirmation of Rev. Moon's ongoing inspiration and exemplary lifestyle. As an official text notes,

> For many decades he wandered in a vast spiritual world in search of the ultimate truth. On this path, he endured suffering unimagined by anyone in human history. God alone will remember it. Knowing that no one can find the ultimate truth to save mankind without going through the bitterest of trials, he fought alone against myriads of Satanic forces, both in the spiritual and physical worlds, and finally triumphed over them all. In this way, he came into contact with many saints in paradise and with Jesus, and thus brought into light all the heavenly secrets through his communion with God.[6]

At least one commentator has placed Rev. Moon's revelation and charisma within the conceptual framework of shamanistic experience, noting, "thus the shaman flew to the 'heavenlies' (cf. Paul, Eph. 1:3, 2:6, 3:10, and the Gnostics) to wrest the secret gnosis from the spirits on behalf of waiting mankind and to wage heroic warfare in the depths (cf. Freud and Jung) so as to become a redeemed redeemer."[7] A third nonnegotiable is the affirmation of Rev. Moon's core teaching, known as "The Principle," as a "completed" testament.

The integrity of these nonnegotiables is essential to the UC's long-term viability. Nonetheless, a second key ideological asset has been the flexibility and adaptability of its belief system. With the continuing leadership of Rev. Moon, fresh departures, modifications, and even reinterpretations are possible according to circumstances and environment. For example, the UC has been transplanted from Korea to the United States, and is now responding to opportunities available as a result of Soviet *glasnost*.[8] Another factor promoting ideological adaptability is the provisional quality of the UC's canonical texts. Since no official edition now existing is understood to have been directly authored by Rev. Moon, and since it is freely acknowledged that more of "The Principle" remains to be published or revealed, there is room for refinement.[9]

This dialectic between adaptability to circumstances and fidelity to a core of beliefs is fundamental to the UC's continuing vitality as a *living* tradition. A third ideological asset of the movement has been the creation of an intellectual class whose primary purpose is "to gain for its tenets a respectable and defensible position in [the] world of higher learning and higher educational values."[10] The UC, using mentors outside the movement, has produced what Lonnie Kliever calls "a second-generation leadership that is highly self-conscious about communication theory, group dynamics, and theological apologetics."[11] John Lofland similarly comments,

> The cognitive systems of dominant elites are studied for the purpose of taking account of their claims, formulating UC principles in response to them, and developing UC arguments that counter these cultural elites. All this has the broader aim of creating an ideology that intellectual and other elites must take seriously.

What, then, are the UC's ideological liabilities? As has been the case for other new religious movements, the UC's core affirmations have elicited profound skepticism and external attacks from rival religionists and secular authorities. Ridicule and attempted repression have had their effect, but more consequential for our analysis are hindrances intrinsic to the movement itself. One of these is a modernist strand implicit in assertions that "man today cannot cognize anything which lacks logic and scientific proof."[13] Hence there is a rational, quasi-scientific overlay to UC ideology that maintains that its "new, ultimate, final truth" has "solved" all the questions of life. As a result, the literary form within which The Principle is embodied tends to be highly specific and technical, lacking in symbol or ambiguity, and thus lacking enchantment.

Quite separately, a latent ethnocentric strand within UC ideology must be counted as a second   ideological liability. This strain deflected most demonstrably in uncritical celebrations of Korean national destiny. A tendency to trade heavily in broad-ranging cultural sterotypes, particularly the spiritual primacy of Oriental culture, is also prevalent. Exclusivist and triumphalist orientations, although common in most religions, are not notably productive of good will or results among outsiders. Thus the universalization of Korean cultural traditions cannot be calculated among the measures likely to enhance the movement's long-term influence.

A third liability is an apocalyptic-spiritualist strand within the movement's ideology. Numerology and specific dispensational timetables figure here, and failures of prophecies to materialize according to schedule have caused cognitive dissonance for some. Finally, the UC has a frequently overlooked history of involvement with spiritualism, given its understanding of an active "spirit world." The potential of "channeling" and other forms of psychic or occult communication in fostering ideological chaos is significant.

Leadership and Organization

Most first-generation religious movements are headed by charismatic figures. For UC adherents, Rev. Moon fits Max Weber's classic description of the charismatic leader as one "endowed with supernatural, superhuman, or at least exceptional powers or qualities."[14] Weber held charisma, in its "pure" form, to be "a specifically revolutionary force." At the same time, he recognized the necessity of "routinization," or setting up a "permanent routine structure" needed after the prophet's death. The transition from "pure" to "routinized" forms of charisma has important organizational consequences.

The most important organizational asset of the UC is its common belief in the founder's exemplary character. One movement scholar, describing "cherished stories" repeatedly narrated in the community, reports that "Theocentric, self-sacrificial love is the most notable virtue manifested in the life of Rev. Moon."[15] Most adherents simply refer to him as a model of "shimjung" (a Korean word for "heart"). Accounts of Rev. Moon's "shimjung" in the face of misery and deprivation help balance the "philosophical treatise" quality of The Principle and promote affective bonds among adherents, particularly as they locate their "stories" within the prophet's exemplary story. If the UC effectively routinizes these stories within a hagiographical tradition, Rev. Moon's "shimjung" will continue to serve as a focal point of shared memory and experience.

A second organizational asset is the accumulated experience of the movement's top and midlevel leadership. Charismatic leaders like Rev. Moon are typically impatient with bureaucracy and frown on undue specialization among their lieutenants, particularly if it hinders their availability for urgent assignments. As a result, charismatically led movements constantly rotate leaders, shuffling them among widely varying assignments and locales. Thus is created a committed, seasoned core of career operatives. Dean Kelley has observed,

> A vigorous, dynamic religious movement can not only attract and hold
> some very impressive and gifted people, but . . . it can and does attract
> a great many more people who are not visibly impressive or gifted
> and install or bring out in them abilities they did not know they
> had. . . .Because new religious movements make higher demands
> . . . .and obtain fuller investment of self in return, they are able to
> accomplish far more with even less promising material.[16]

Adherents with limited backgrounds in public relations, law, lobbying,
and the like, in addition to implementing the movement's charismatic
agenda, have helped ward off threats and gain the UC recognition as
a *bona fide* religion with the privileges, including tax exemption and
access to missionary visas, other faiths enjoy.

Such public gains, however, are insufficient to avert what Rodney
Stark calls "the crisis of confidence that awaits most new religious
movements as members of the founding generation reach the end of
their lives." According to Stark, "the record of new faiths suggests that
unless the movement achieves a persuasive appearance of major success
within the first generation, the founders will lose hope and turn the
movement inward—adopt a new rhetoric that de-emphasizes growth
and conversion."[17] The UC in one generation has become a complex,
diversified, multinational conglomerate with numerous churches, an
imposing array of educational and cultural foundations, and an aston-
ishing number of businesses. Whether or not this comprises "success"
in Stark's terms is not immediately clear. It is clear, however, that
charismatic leadership has fueled the movement's initial advance. Rev.
Moon has had few internal constraints in making policy decisions and
allocating movement resources. More significant is Weber's insight that
personal charisma survives only so long as it is "proved."[18] Hence
prophets must "produce" in order to satisfy followers. This emphasis
on results energizes first-generation development and, if Stark is correct,
has long-term institutional consequences.

What are the UC's organizational liabilities? Despite its importance
as an engine of development, the emphasis on results is also an important liability. It has led to, for example, "a tendency to rely on showy,
visual depictions of success." It also has tended to shorten the movement's attention span and promote numerous short-term projects. The
UC's sense of urgency in evidencing its claims has led to additional
problems; in particular, the pressure on leaders to succeed and report
success has encouraged reportage of inflated results and thus undermined the movement's access to accurate information. Also, since
charismatic authority implies a flawless performance, *ex post facto*
interpretations neutralizing attributions of failure have hindered the UC's

confrontation with obstinate facts.[19] Finally, an emphasis on results has led to monetary debts. High profile projects such as *The Washington Times* have absorbed huge operating losses.

Weber states that the disappearance of the personal charismatic leader inevitably raises the problem of succession.[20] Therefore the concentration of authority in a single individual, no matter how worthy, is an organizational liability. The UC has survived Rev. Moon's imprisonment, and certain branches of the movement function with relative autonomy. However, Rev. Moon's presence has enabled the movement to survive infighting among the top leaders and factionalism between departments, as well as a climate of distrust between leaders and members. Rank and file members, when confronted with disillusioning experiences, for example, typically contend that Rev. Moon "was unaware of the inequities" and that "other leaders were either mistranslating his speeches or misinterpreting his intentions."[21] The succession problem is further complicated by a multiplicity of candidates from the same charismatic family. Much current expectation focuses on Rev. Moon's eldest living son. However, a UC scholar has argued, "It is usually very difficult for hereditary charisma to demand the same or stronger dedication from the original founder's followers. . . .Few biographical stories about Rev. Moon's children. . . .are likely to match the dramatic and extraordinary quality of their father's story."[22]

Despite heavy investment in the theme of "Unification," cross-cultural conflict is another UC organizational liability. Part of this has been due to the UC's diverse membership base and separately incorporated national churches. David Bromley writes that "the more significant ongoing conflicts" have been "those between oriental (Korean and Japanese) and American components" of the UC and "those between the Koreans and Japanese." He contends the East-West conflict has figured "in the exodus of some of the more talented and creative American. . . .members" and conjectures that eventually either the American UC "will become overwhelmingly 'orientalized' or that a schism will occur." Historic Japanese-Korean enmity and the Japanese movement's economic power may prove more significant. Bromley doubts that the Japanese UC "would be willing to accept its current subordinate status and financing of deficit producing international operations absent Moon's charismatic authority."[23]

Recruitment and Socialization

To survive, a religious movement must be able to recognize and win a constituency. Further, it must bolster group cohesion and commitment within that constituency. It must also develop mechanisms that resist, or ameliorate, secularization. In each of these areas the UC has both assets and liabilities.

In recruitment, the UC's greatest asset is its ability to cast a wide net. A multinational organization, the UC is not tied to any single geopolitical setting. The movement's losses in one locale generally have been balanced by gains in another. For example, the leveling off of conversion rates in the United States have been more than offset by high rates of conversion in Japan. At present the UC stands poised to move into the rapidly changing Communist world. A recent op-ed piece in the *Wall Street Journal* reported that in exchange for helping fund a joint venture with the Chinese government for an automobile parts plant (and keeping the profits in China), the movement "has the government's blessing to build churches and spread Unificationism in that country."[24]

A second major asset in recruitment and socialization is the UC's still solid standing as a "high demand" religion, with high levels of cohesion and commitment in its followers. Several factors figure here. First, largely due to its founder, the movement has a strong system of central authority. Second, it has managed to create a strong network of internal attachments without unduly impeding the ability of members to maintain connections with outsiders (although this point may be debatable, given the tendency of some persons within UC communal enclaves to distance themselves from secular culture). Third, the UC has promoted a world-transforming social agenda, delineating itself as a strenuously public faith.

A final asset in recruitment is the UC's strong demographic profile. As Stark notes, a religion can grow through fertility alone, given an "appropriate age and sex composition pattern."[25] Christian Science, Stark argues, declined because it overrecruited older women in its first generation; the early Mormons thrived because of their appeal to young people of both sexes.[26] Yoshihiko Masuda points out that the UC has a rough global balance between unmarried male and female members, and that despite the fact that first-generation adherents "have had children at an older age than is the case with the average American, they are still encouraged to have a larger than average number of children."[27]

There are liabilities in these areas as well. A lack of continuity and development in recruitment strategy is one. Due to the constant rotation of leadership and changes of direction that typify charismatically led movements, UC local operations tend to be transient and lack adequate contextualization. In addition, as recruitment pools have dried up in one area, the movement has found it easier to switch locales than to develop alternative mission strategies. Thus street witnessing and workshops that press prospective converts for immediate affiliation (as well as for the severance of nonmovement ties) have continued as staples in the UC's recruitment arsenal. On occasion the movement has tried parish-style "Home Church" ministries, with adherents moving into and taking responsibility for certain neighborhoods. These efforts, however, have been interrupted by periodic "emergency" mobilizations requiring that members join mobile witnessing teams for months at a time.

Some would term authoritarianism a liability in UC recruitment and socialization, citing it as a reason for the movement's high turnover rate. However, voluntary organizations are highly permeable. In fact, there is probably no more switching or defection in the most stridently "militant" faith than there is in the most permissive New Age religion. More significant for the UC's future than its apostates are those who have opted out of active participation while staying nominally affiliated. Reasons for declining levels of participation vary; some members have objected to being given "quotas of 'spiritual children' (converts) which had to be achieved before family formation could begin."[28] Beyond that, J. Stillson Judah notes, "The disruption and separation of families with children to perform special missions, when members had worked sacrificially for years and were expecting a more settled life" has led others to become inactive.[29]

Secularizing tendencies implicit within the UC's recruitment and socialization model are a third liability in these areas. Simply put, adherents commonly understand that they are on the ground floor of the New Age, implying that they or their posterity will eventually become a ruling elite while opponents will suffer reversals. Systems of rewards and punishment are common in religious traditions; the problems arise when hope for reward fades or fear of punishment recedes. Then adherents typically seek compensators in the here and now. The UC has not been exempt from this trend. In the 1980s, for example, many adherents began to desire what during that decade was called "yuppie respectability." Some began to plot personal career paths inside or outside the movement. More troubling has been a tendency for some adherents to incorporate alternative, even secular, models for understanding their experience. This tendency has been especially apparent in recent disagreements over the use of psychological counseling techniques.[30]

Public Identity

So far we have dealt primarily with the UC's internal components—its ideology, its leadership and organization, its recruitment and

socialization style. Now we must examine the movement's relations with
the broader social milieu. Movements like the UC face two major
challenges with respect to their host societies. First, they must attain
public visibility. In order to survive, movements need to escape
anonymity and become known. Most never do. However, should a
movement be fortunate enough to be noticed, it faces a second
challenge: It must gain legitimacy. A dilemma of world-transforming
movements, according to David Bromley and Anson Shupe, "lies in
trying to promote change in the status quo" while not engendering
"hostility among those who must accommodate or participate in that
change." Most movements fail to resolve the dilemma and fall prey to
"social control measures either through formal legal channels or
through *ad hoc* vigilante-style countermovements."³¹

The UC has had decidedly mixed results with its public identity.
Its ability to attain public visibility is an important asset. Some of this
may be attributed to the media hype of unconventional new religions
in the United States. Equally telling, however, has been the movement's
shrewdness, political savvy, and sophistication in building on this base.
The UC has, for example, conducted its most intense campaigns in the
nation's media centers. It has tirelessly pursued high-level contacts with
civic leaders and intellectuals. It also has been willing to spend money.
Indeed, the UC discovered that large expenditures were a means of
attaining public visibility. Hence movement spokespersons readily
released budgets for evangelistic tours and real estate acquisitions.
Speculation about the sources of this income generated additional
publicity. Finally and most importantly, the UC has developed a
formidable infrastructure of local leaders, itinerant workers, mobile unit
"commanders," evangelistic bus teams, training sites and programs,
internal newsletters, mobile fundraising teams, and regular directors'
conferences.

The movement's attainment of legitimacy is another asset in terms
of public identity. The gradual public acceptance of the UC as a *bona
fide* religion and the movement's well-defined corporate identity have
helped it extend constitutional protections to its members and counter
the work of deprogrammers. Due in large measure to its cultivation of
intellectual and other elites, the UC has also made a growing number
of friends. Others, while not directly sympathetic, have defended the
UC on civil libertarian grounds. The UC, for its part, effectively parlayed
such sentiment into a variety of alliances, public forums, and *amicus
curiae* briefs. Recognition has also come from other public institutions;
the New York State Board of Regents, for example, recently awarded
the movement's seminary a permanent charter.

What are the UC's liabilities in matters of public identity? A negative public image is one. A 1977 Gallup poll found that Sun Myung Moon "elicited one of the most overwhelmingly negative responses ever reported by a major poll," so much so that "in the more than twenty years the Gallup Poll has been asking Americans to rate various people, only Nikita Khruschev and Fidel Castro have received more negative ratings."[32] Apart from stigmas associated with "cult" membership, adherents have also faced a variety of specific disabilities including efforts of families and their agents to extricate them from the UC. At the same time, sectarian attitudes of the UC toward the "outside" may have helped precipitate this conflict.

"Persecution" is not the only problem; movements often fall victim to their own successes. The UC, by its very success in attaining public visibility, may have created false expectations. It could find itself typecast as a "boom and bust" millennial movement.[33] More seriously, movements that have attained a measure of visibility tend to become primarily concerned with preserving what has been gained. What had been transformative activity becomes more a matter of increasing organizational power to displace dominant elites. Short of that, a movement may seek accommodation, looking to carve out a denominational niche within which it might self-perpetuate. The UC has created a formidable institutional infrastructure; whether it maintains its transformative fervor while serving its legitimate organizational interests, or whether its organizational interests become primary, remains to be seen.

Conclusion

Having investigated the UC's internal components and social relations, it is tempting to conclude by suggesting that the UC seek to improve its postcharismatic odds by maximizing its assets and minimizing its liabilities. For several reasons, however, that would be a mistake. First, assets and liabilities vary according to circumstance. For example, under conditions of repression or utter anonymity, an apocalyptic-spiritualist strand might be an asset and intellectualizing a liability in terms of basic survival.

Second, traits identified as assets or liabilities tend to merge. For example, an emphasis on results is both an asset (as an engine of development) and a liability (fostering an inclination to trade on appearances). Similarly, the UC's ability to recruit widely (an asset) has led to a lack of continuity and development in some locales (a liability). In actual practice assets and liabilities often comprise a single fabric.

Third (here our initial market analogy is apt), assets and liabilities together stimulate growth. The UC did not gain public visibility (an asset) without controversy over its sectarianism (a liability). Determining the movement's longevity, therefore, is not simply a matter of subtracting liabilities from assets but a more complex computation of their interrelatedness. The configuration of UC assets and liabilities is dynamic. The movement's postcharismatic fate will depend on its continued effectiveness in balancing the two.

Afterword

Some religions may indeed die not too long after the passing of the charismatic founder or leader, but it now seems clear that the great majority do not. Several of those studied in the preceding pages are over a century old; in some cases they are healthier than they have ever been. For some movements, such as Theosophy and Mormonism, new offshoots continue to appear from time to time, indicating a basic vitality in the religion itself, if not always in all branches of it. Some, such as the Amana Society, seem destined to continue to stay small and marginal in the vastness of American society. Some, notably Mormonism, are booming today. Some, such as Shakerism, have dwindled substantially but continue to cling to a thin reed of life. Some, such as the Spirit Fruit Society, indeed have eventually passed from the scene. But the Spirit Fruit Society may be the exception that proves the rule.

Nothing we have written should be construed to mean that the transition to second-generation leadership is painless. These essays suggest that conflict of some sort is a common component of the process of succession. It is not, however, in most cases fatal. On balance, life continues for new religions.

We are living in a time of religious decentralization. A culture with a single pervasive religiosity seems distant, either temporally (medieval Western Europe) or geographically (Saudi Arabia today). Most of America's largest denominations are currently either stable or declining; much of the vitality in American religion is in the smaller groups. Methodism and Presbyterianism lose members while Pentecostalism and Mormonism—and apparently even Unitarianism—grow.[1]

The continued emergence of small religious movements is not, and has never been, free of controversy or conflict. There was mob violence against Catholics when their numbers were few but Protestants saw them as a looming menace; Mormons suffered terrible persecutions for decades before they finally found a refuge in remote Utah. Shakers were whipped and ridiculed; the early Pentecostalists were derided as hicks and rubes. Persecuting minorities and dumping sins on scapegoats are age-old human enterprises.

Violence and even criminal acts against new religions continue to be tolerated, even promoted, in the larger culture. In the 1970s and 1980s deprogramming emerged as the tactic of choice in combatting the "cult menace." Principled opposition to deprogramming from scholars and some civil libertarians, as well as a few convictions for kidnapping, have slowed the program of physical, involuntary seizure of dissenting religionists, and at this writing deprogramming seems to be on the decline. However, lawsuits brought by deprogrammed members against the groups they formerly adhered to are very much with us, and the huge damages those suits could win for the plaintiffs may turn out to do more damage to new religions than deprogramming ever did. We pride ourselves, as a nation, on our diversity, but we have not yet learned very well how to welcome new additions to the melting pot.

We might as well learn to live with religious diversity, however, because it is bound to be with us for a long time to come. New charismatic leaders will appear, new movements will spring up, and existing movements will continue to survive in our midst. The American appetite for religion is a hefty one, and although specific prophets may die, spiritual needs will continue to need to be fulfilled.

Notes

Introduction. When Prophets Die:
The Succession Crisis in New Religions

1. Max Weber, *The Theory of Social and Economic Organization* (New York: Oxford University Press, 1947), 358–59. Quoted in Keith A. Roberts, *Religion in Sociological Perspective* (Homewood, IL: Dorsey Press, 1984), 184.

2. The attention given to religious founders as examples of charismatic leaders is in large part due to the lack of a preexisting structure that supports the new group founder; hence his/her achievements can be more clearly seen to be a direct result of individual effort.

3. J. Milton Yinger, *Religion, Society and the Individual* (New York: Macmillan Company, 1957), 154–55.

4. There is every reason to believe that this paragraph was written in haste and that Yinger gave it little thought. It appears at the very end of a chapter and was possibly added only to supply a sixth catch-all category to complete the more rigorous classification scheme he had worked out for the various Christian bodies (which dominate the rest of the typology). He would largely abandon this definition in his later volumes *Sociology Looks at Religion* (1962) and particularly *The Scientific Study of Religion* (1970), where he further develops his typology. In his revised typology, he retains the idea of the cult as a religious innovation that breaks continuity with the major religious format of the society, and understands it to be small and under the direction of a charismatic leader. While Yinger continues to see a cult as being led by a charismatic person, however, there is no mention in the later volumes of the problems of succession following the death of that leader.

5. G. K. Nelson, *Spiritualism and Society* (New York: Schocken Books, 1969).

6. See the discussion of cults in Rodney Stark and William Simms Bainbridge, *The Future of Religion* (Berkeley, CA: University of California Press, 1985).

7. Thus while a sect of whatever variety (because it shares the religious symbols, thoughts, and paraphernalia of dominant culture) can change into a church or denomination, the cult, no matter how successful, cannot. The Church of Scientology and the Nation of Islam will never become denominations in America, simply because they do not share the dominant Christian symbols possessed by all denominations according to Yinger. In like measure, by definition, the United Methodist Church cannot be anything but a "cult" (i.e., a group that makes a sharp break from the dominant religious pattern of the culture) in Japan since it does not share nor is it willing to more than superficially accommodate to the symbols of the dominant Buddhist and Shinto religions.

8. While frequently stated verbally, the assumption is rarely mentioned in print. For some recent examples, however, see the essays by Michael L. Mickler and Benton Johnson in David C. Bromley and Phillip E. Hammond, *The Future of New Religious Movements* (Macon, GA: Mercer University Press, 1987), and the discussion of the death of the founder of the International Society of Krishna Consciousness in Larry Shinn, *The Dark Lord* (Philadelphia: Westminster Press, 1987).

9. Charles Y. Glock and Robert N. Bellah, *The New Religious Consciousness* (Berkeley, CA: University of California Press, 1976).

10. For a discussion of this point see J. Gordon Melton, "Spiritualization and Reaffirmation: What Really Happens When Prophecy Fails," *American Studies* 26, 2 (Fall 1985): 17–29.

Chapter 1. The Shakers: The Adaptation of Prophecy

1. Today, fewer than a dozen Shakers remain at Sabbathday Lake, Maine and Canterbury, New Hampshire.

2. Since the story of Ann Lee's early life and the migration of Believers to America is well known and available in general histories of the Shakers, it will not be recounted here.

3. *A Summary View of the Millennial Church, or United Society of Believers, (Commonly Called Shakers.)* (Albany: Published by Order of the Ministry, in Union with the Church, Printed by Packard & Van Benthuysen, 1823), 10.

4. Niskeyuna was later known as Watervliet.

5. Edward Deming Andrews, *The People Called Shakers* (New York: Dover Publications, Inc., 1963), asserts that her "insistence on industry was further proof that Ann thought of the church as an organization having socio—economic as well as strictly religious functions," 47. I find little evidence that Ann Lee's understanding of church organization went beyond the analogy of the society to a "family" with its attendant domestic concerns.

6. When traveling across New England, Mother Ann established a base in the home of a local convert where inquirers (often relatives and acquaintances of the convert) visited and where she heard their confessions of sin. Her greatest influence was through personal contacts, not public preaching.

7. During this charismatic phase, Shakers may have danced or bathed naked in order to demonstrate that they had eradicated all sexual desire. Clarke Garrett, *Spirit Possession and Popular Religion: From the Camissards to the Shakers* (Baltimore and London: The Johns Hopkins University Press, 1987), concludes that spiritual "gifts" got out of hand during the last two years of Ann Lee's life and that, after her decease, Whittaker and Meacham brought inspiration under control, "making it a vehicle for collective rather than individual religious experience," 196.

8. *A Summary View,* chapter V, 38ff., presents a sketch of William Lee.

9. Ibid., chapter VI, 42ff., presents a sketch of Whittaker.

10. Daniel Rathbun, *A Letter from Daniel Rathbun, Richmond, in the county of Berkshire to James Whittacor, Chief Elder of the Church, called Shakers* (Springfield, MA: Printed at the Printing-office, near the Great Ferry, 1785), 37, relates with indignation an incident when Whittaker had promised to answer inquirers' questions, but Mother demanded his presence and so forced him to break his promise.

11. Thomas Brown, *An Account of the People Called Shakers* (Troy: Printed by Parker and Bliss, 1812; reprint edition, New York: AMS Press Inc., 1972), 343.

12. Reuben Rathbone, *Reasons Offered for Leaving the Shakers* (Pittsfield: Printed by Chester Smith, February 1800), 6. To be sure, Rathbone includes this incident as further evidence of drunken behavior by Mother and Father William. Yet his description of the competition for leadership between William Lee and James Whittaker seems very probable.

13. From the time of the Great Awakening to the first quarter of the nineteenth century, New England Congregational ministers split between the "New Lights" and the "Old Lights." The "New Lights" emphasized the need for a "conviction" of sin and a "new birth," and they favored revivalism, some insisting upon emotional manifestations as evidence of conversion. The "New Lights" formed at least ninety-eight "Separate" churches, many of which subsequently became Baptist. It was from the "Separates" that the Shakers drew large numbers of converts. For more information, see Winthrop S. Hudson, *Religion in America*, 3rd ed., (New York: Charles Scribner's Sons, 1981), Chapter III, "The Great Awakening," 59–82.

14. Rodney Stark, "How New Religions Succeed: A Theoretical Model," in *The Future of New Religious Movements*, David G. Bromley and Phillip E. Hammond, eds. (Macon, GA: Mercer University Press, 1987), 17.

15. Stephen A. Marini, *Radical Sects of Revolutionary New England* (Cambridge, MA, and London: Harvard University Press, 1982), 56, points out that although religious fervor was widespread, it was not easily routinized because New England was fragmented by isolation, war, and a sagging economy. Consequently, separatist churches and local sects proliferated.

16. Garrett, 194.

17. Priscilla J. Brewer, *Shaker Communities, Shaker Lives* (Hanover and London: University Press of New England, 1986), 7.

18. C. C. Goen, *Revivalism and Separatism in New England, 1740–1800* (New Haven: Yale University Press, 1962), concludes that Congregational "separatists" were not from the lower class, but that they represented a cross section of the population and included many prominent citizens. More recently, Garrett has taken a similar position, asserting that Shaker converts were not responding to displacement caused by industrialization and poverty, 129.

19. For example, Samuel Johnson, a New England clergyman, had graduated from Yale University in 1769.

20. James Whittaker, *The Shaker Shaken: or, God's Warning to Josiah Talcott, as Denounced in a Letter from James Whittaker, One of the United Society of Believers in Christ's Second Appearing, (Vulgarly Known as Shakers). From an Original Manuscript* (New Haven: Printed at the Bibliographical Press, over against Linonia & Brothers, 1938).

21. Andrews, 48.

22. Calvin Harlow, MS, Western Reserve Historical Society Shaker Collection, VII:A–9.

23. *A Summary View*, 36–37.

24. Benjamin West, *Scriptural Cautions Against Embracing a Religious Scheme* ...(Hartford: Printed and sold by Basil Webster, 1783), 14. Such beliefs might have been held by followers of Shadrack Ireland who subsequently became Shakers. There is little indication, however, that they were widespread.

25. Brown, 325.

26. William Sims Bainbridge, "The Decline of the Shakers: Evidence from the United States Census, "*Communal Societies* 4 (Fall 1984): 19–34; and Brewer, 228–38, question estimates of Shaker membership. Brewer cites data to show 1,373 members in eleven communities in 1800. Thomas Brown states, 328, that there were about three thousand Shakers in 1787, while contemporary

scholars often estimate two thousand members at this period. If either estimate is correct, a considerable number of converts left the movement after Ann Lee's death.

27. *A Summary View*, 35.

28. Ibid., 43.

29. Henri Desroche, *The American Shakers: From Neo-Christianity to Presocialism*, translated from the French and edited by John K. Savacool (Amherst: The University of Massachusetts Press, 1971), 213.

30. *A Summary View*, 45.

31. Brown, 325.

32. The late Brother Theodore Johnson made such a suggestion in a talk he gave at a conference at Pleasant Hill, Kentucky, 3 May 1984.

33. *A Summary View*, 48.

34. Joseph Meacham, *Concise Statement of the Principles of the Only True Church...Together with a Letter from James Whittaker, Minister of the Gospel in This Day of Christ's Second Appearing—to His Natural Relations in England. Dated October 9th, 1785.* (Bennington, VT: Haswell & Russell, 1790).

35. See Andrews, 58, for a description of the "order of families."

36. This position has been misinterpreted by some writers. See, for example, Raymond Lee Muncy, *Sex and Marriage in Utopian Communities* (Bloomington and London: Indiana University Press, 1973), 20. For a exposition of celibacy as the organizing symbol of Shakerism, see Sally L. Kitch, *Chaste Liberation: Celibacy and Female Cultural Status* (Urbana and Chicago: University of Illinois Press, 1989).

37. Andrews, 52.

38. *A Summary View*, 47.

39. Brown, 329.

40. Anna White and Leila Taylor, *Shakerism, Its Meaning and Message* (Mount Lebanon, NY: The United Society of Believers, 1905), 70.

41. Brown, 333.

42. Andrews, 54.

43. For further information, see Andrews, 57ff.

44. Thus, in retrospect, Shakers asserted that Ann Lee had appointed James Whittaker as her successor, while Whittaker had designated Joseph Meacham to succeed him.

45. Garrett, 230.

46. Joseph Meacham, MS, Western Reserve Historical Society, VII A–12.

47. Reuben Rathbone, 9.

Chapter 2. Postcharismatic Authority in the Amana Society: The Legacy of Christian Metz

1. *Inspirations-Historie/oder Auszuege aus den Tagebuechern von Br. Christian Metz,* etc. [on spine: *Tagebuch von Br. C. Metz*] (Amana, Iowa: [Amana Society], 1875), 902–26. Metz's obituary was twenty-five pages long. By comparison, the longest obituary prior to his (Br. C. L. Meyer, d.1862) was five pages, the longest afterward nine (Br. C. Winzenried, d.1886).

2. *Inspirations-Historie/oder Auszuege aus den Tagebuechern von Br. Christian Metz* (1875), 919–29.

3. Ibid., 921.

4. Ibid., 924.

5. *Jahrbuecher der wahren Inspirations-Gemeinden/oder Bezeugungen des Geistes des Herrn, ausgesprochen im Jahr 1867* [Volume 42] (Amana, Iowa: [Amana Society], 1871), 78.

6. *Inspirations-Historie/oder Auszuege aus den Tagebuechern von Br. Christian Metz,* 925.

7. Manuscript of *Bruderraths Beschluesse 1850–1900* [Resolutions of the Board of Trustees], used by the author in 1973 courtesy of Mr. Don Shoup, Secretary of the Amana Society.

8. Although not specified in the constitution, a third level of authority existed in each of Amana's seven villages, namely the village *Bruderraths.* These local councils, appointed by the trustees, implemented Board policies and dealt with the members on a day to day basis, assigning them their work, lodging, and dining hall. They were the first to deal with transgressions against the rules, usually by summoning the offending parties to appear before them for a reprimand; serious cases were referred to the board of trustees. The local councils also oversaw all business and production activities within each village, and for that reason were made up of elders with some business experience.

9. *Bruderraths Beschluesse,* 127.

10. Ibid., 127.

11. Ibid., 128. Presumably, this meant that testimonies given by the eighteenth-century *Werkzeuge,* and also ones given earlier by Metz and Landmann, would not be read.

12. Ibid., 170.

13. See the various *Sammlungen* [Collections] of inspired testimonies, for example *Jahrbuecher der wahren Inspirations-Gemeinden, Oder Bezeugungen des Geistes des Herrn, ausgesprochen im Jahr 1865 durch Christian Metz und Barbara Landmann*, Volume 42 (Amana, Iowa: [Amana Society], 1870) and earlier volumes.

14. Ibid., Volume 41, 194.

15. *Bruderraths Beschluesse*, 129. Although the church did not actually adhere to this schedule, the important point is that they announced a schedule almost immediately.

16. The source of the decision to regularize the Communion service has not been found, though it almost certainly was the board of trustees. Barbara Landmann was regularly inspired in Communion services, but none of her testimonies prescribes a scheduling pattern.

17. *Inspirations-Historie*, 1867–1876 (Amana, Iowa: [Amana Society], 1900), 22.

18. For example, in consecutive years from 1868 to 1882 Landmann delivered in West Amana (5,5,5,5,6,5,5,4,4,4,3,3,3,3,3,3) testimonies. Between 1858 and 1867, Metz gave (5,7,9,3,6,3,2,3,2). A comparable difference can be found in the monthly output of testimonies; for example, in successive Augusts from 1868 to 1882 Landmann gave (2,2,2,2,1,3,1,1,2,2,2,1,1,4,2) testimonies, while between 1858 and 1867 Metz gave (6,0,4,7,6,3,7,4,3). Landmann also gave a consistent number of testimonies at particular church rituals from year to year; at the Yearly Spiritual Examination (*Unterredung*) services from 1868 to 1882 she gave (16,13,13,12,15,14,14,14,13,15,14,14,14,14,14,14) testimonies, and at Holy Communion (7,0,7,0,7,0,8,0,7,0,7,0,7,0,7). At *Unterredung* services Metz became inspired (13,9,2,20,15,10,11,22,6) times. (Holy Communion was held only once between 1858 and 1867.) See Jonathan G. Andelson, "Routinization of Behavior in a Charismatic Leader," *American Ethnologist* 7(4):716–33 (November 1980) for a fuller discussion of this evidence.

19. Evidence on these points can be found in the various *Jahrbuecher* (collections of testimonies) from Landmann's years. Her testimony about the railroad is from Volume 46, 44 (25 March 1871); that about photographs is in Volume 49, 3 (12 January 1874). The one about useful and decorative trees is in Volume 55, 62 (27 April 1880).

20. *Jahrbuecher*, Volume 42, 85.

21. Ibid., 96.

22. G. Scheuner. *Inspirations-Historie* (Amana, Iowa: [Amana Society] 1900), 9.

23. *Jahrbuecher*, Volume 42, 88.

24. Ibid., 92.

25. Ibid., 96.

26. Ibid., 84.

27. Ibid., 91.

28. Ibid., 92.

29. Ibid., 88.

30. *Jahrbuecher*, Volume 43 (Amana, Iowa: [Amana Society], 1872), 26.

31. *Jahrbuecher der wahren Inspirations-Gemeinden*, Volume 42, 78.

32. The possibility exists that these net gains might be masking large emigra-tion rates so long as immigration was larger. Census records reveal that over forty adults (plus their children) left the community between 1860 and 1870, although unfortunately we cannot determine what proportion of them did so after Metz died.

33. See Charles Nordhoff, *The Communistic Societies of the United States* (New York: Hillary House Publishers, Ltd., 1960 [orig. publ. 1875]), 57.

34. *Inspirations-Historie oder Beschreibung des Gnadenwerks des Herrn in den Gemeinden der wahren Inspiration* [on spine: *Inspirations-Historie 1877–1883]* (Amana, Iowa: [Amana Society], 1916), 433–34.

Chapter 3. American Indian Prophets

1. Leslie Marmon Silko, *Ceremony* (New York:Signet, 1978), 132–133.

2. E.g., "These forms of religion, like the culture out of which they spring, have no possibility of any significant and conscious progress. A traditional civilization is always stationary." Edmund Davison Soper, *The Religions of Mankind* 3rd ed., revised (New York: Abingdon, 1951). With respect to native Americans, the image of the "timeless Indian" persisted in academic studies until the early 1970s—not coincidently the same period during which American Indian activist groups began to make an impression on this country's con-sciousness. Robert F. Berkhofer, Jr., *The White Man's Indian: Images of the American Indian from Columbus to the Present* (New York: Vintage, 1979), 67.

3. It also serves to legitimate the physical and cultural conquest of another people. With respect to the North American context, refer to Berkhofer and to the introductory discussion in Francis Jennings, *The Invasion of America: Indians, Colonialism, and the Cant of Conquest* (Chapel Hill: University of North Carolina Press, 1975).

4. E.g., refer to the discussion in Andrew Walls, "Primal Religious Traditions in Today's World," in Frank Whaling, ed., *Religion in Today's World: The Religious Situation of the World from 1945 to the Present Day* (Edinburgh: T & T Clark, 1987), 250–278.

5. Sam D. Gill, *Beyond "The Primitive": The Religions of Nonliterate Peoples* (Englewood Cliffs:Prentice-Hall, 1982), 107–108.

6. Dale Van Every, "Cherokee Removal," in Francis Paul Prucha, ed., *The Indian in American History* (Hinsdale:Dryden, 1971), 29–38. This selection is excerpted from Every's *Disinherited: The Lost Birthright of American Indians.*

7. Although its importance as a factor would be difficult to deny, the connection between a state of "deprivation" and the emergence of new religious movements is not a simple one. Taken by itself, it explains neither why millenarian movements fail to develop among *all* demoralized groups, nor why such movements sometimes emerge among groups that are relatively well off. With respect to this latter point, refer to the discussion in Joel Martin, *Cultural Hermeneutics on the Frontier* (diss., Duke University, 1988).

8. On this point, Durkheim's classical analysis of the social function of group ritual is still useful. Emile Durkheim, *The Elementary Forms of the Religious Life* (New York: Free Press, 1965; reprint of 1915).

9. The Ghost Dance of 1870 was the prototype of the more well known Ghost Dance of 1890. In much the same way that Wovoka's Ghost Dance spread eastward and revitalized many eastern tribes, the Ghost Dance introduced by the earlier prophet Wodziwob spread beyond the Paiute to stimulate religious revivals among western tribal groups. An overview of Wodziwob's less familiar movement can be found in Michael Hittman, "The 1870 Ghost Dance at the Walker Reservation: A Reconstruction," *Ethnohistory* 20:3 (Summer 1973), 247–278. For a survey of its broader impact, refer to Cora Du Bois, "The 1870 Ghost Dance," *University of California Anthropological Records* 3 (Berkeley: University of California Press, 1939).

10. James R. Lewis, "Shamans and Prophets:Continuities and Discontinuities in Native American New Religions," *American Indian Quarterly* 12:3 (Summer 1988), 221–228.

11. The shamanic call and its accompanying deathlike states, such as initiatory sicknesses, is a well studied phenomenon; e.g., Mircea Eliade, *Shamanism* (Princeton: Princeton University Press, 1972).

12. The similarities and dissimilarities between shamans and prophets are outlined fairly lucidly in Grim's analysis of shamanism. John A. Grim, *The Shaman* (Norman: University of Oklahoma Press, 1983).

13. John Heckewelker, *History, Manners, and Customs of the Indian Nations Who Once Inhabited Pennsylvania and the Neighbouring States* in

Memoirs of the Historical Society of Pennsylvania, Vol. 12 (Philadelphia: Historical Society of Pennsylvania, 1876), 291.

14. Joseph B. Herring, *Kenekuk, the Kickapoo Prophet* (Lawrence: University Press of Kansas, 1988), 36.

15. Cited in R. David Edmunds, *The Shawnee Prophet* (Lincoln: University of Nebraska Press, 1983), 38.

16. Vittorio Lanternari, *The Religions of the Oppressed: A Study of Modern Messianic Cults* (New York: Mentor, 1965), 101.

17. Cited in James Mooney, *The Ghost-Dance Religion and the Sioux Outbreak of 1890* (Chicago: University of Chicago, 1965; abridged reprint of original 1896 edition), 23.

18. Omer C. Stewart, "The Ghost Dance" in W. Raymond Wood and Margot Liberty, eds., *Anthropology on the Great Plains* (Lincoln: University of Nebraska Press, 1980), 179–187.

19. This assertion needs to be qualified, however, with the observation that even war prophets often left permanent traces in their cultures' traditions. Recently, one scholar has argued that the activities of the Delaware prophets led, in spite of Pontiac's defeat, to a lasting "internal reordering of Delaware society." Duane Champagne, "The Delaware Revitalization Movement of the Early 1760s: A Suggested Reinterpretation," *American Indian Quarterly* 12:2 (Spring 1988), 107.

20. Edmunds, *The Shawnee Prophet*, 33–34.

21. Letter of Thomas Jefferson to John Adams, 20 April 1812. Cited in Carl F. Klinck, ed., *Tecumseh:Fact and Fiction in Early Records* (Englewood Cliffs: Prentice-Hall, 1961), 53.

22. Edmunds, *The Shawnee Prophet*, 40.

23. Edmunds, *The Shawnee Prophet*, 110.

24. Tenskwatawa's post-Tippecanoe career was actually fairly complex, and he remained a minor leader until his death. The fate of the prophet's religious innovations was also more complex than I am portraying it. For example, field workers in the early part of the present century discovered that traditional Shawnees *continued* to identify the Evil Spirit with Euro-americans, an identification that might well have originated with Tenskwatawa. Noel William Schutz, Jr., *The Study of Shawnee Myth in an Ethnographic and Ethnohistorical Perspective* (diss., Indiana University, 1975), 92–93.

25. Anthony F. C. Wallace, *The Death and Rebirth of the Seneca* (New York: Vintage, 1972; reprint of 1969), 244.

26. Wallace, *The Death and Rebirth of the Seneca*, 281.

27. Although some reports of Wovoka's teachings portrayed them as being one-sidedly antiwhite, the prophet's personal attitude was more complex. For instance, although he predicted the destruction of Anglo civilization, such items of information as the fact that "he saw both Indians and whites" during his visit to/vision of heaven indicates that he distinguished between good and evil Euro-Americans, and felt no unusual antipathy toward the former. Cited in Edward C. Johnson, *Walker River Paiutes: A Tribal History* (Schurz, NV: Walker River Paiute Tribe, 1975), 47.

28. Lanternari, *The Religions of the Oppressed*, 129–130.

29. Peggy V. Beck and A. L. Walters, *The Sacred: Ways of Knowledge, Sources of Life* (Tsaile, AZ: Navajo Community College Press, 1977), 180. This is a debatable point. For a recent survey of interpretive scholarship on the Ghost Dance refer to Part Two of Alice Beck Kehoe, *The Ghost Dance: Ethnohistory and Revitalization* (New York: Holt, Rinehart and Winston, 1989).

30. Ake Hultkrantz, *Native Religions of North America* (New York: Harper and Row, 1987), 83. Also note that Kehoe discovered a Ghost Dance "congregation" in Saskatchewan in the 1960's; refer to her *The Ghost Dance.*

31. E.g., among the Pawnee. Alexander Lesser, *The Pawnee Ghost Dance Hand Game: A Study of Cultural Change* (New York: Columbia University Press, 1933).

32. Wallace, *The Death and Rebirth of the Seneca.*

33. Herring, *Kenekuk.*

34. H. G. Barnett, *Indian Shakers: A Messianic Cult of the Pacific Northwest* (Carbondale: Southern Illinois University Press, 1957). A more recent study of the Tolowa Shakers indicates that the group is alive and well. Al Logan Slagle, "Tolowa Indian Shakers and the Role of Prophecy at Smith River, California," in Clifford E. Trafzer, ed., *American Indian Prophets* (Newcastle, CA: Sierra Oaks, 1986), 115–136.

35. Although the fieldwork for Clement W. Meighan and Francis A. Riddell's *The Maru Cult of the Pomo Indians: A California Ghost Dance Survival* (Los Angeles: Southwest Museum, 1972) was carried out in the late forties, the authors noted that the ceremonies were still being carried out in the early seventies, and furthermore asserted that "unless some action disbands the Pomo community we may anticipate continuance of Maru ceremonialism indefinitely" (p. 81).

36. Unlike the above movements for which few book-length studies exist (and for which it is easy to cite *the* one major study), the Peyote Religion has attracted many scholars. One of the classic studies in this area is Weston LaBarre, *The Peyote Cult* (New Haven: Yale University Publications in Anthropology, 1938).

37. John G. Neihardt, *Black Elk Speaks* (1959; New York: Washington Square Press, 1972). Even scholars with more than a superficial acquaintance with the Ghost Dance have made this mistake; e.g., as recently as 1969 one author asserted that the Wounded Knee massacre "put an end to the Ghost Dance." John Greenway, "Ghost Dance," *The American West* 4:4 (1969), cited in Omer C. Stewart, "Contemporary document on Wovoka (Jack Wilson) Prophet of the Ghost Dance in 1890," *Ethnohistory* 24:3 (Summer 1977), 219.

38. Leon Festinger, Henry W. Riecken, and Stanley Schachter, *When Prophecy Fails* (Minneapolis: University of Minnesota Press, 1956).

39. Hittman, "The 1870 Ghost Dance," 247–278. Although the Paiute eventually rejected it, Wodziwob's movement spread to California where it "was institutionalized into beliefs and practices that continue today." Kehoe, *The Ghost Dance*, 34.

40. Lanternari, *The Religions of the Oppressed*, 119.

41. Margery Ann Beach, "The Waptashi Prophet and the Feather Religion: Derivative of the Washani" in Clifford E. Trafzer, ed., *American Indian Prophets* (Newcastle, CA: Sierra Oaks, 1986), 87–95.

42. This is the theoretical perspective, formulated by Weber and perpetuated by Yinger, that was discussed in the introductory essay of this volume. Max Weber, *The Theory of Social and Economic Organization* (New York: Oxford University Press, 1947), 363–387. The same analysis has often been applied to such prophet religions as the Ghost Dance of 1890; e.g., in one otherwise careful analysis, the author asserts that "Only the magnetic appeal of a charismatic leader could bring about a revitalization movement which could periodically draw the Paiute groups together. Similarly only such a leader could maintain the momentum of this movement." Brad Logan, 'The Ghost Dance Among the Paiute: An Ethnohistorical View of the Documentary Evidence, 1889–1893," *Ethnohistory* 27:3 (Summer 1980): 281.

43. One of the principal conclusions of Barker's excellent study of converts to the Unification Church was that the members who remained with the movement more than a short period of time were the members whose primary concerns were addressed by the group's ideology, a conclusion that supports the present argument. Eileen Barker, *The Making of a Moonie* (New York: Basil Blackwell, 1984).

44. Peter L. Berger and Thomas Luckmann, *The Social Construction of Reality: A Treatise in the Sociology of Knowledge* (Garden City, NY: Doubleday Anchor, 1967).

45. Even under peculiar conditions, such as when Kenekuk prophesied that he would be resurrected three days after his death, the faith of a community is frequently not shattered. Herring, *Kenekuk*, 126.

Chapter 4. The Latter Day Saint Movement:
A Study in Survival

1. For an overview of the various churches that have comprised the Latter Day Saint movement through the years, see Steven L. Shields, *Divergent Paths of the Restoration* (Los Angeles, CA: Restoration Research, 1990). A detailed bibliography of the various Latter Day Saint churches also provides pertinent information. See Steven L. Shields, *The Latter Day Saint Churches: An Annotated Bibliography* (New York: Garland Publishing, Inc., 1987). Chad J. Flake provides a comprehensive bibliography of all Latter Day Saint publications from 1830 to 1930 in *A Mormon Bibliography* (Salt Lake City: University of Utah Press, 1978).

2. Joseph Smith expressed his story of the coming forth of the church he organized in several different versions. The most commonly known story was first published in 1842. See *Times and Seasons*, Volume 3, Number 9, 1 March 1842, pages 706–710, and *Times and Seasons* Volume 3, Number 11, 1 April 1842, page 748. Succeeding issues of this periodical contained installments of Joseph Smith's history and the history of the church. This record has formed the basis for much of the history of the Latter Day Saint church from its inception up to Smith's death in 1844.

In Smith's interpretation and practice of priesthood, any male member of the church who was deemed worthy could be ordained as a minister without requirements of a seminary degree or other formal education. Certain of the priesthood were designated to officiate in sacramental roles that were reserved only to those so appointed. However, the responsibility of all members of the church, by virtue of their baptism, to provide ministry to other persons has been an important concept in the church since its earliest days.

3. The fourteen years is marked from the legal organization of the church as of 6 April 1830. Contemporary records of persons associated with the church at that time contend that the church existed prior to that date by at least a year or possibly more, and that the action on 6 April 1830 was taken in order to satisfy the requirements of the law. See David Whitmer, *An Address to All Believers in Christ* (Richmond, MO: author, 1887), 32–33.

4. Shields, *Divergent Paths of the Restoration*, 21–29.

5. Ibid., 22

6. This period was a time of great crisis in the church. All of the Three Witnesses to the Book of Mormon, four apostles, several presidents of seventy and one member of the First Presidency left the church. See Milton V. Backman, Jr., *The Heavens Resound: A History of the Latter-Day Saints in Ohio* (Salt Lake City: Deseret Book Company, 1983), 327–329.

7. Shields, *Divergent Paths*, 23. See *Elders Journal 1* (August 1838):55–60 for a contemporary narrative regarding Parrish's separatist movement.

Notes

8. The "First Presidency" is a group of three persons, who, including the Prophet Joseph, represented the highest authority in the church. Several present-day Latter Day Saint churches maintain this tradition and base it on scriptures contained in the various editions of the *Doctrine and Covenants*.

9. See James B. Allen and Glenn M. Leonard, *The Story of the Latter-day Saints* (Salt Lake City: Deseret Book Company, 1976), 170–171. Information relating to the renunciation of the practice is found in the same volume on pages 413–415, as well as numerous other sources. See Shields, *Divergent Paths*, 104–106.

10. For an interesting and scholarly analysis, see Richard P. Howard, "The Changing RLDS Response to Mormon Polygamy: A Preliminary Analysis," *John Whitmer Historical Association Journal 3* (1983), 14–29.

11. Shields, *Divergent Paths*, 29–30, quotes Thomas C. Sharp's stinging renunciation of Smith's actions and a call to arms.

12. Joseph Smith manustript 1832–1834 Journal, 19 April 1834, 79, LDS Historical Department.

13. *Times and Seasons* 5 September 1844, 651. The "Quorum of Twelve Apostles" was a "restoration" of the body that Jesus called to assist him in his ministry. In the original organization of the church under Joseph Smith, the first body of twelve men was selected by a committee of three who had been appointed by Joseph Smith. The first "twelve apostles" were organized and ordained in 1835. At the time of Joseph Smith's death, Brigham Young was president of this group of church leaders. Next to the First Presidency, the Quorum of Twelve was the most influential group of church leaders in Joseph Smith's time. This tradition is based on revelations issued by Smith, and is maintained by several Latter Day Saint churches. Persons who become members of the Twelve Apostles in any of the various Latter Day Saint churches are called by revelation and ordained according to the authority of the particular church. The body of membership is usually called upon to ratify the action by a sustaining vote. Apostles in the Utah LDS tradition generally serve for life; apostles in the RLDS tradition may be released by revelation and permitted to retire from public life. In some cases, apostles are called upon to assume other leadership functions in the church and thus are released from the "Twelve." In the RLDS and LDS Churches, the president of the quorum is generally the most senior member according to date of ordination. The First Presidency, in both cases, would either select the president of the twelve, or approve the selection of a president by his peers. Again, the body of membership would eventually ratify this by a voting process. Procedures in the different churches vary. The Twelve Apostles function under the direction of the First Presidency, and according to the *Doctrine and Covenants*, the Twelve are the "second" presidency, and have administrative jurisdiction in some areas of the church. The "keys of the kingdom" are referred to in various places in the Doctrine and Covenants, and are defined as the "right of presidency; they are the power and authority to govern and direct all of the Lord's affairs on earth."

14. See D. Michael Quinn, "Joseph Smith III's 1844 Blessing and the Mormons of Utah,"*John Whitmer Historical Association Journal 1* (1981), 13–14.

15. See *Doctrine and Covenants* [RLDS 104:11c; 105:12]; [Utah 107:24; 118:30].

16. See Roger D. Launius, *Joseph Smith III: Pragmatic Prophet* (Urbana and Chicago: University of Illinois Press, 1988), 31–32. Various contemporaries recorded one or more of the blessings pronounced on Joseph Smith III as his father's successor. The most lengthy account was left by James Whitehead in his testimony in the Temple Lot Suit of the 1890s. Whitehead's testimony begins on page 28 of the *Complainant's Abstract of Pleading and Evidence* (Lamoni, IA: Herald Publishing House and Bindery, 1893). Even though Whitehead's testimony on other matters, notably polygamy, are in error, his comments regarding the selection of Joseph Smith III has been corroborated by other evidence and witnesses.

17. The "stake" was an ecclesiastical unit of church organization that is similar to a diocese. Both the Utah LDS and the RLDS churches utilize the "stake" as a format for local organization of the church.

18. See D. Michael Quinn, 21.

19. F. Mark McKiernan, *The Voice of One Crying in the Wilderness: Sidney Rigdon, Religious Reformer* (Independence, MO: Herald House, 1979), 113–119. McKiernan details the strained relations between Smith and Rigdon.

20. Allen and Leonard, 200.

21. Ibid.

22. *Wilford Woodruff's Journal (Typescript)* Volume 2 (Midvale, UT: Signature Books, 1983), 434.

23. *History of the Church (LDS)*, 7:229–30. This multivolume set was published in Salt Lake City between 1902 and 1912. Volume 7 was added in 1932. Although written in the first person, Joseph Smith actually did very little of the writing himself. And, when the bulk of the work first appeared in church periodicals in the mid to late 1800s, the editors of the work stated that the history has been carefully revised under the strict inspection of President Brigham Young, and approved by him (Preface, Volume 1, pp. v–vi).

24. "History of Brigham Young," *LDS Millennial Star 26* (4 June 1864), 359.

25. See *Wilford Woodruff's Journal* Volume 2, 434–440 for a detailed narrative of the proceedings of the conference. The office of "patriarch" to the church was established early in the 1830s by Joseph Smith. A common practice in the early Latter Day Saint church, one that was modeled after stories in the Bible and Book of Mormon, was for fathers to pronounce special

"patriarchal" blessings on their children. The church patriarch was to serve this function for the fatherless of the church. Several Latter Day Saint churches continue this practice today, but in various formats.

26. Allen and Leonard, 201–202. See also Shields, *Divergent Paths*, 36.

27. See Quinn, 20.

28. *Times and Seasons* 5 (15 August 1844), 618.

29. Quinn, 19–20.

30. These religious ceremonies were said to have power to "seal" in heaven the relationships forged on earth. The Utah LDS Church and a number of groups that have separated themselves therefrom, along with a few others, continue to practice these "endowments" in some format. Considerable research has been done on the connection between these and Masonic ritual. See Jack Adamson and Reed C. Durham, Jr., *No Help for the Widow's Son* (Nauvoo, IL: Martin Publishing Company, 1980).

31. In 1844 Joseph Smith made a bid for the presidency of the United States. At the time of his death, most of the church's leaders and missionaries were campaigning for his candidacy in many parts of the country. Joseph's vision for a political kingdom of God has been described in a number of books, including Klaus J. Hansen, *Quest for Empire* (Lincoln: University of Nebraska Press, 1974) and Robert Bruce Flanders, *Nauvoo: Kingdom on the Mississippi* (Urbana, IL: University of Illinois Press, 1965).

32. See Quinn, 20. His footnotes are especially germane to the issue for they demonstrate that records were kept long after the fact.

33. Ibid.

34. See Shields, *Divergent Paths*, for various Latter Day Saint beliefs.

35. The Reorganized Church of Jesus Christ of Latter Day Saints. This church began to emerge in the early 1850s, but became formally established in 1860 when Joseph Smith III, son of the martyred prophet, became president.

36. Brigham Young's church continued the name "Church of Jesus Christ of Latter-day Saints," formalizing the hyphenated spelling of "Latter" and "Day," even though in the original church it had been written variously. Strang's church adopted the name "Church of Jesus Christ of Latter Day Saints" with more modern manifestations including "Strangite" at the end. Alpheus Cutler's group adopted "The Church of Jesus Christ," as did William Bickerton's. Granville Hedrick's movement opted for the original name of the church as stated in 1830. "Church of Christ." Since the late 1800s that church has attached "Temple Lot" to its name to distinguish itself from other groups of similar name. The "Temple Lot" is the name of the property in Independence where this group has its headquarters. The RLDS Church adopted the name "Church of Jesus Christ of Latter Day Saints" and formally attached the prefix

"Reorganized" in the late 1860s or early 1870s in order to distinguish the movement from the church in Utah, which was then being scandalized nationally for its practice of polygamy.

37. In other words, those who still maintain the practice of polygamy, etc.

38. For an interesting discussion of this issue, see Fred C. Collier, "The Nauvoo Doctrine on Priesthood," *Restoration: The Journal of Latter Day Saint History 6* (January 1987), 8–15.

39. This document is in the collections at Yale University.

40. A number of excellent materials provide information on Strang, his organization, and the doctrines that made the church unique. See Shields, *Divergent Paths*, 40–46; also Shields, *The Latter Day Saint Churches: An Annotated Bibliography*, 41–70.

41. William Shepard, Donna Falk, Thelma Lewis, *James J. Strang: Teachings of a Mormon Prophet* (Burlington, WI: Church of Jesus Christ of Latter Day Saints (Strangite), 1977), 6,7.

42. Ibid., iii.

43. *Wilford Woodruff's Journal 3*, 283.

44. Ibid., 293–301.

45. Ibid., 249–251

46. Allen and Leonard, 279. See also Leonard J. Arrington and Davis Bitton, *The Mormon Experience* (New York: Alfred A. Knopf, 1979), 212–213.

47. *Journal of Discourses 4* (1857), 6.

48. As quoted in Quinn, 21.

49. As quoted in Quinn, 23.

50. Quinn, 23–24.

51. One has but to review current literature, published by numerous official and independent presses to the Utah church market, to have a clear understanding of the tremendous weight that Utah Mormons place in all that Joseph Smith said or was alleged to have said. See Shields, *The Latter Day Saint Churches: An Annotated Bibliography* for listings of much of the current and past literature of the movement.

52. Bruce R. McConkie, *Mormon Doctrine* (Salt Lake City: Bookcraft Inc., 1966), 650.

53. Arrington and Bitton, photo plate prior to page 201, the caption under David O. McKay reads that he was a "member of the Quorum of Twelve Apostles from 1906 until his death [in 1970] and member of the First Presidency from 1934 to 1970."

54. Allen and Leonard, 201.

55. Bruce R. McConkie, *A New Witness for the Articles of Faith* (Salt Lake City: Deseret Book Company, 1984), 3.

56. The high council was a judicial body within the leadership of the stake comprised of twelve high priests. In the days of Nauvoo, the high council wielded considerable authority in the community.

57. Shields, *Divergent Paths*, 60–65.

58. Rupert J. Fletcher and Daisy Whiting Fletcher, *Alpheus Cutler and the Church of Jesus Christ* (Independence, MO: The Church of Jesus Christ, 1974), 36, 37. See Shields, *The Latter Day Saint Churches: An Annotated Bibliography.*

59. See Shields, *Divergent Paths*, 65; Arrington and Bitton, 91; Inez Smith Davis, *The Story of the Church* (Independence, MO:Herald House, 1981), 392–393.

60. Shields, *Divergent Paths*, 65.

61. RLDS D&C 43:2a; LDS D&C 43:4; Book of Commandments 45:4.

62. Joseph Smith III is quoted as having stated, in regard to lineal succession, that "no son of mine will be entitled to follow me as my successor, unless at the time he is chosen he is found to be worthy in character." Roger D. Launius, 341–342. Three of Joseph Smith III's sons succeeded him in presiding over the church.

63. Arrington and Bitton, 92.

64. Current editions of the RLDS Doctrine and Covenants are kept up to date with sections as they are added by the conferences of the church.

65. Quinn, 24.

66. W. H. Cadman, *A History of the Church of Jesus Christ* (Monongahela, PA: The Church of Jesus Christ, 1945), 7–9; 28–31.

67. Ibid., 31–34.

68. See Shields, Divergent Paths, 89–98 for a brief historical summary and overview of beliefs.

69. V. James Lovalvo, *A Dissertation on the Faith and Doctrine of the Church of Jesus Christ* (1986), 114–117. See also Shields, *The Latter Day Saint Churches: An Annotated Bibliography.*

70. B. C. Flint, *An Outline History of the Church of Christ (Temple Lot)* (Independence, MI: Church of Christ (Temple Lot), 1953), 102.

71. Shields, *Divergent Paths*, 76–77. See 78–83 for doctrinal summary of this church.

72. *A Brief History of the Church of Christ* (nd, np, but issued by the Church of Christ (Temple Lot)).

73. B. C. Flint, 68. See also Shields, *The Latter Day Saint Churches: An Annotated Bibliography.*

Chapter 5. They Found a Formula: 450 Years of Hutterite Communitarianism

1. Rosabeth Moss Kanter has argued that the proper test of communal success is survival for twenty-five years, a sociological generation. By that standard the great majority of communes are not successful. Kanter herself, measuring the success of the ninety-one communal movements and societies she counted as having been founded between 1780 and 1860, found eleven successful, seventy-nine unsuccessful, and one unclassifiable. (See Rosabeth Moss Kanter, *Commitment and Community* [Cambridge: Harvard University Press, 1972], 244–248.) My own survey of 150 communes and communal movements founded in America between 1860 and 1960 suggests that about 10 percent of them have been successful in Kanter's terms. (See Timothy Miller, *American Communes, 1860–1960: An Annotated Bibliography* [New York: Garland, 1990].

2. See Leonard Gross, *The Golden Years of the Hutterites* (Scottsdale, PA: Herald Press, 1980).

3. That group was the Society of Brothers, or Bruderhof, now known as the Hutterian Society of Brothers. The most detailed account of its history and life is Benjamin Zablocki, *The Joyful Community* (Chicago: University of Chicago Press, 1971).

4. This overview of early Hutterite history is based on several secondary accounts written by various authors. In the past several decades much has been published on Hutterite origins. Examples of general histories that cover the early phases of Hutterism include John A. Hostetler, *Hutterite Society* (Baltimore: Johns Hopkins University Press, 1974), 5–118, and Victor Peters, *All Things Common: The Hutterian Way of Life* (New York: Harper and Row, 1965), 9–37. For an excellent essay review of works on early Hutterite history see Robert Friedmann, "Comprehensive Review of Research on the Hutterites 1880–1950," *Mennonite Quarterly Review* 24 (October, 1950): 353–363; for a bibliographical list see John A. Hostetler, "Bibliography of English Language Materials on the Hutterian Brethren," *Mennonite Quarterly Review* 44 (January, 1970): 106–113.

5. Hutterian Brethren, trans. and ed., *The Chronicle of the Hutterian Brethren*, vol. I (Rifton, NY: Plough Publishing House, 1987), 80–81.

6. Many have assumed that Hutter's name derived from his trade (see, for example, George Huntston Williams, *The Radical Reformation* [Philadelphia:

Westminster, 1962], 419). John Hostetler, however, finds that conclusion "doubtful" (see Hostetler, *Hutterite Society*, 17).

7. Peter Riedemann (Rideman), *Account of Our Religion, Doctrine and Faith, Given by Peter Rideman of the Brothers Whom Men Call Hutterians*, trans. Kathleen E. Hasenberg (London: Hodder and Stoughton, with Plough Publishing House, 1950).

8. *Chronicle of the Hutterian Brethren*, 319–520.

9. For a discussion of Hutterite population estimates for this period, see Hostetler, *Hutterite Society*, 29.

10. On Hutterite ceramics, see two articles by Robert Friedmann: "Hutterian Pottery or Haban Fayences," *Mennonite Life* 13:4 (October, 1958): 147–152, 182; and "More About Habaner Pottery, *Mennonite Life* 14:3 (July, 1959): 129–130.

11. See Robert Friedmann, "Hutterite Physicians and Barber—Surgeons," *Mennonite Quarterly Review* 27:2 (April, 1953): 128–136.

12. For an overview of the mistreatment of Hutterite conscript prisoners, see John D. Unruh, "The Hutterites During World War I," *Mennonite Life* 24:3 (July, 1969): 130–137. For a first-person account, see Theron Schlaback, ed., *"An Account*, by Jakob Waldner: Diary of a Conscientious Objector in World War I," *Mennonite Quarterly Review* 48 (January, 1974): 73–111.

13. John Hofer, *The History of the Hutterites* (Elie, Manitoba: Hutterian Educational Committee, James Valley Colony, 1988), 92–99.

14. Lawrence Anderson, "List of Hutterite Colonies, 1983." Copy at Center for Communal Studies archives, University of Southern Indiana, Evansville.

15. Robert C. Cook, "The North American Hutterites: A Study in Human Multiplication," *Population Bulletin* 10:8 (December, 1954): 97–107.

16. Robert Friedmann, "A Hutterite Census for 1969: Hutterite Growth in One Century, 1874–1969," *Mennonite Quarterly Review* 44:1 (January, 1970): 100–105.

17. Karl A. Peter, "The Decline of Hutterite Population Growth," *Canadian Ethnic Studies* 12:3 (1980): 97–110. Reprinted in *The Dynamics of Hutterite Society: An Analytical Approach* (Edmonton: University of Alberta Press, 1987), 152–170.

18. Rodney Stark, "How New Religions Succeed: A Theoretical Model," in David G. Bromley and Phillip E. Hammond, eds, *The Future of New Religious Movements* (Macon, GA: Mercer University Press, 1987), 13.

19. Kenneth Rexroth, *Communalism: From Its Origins to the Twentieth Century* (New York: Seabury, 1974), 283.

20. John W. Bennett, "The Managed Democracy of the Hutterites." *Communes: Creating and Managing the Collective Life*, ed. Rosabeth Moss Kanter (New York: Harper and Row, 1973), 192–205. Reprinted, slightly revised, from Bennett's *Hutterian Brethren: The Agricultural Economy and Social Organization of a Communal People* (Stanford, CA: Stanford University Press, 1967). Bennett provides an organizational chart for a typical Hutterite colony on page 195.

21. Pierre L. van den Berghe and Karl Peter, "Hutterites and Kibbutzniks: A Tale of Nepotistic Communism," *Man* n.s. 23 (September, 1988): 536.

22. Karl Peter reports that since perhaps the 1970s birth control has come into some use; the Hutterites have relied increasingly on modern medicine, and thus birth control has become something decided by a woman and her doctor, not by the community. See Karl A. Peter, "A 'Demographic' Theory of Hutterite Population Growth," *Dynamics of Hutterite Society*, 150.

23. For a discussion of the increase in the growth rate after 1910, see Joseph W. Eaton and Albert J. Mayer, *Man's Capacity to Reproduce: The Demography of a Unique Population* (Glencoe, IL: Free Press, 1954). Reprinted from *Human Biology* 25:3 (1954), where it was titled "The Social Biology of Very High Fertility Among the Hutterites."

24. Hostetler, *Hutterite Society*, 273.

25. See Joseph W. Eaton, "Controlled Acculturation: A Survival Technique of the Hutterites," *American Sociological Review* 17:4 (June, 1952): 331–340.

26. Hostetler, *Hutterite Society*, 117.

27. For the text of the Communal Property Act, see Province of Alberta, *Report of the Hutterite Investigation Committee* (Edmonton: Government of Alberta, 1959). For government findings that led to the repeal of the Act see Province of Alberta, *Report on Communal Property, 1972* (Edmonton: Select Committee of the Alberta Assembly, 1972).

28. For an account of the conflict in Alberta, see Howard Palmer, "The Hutterite Land Expansion Controversy in Alberta," *Western Canadian Journal of Anthropology* (July, 1971): 18–46.

29. See, for example, "Can't Buy Land in Alberta; Hutterites Eye Washington," *Financial Post* 50 (16 June 1956): 39.

30. See *Dominion Law Reports* (Canada), Second series, v. 59 (1967): 723–736.

31. Karl Peter, Edward D. Boldt, Ian Whitaker, and Lance W. Roberts, "The Dynamics of Religious Defection Among Hutterites," *Journal for the Scientific Study of Religion* 21:4 (December, 1982): 327–337. Reprinted in Peter, *Dynamics of Hutterite Society*, 45–58.

32. Edward D. Boldt, "The Death of Hutterite Culture: An Alternative Interpretation," *Phylon* 41:4 (December, 1980): 390–395.

33. Peter, "A 'Demographic' Theory of Hutterite Population Growth," 147.

34. Ibid., 148–149.

35. Karl Peter and Ian Whitaker, "Changing Roles of Hutterite Women". *Prairie Forum* 7:2 (Fall, 1982): 267–77. Reprinted in Peter, *Dynamics of Hutterite Society*, 197–207.

36. See, for example, James S. Frideres, "The Death of Hutterite Culture," *Phylon* 33:3 (Fall, 1972): 260–265.

Chapter 6. Democracy vs. Hierarchy:
The Evolution of Authority in the Theosophical Society

1. H. P. Blavatsky, "The Original Programme of the Theosophical Society," in *The Original Programme of the Theosophical Society and Preliminary Memorandum of the Esoteric Section* (Adyar, Madras: The Theosophical Publishing House, 1974), 5.

2. Henry S. Olcott, *Old Diary Leaves: The History of the Theosophical Society*, Third Series, 1883–87 (Adyar, Madras: The Theosophical Publishing House, 1972), 231.

3. Josephine Ransom, *A Short History of the Theosophical Society* (Adyar, Madras: Theosophical Publishing House, 1938), 81.

4. Ibid., 105, 155, 545–553.

5. Henry S. Olcott, *Old Diary Leaves: The History of the Theosophical Society As Written By the President-Founder Himself*, First Series, America 1874–1878 (Adyar, Madras: The Theosophical Publishing House, 1974), 267–69.

6. Constance Wachtmeister, et al, *Reminiscences of H.P. Blavatsky and The Secret Doctrine*, Quest Book (Wheaton, IL: The Theosophical Publishing House, 1976), 25, 27.

7. Ransom, *A Short History*, 97; Olcott, *Old Diary Leaves*, I, 379–82.

8. See Ransom, *A Short History*, 170, 177, 196, 202, 220, 232, 248, 251 concerning appearances of the Masters. The "Mahatma Letters" to A. P. Sinnett are now in the British Museum. Olcott coined the term "precipitation." See *Old Diary Leaves* I, 362.

9. Henry S. Olcott, "The President-Founder's Address" in *General Report of the Thirteenth Convention and Anniversary of the Theosophical Society at the Head-Quarters, Adyar, Madras, December the 27th, 28th, and 29th—1888* (N.p.:No Publisher, n.d.). Although this report is not listed as part of *The*

Theosophist, it can be located after the issue for September 1889 in Vol. X. Olcott always cited membership statistics by branches, and not by individuals.

10. The "Introductory Explanations" to the Revised Rules are simply signed as being written by "F. T. S.," i.e., "Fellow of the Theosophical Society," in the *General Report of the Thirteenth Convention and Anniversary of the Theosophical Society.*

11. See J. N. Farquhar, *Modern Religious Movements in India*, 1st Indian ed., (Delhi: Munshiram Manoharlal, 1967), 232–55 for an examination of the evidence. Vernon Harrison of the SPR reexamined the Hodgson Report in *Journal of the Society for Psychical Research*, 53 (April 1986), and concluded that Hodgson ignored evidence that favored Blavatsky's case, and that the SPR owed an apology to Blavatsky. Joy Mills, *100 Years of Theosophy: A History of the Theosophical Society in America* (Wheaton, IL: The Theosophical Publishing House), 210.

12. Ransom, *A Short History*, 247–252. H. P. Blavatsky, "The Esoteric Section of the Theosophical Society, Preliminary Memorandum," in *The Original Programme of the Theosophical Society and Preliminary Memorandum of the Esoteric Section*; Henry S. Olcott, *Old Diary Leaves: The History of the Theosophical Society*, Fourth Series, 1887–92 (Adyar, Madras: The Theosophical Publishing House, 1975), 54–65.

The Esoteric Section, now known as the Esoteric School, as its name indicates, is a secret organization. Blavatsky's "Preliminary Memorandum" for the Esoteric Section explained that its purpose was to bring together a select group for the study of practical occultism, which would help promote growth toward the first object of the Theosophical Society: brotherhood. She stressed that E. S. members would *not* be taught the magic arts or how to produce physical phenomena. She warned that those wishing to receive direct orders from the Masters would probably be disappointed. To become an E. S. member, one must be prepared to abstain from meat, tobacco, alcohol, and nonprescription drugs, and to be chaste (but not necessarily celibate).

13. Ransom, *A Short History*, 248.

14. "Introductory Explanations" to the Revised Rules, 48.

15. Earlier Rules drawn up in 1879, just after the founders had come to India, stated that the president was under the authority of the Masters who constituted the "First Section" of the Society. The Rules were revised in 1885 to drop this reference to the Masters. See "The Theosophical Society, or Universal Brotherhood. Principles, Rules, and Bye-Laws, as revised in General Council, at the meeting held at the Palace of H. H. the Maharajah of Vizianagram, Benares, 17th December, 1879)" in *The Theosophist*, 1 (April 1880): 179–80; Ransom, *A Short History*, 123, 229.

Presently, the membership of the General Council consists of the president, vice president, treasurer, secretary, and general secretaries of the national sections (the post of president of the Theosophical Society in America is equivalent to the position of general secretary). The General Council may also include not fewer than five, and not more than twelve, additional members, which will include all past presidents. Other additional members are elected to terms of three years by the General Council. "Rules and Regulations for the Management of the Association Named 'The Theosophical Society', Adyar, Madras," *Hundred and Twelfth Annual General Report of the Theosophical Society 1987* (Adyar, Madras: The International Secretary, 1987), 77.

16. "Introductory Explanations" to the Revised Rules, 46.

17. Arthur H. Nethercot, *The First Five Lives of Annie Besant* (Chicago: The University of Chicago Press, 1960), 358.

18. Ransom, *A Short History*, 282. Joy Mills, Director of the Krotona Institute, School of Theosophy, in Ojai, California, states that it is unclear whether Blavatsky appointed solely Besant, or both Besant and Judge to be the Outer Heads of the Esoteric Section. From her reading of the Esoteric Section records, she believes that Blavatsky appointed Besant and Judge to be joint Outer Heads. Conversation with Joy Mills, 4 January 1989.

19. Arthur H. Nethercot, *The Last Four Lives of Annie Besant* (Chicago: The University of Chicago Press, 1963), 28; Olcott, *Old Diary Leaves*, IV, 524.

20. Ransom, *A Short History*, 286–90; Olcott, *Old Diary Leaves*, IV, 441–47.

21. Henry S. Olcott, *Old Diary Leaves: The History of the Theosophical Society*, Fifth Series, Jan. 1893–April 1896 (Adyar, Madras: The Theosophical Publishing House, 1975), 202–03.

22. Ibid., 272.

23. Ibid., 273

24. Ibid., 252, 268, 286–300, 314–16. Judge died within a year of the secession and his leadership passed to Katherine Tingley, who changed the name to Universal Brotherhood and Theosophical Society, and concentrated her efforts on the community at Point Loma, California. Currently, the American section of the Theosophical Society (Adyar) is officially known as the Theosophical Society in America.

25. Olcott, *Old Diary Leaves*, V, 206; Mills, 29.

26. Bruce F. Campbell, *Ancient Wisdom Revived: A History of the Theosophical Movement*, (Berkeley: University of California Press), 131–35, 150–53, 158–63.

27. Olcott, *Old Diary Leaves*, V, 82.

28. Olcott, *Old Diary Leaves*, IV, 521; Olcott, "President's Address" in *General Report of the Thirtieth Anniversary and Convention*, 4.

29. "Rules and Regulations for the Management of the Association named The Theosophical Society, Adyar, Madras," in *General Report of the Thirtieth Anniversary and Convention*, 81.

30. Ransom, *A Short History*, 366. See also Nethercot, *Last Four Lives*, 99–112; Henry S. Olcott, "To the Theosophical Society," *Supplement to the Theosophist*, February 1907, xx.

31. Ransom, *A Short History*, 368-71.

32. Upendranath Basu, " 'A Conversation with the Mahatmas, ' " in *Supplement to The Theosophist*, March 1907, xxxi–xxxvii.

33. Bertram Keightley, "To My Fellow Members of the T. S., "*Supplement to the Theosophist*, April 1907, xxxvi–xxxvii.

34. G. R. S. Mead, "The Coming Election to the Presidency," *Supplement to The Theosophist*, April 1907, lix. See Ransom, *A Short History*, 370–73, for A. P. Sinnett's opinion that the figures who stood by Olcott's bed were not whom they seemed to be.

35. Annie Besant, "To the members of the Theosophical Society," *Supplement to The Theosophist*, March 1907, xxviii.

36. Annie Besant, "The Presidency of the T.S. To the Members of the British Section," in *Supplement to The Theosophist*, May 1907, lxxii.

37. Ransom, *A Short History,* 372.

38. Besant began reporting her statistics in terms of individual members, rather than branches. See Michel R. Chapotin, "The Theosophical Society in the World." This is an unpublished compilation of statistics drawn from the Annual Reports of the Theosophical Society. M. Chapotin can be reached at 4 Square Rapp, 75007 Paris, France. My sincere thanks go to Bing Escudero, national lecturer for the Theosophical Society in America, for sharing this material with me.

39. "Freedom of Thought," resolution passed by the General Council of the Theosophical Society on 23 December 1924, *The Theosophist*, 74 (October 1952): ii.

40. Catherine Lowman Wessinger, *Annie Besant and Progressive Messianism* (Lewiston, NY: The Edwin Mellen Press, 1988).

41. Campbell, 128.

42. Nethercot, *Last Four Lives*, 361–375.

43. See Mary Lutyens, *Krishnamurti: The Years of Awakening*, (New York: Farrar, Straus and Giroux, 1975); Mary Lutyens, *Krishnamurti: The Years of Fulfillment,*, (New York: Farrar, Straus and Giroux, 1983); Mary Lutyens, *Krishnamurti: The Open Door,* (New York: Farrar, Straus and Giroux, 1988); Pupul Jayakar, *Krishnamurti: A Biography,* (San Francisco: Harper & Row, 1986).

44. Michel Chapotin, "The Theosophical Society in the World."

45. Josephine Ransom, *The 75th Anniversary Book of the Theosophical Society: A Short History of the Society's Growth 1926–1950*, (Adyar, Madras: The Theosophical Society, 1950), 52.

46. See, for example, "The Transfer of the Presidential Ring, February 17, 1953", *The Theosophist* 74 (March 1953): 387.

47. Marie Minor, Department of Education, Theosophical Society in America, Linda Jo Pym, Director of Fieldwork and Assistant to the President, Theosophical Society in America, and Nancy Harper, National Secretary of the Theosophical Society in America, report that no one today is claiming to be in direct contact with the Masters. All three expressed polite skepticism about the claims of other individuals outside the Theosophical Society, but within the Theosophical movement, concerning their representation of the Masters. These conversations took place on 31 December 1988, and 3 January 1989.

Chapter 7. Charisma and Covenant: The Christian Science Movement in its Initial Postcharismatic Phase

1. Stated in a letter to the Christian Science Board of Directors, 27 February 1903: cited in Norman Beasley, *The Continuing Spirit* (New York: Duell, Sloan and Pearce, 1956), 7.

2. For those readers unfamiliar with the Christian Science movement, along with Mormonism, the Adventist groups, New Thought groups, and Pentecostalism, Christian Science is a "made in America" religion. It was founded by Mary Baker Eddy in the later decades of the Nineteenth century after she experienced a "miraculous" healing and, thereafter, surmised that all material limitations were surmountable through the attainment of Christ-consciousness. Though devout Christian Scientists insist that Mrs. Eddy's revelation was unique, the worldview reverberates with traditions dating back to Plato. God is Mind, the material realm is illusory, all is spirit, and health, wealth, and happiness are available to anyone who gives up negative, limited thinking and recognizes his or her self as a perfect thought reflected in the Divine Mind. The "Christian" element emerges in the teaching in that Jesus was the ultimate "Christian Scientist" who demonstrably overcame sin, sickness, and death through his superior perception of the allness of Spirit and the nothingness of matter.

3. Annie C. Bill, *Message of Life, Liberty, and Happiness* (Washington, D.C.: A. A. Beauchamp, 1926), 109.

4. In a chapter from her "miscellaneous writings" entitled "Personality," Mrs. Eddy writes, "There was never a religion or philosophy lost to the centuries except by sinking its divine Principle in personality." *The First Church*

of Christ, Scientist and Miscellany (Boston: Christian Science Publishing Co., 1913), 117.

5. One rather extreme example of her control of church members may be found in Article 22, section 11 of *The Church Manual*, which requires that, upon ten days notice, a Christian Scientist must leave home and family to serve Mrs. Eddy *for three years*. Refusal results in "excommunication." Apparently such servitude was considered a blessing, and many early Christian Scientists were more than happy when they received the call to serve. Mary Baker Eddy, *Manual of The Mother Church* (Boston: Trustees Under The Will of Mary Baker Eddy, 1936), 67.

6. The only hope in trying to arrive at an unbiased appraisal of the Christian Science movement is to read biographies at the two extremes—then make your own conclusions. Robert Peel, the premier "in-house" biographer of Mary Baker Eddy, is an excellent source—well-documented, comprehensive, etc.— for the pro–Christian Science rendition of the historical emergence of the movement.
   On the other hand, in 1906 and 1907, *McClure's Magazine*, the most prominent of the muckraking journals of the time, published a series of articles on Mrs. Eddy by Georgine Milmine that were reissued in revised form as a book in 1909 (Georgine Milmine, *Life of Mary Baker G. Eddy)*. Milmine's book is also well documented, containing many eyewitness accounts of life in the early Christian Science movement, but is radically biased against its subject and is the first in a long line of debunking biographies of the founder of Christian Science.
   There is no better compilation and explanation of the theologically intricate teachings of Christian Science than in Stephen Gottschalk's *The Emergence of Christian Science in American Religious Life* (Berkeley: University of California, 1973). While Gottschalk is obviously a pro–Christian Science historian, he has the understanding and writing skills to make Christian Science comprehensible to the uninitiated.

7. Gottschalk, 184.

8. Cf. Max Weber, *The Theory of Social and Economic Organization*, ed. Talcott Parsons (New York: The Free Press, 1947), 328ff.

9. Cf. Robert Peel, *Mary Baker Eddy*, 3 Vols. (New York: Holt, Rinehart and Winston, 1971).

10. Gottschalk, 184.

11. Quoted in Gottschalk, 185.

12. Beasley, 5–6.

13. Eddy, *The Manual*, 26.

14. From Francis J. Mott, *Spiritual Organization* (New York: The Integration Publishing Co., 1946), 10.

15. Robert Peel, *Mary Baker Eddy: The Years of Authority* (New York: Holt, Rinehart and Winston, 1977), 346.

16. Eddy, *The Manual*, 72.

17. Helen M. Wright, *If Mary Baker Eddy's Manual Were Obeyed* (self published, 1984), 23–24.

18. Francis J. Mott, *The Christ Seed* (Boston: A. A., Beauchamp, 1939), 5.

19. See Gottschalk, Peel.

20. Braden, 70.

21. Eddy, *The Manual*, 81–82.

22. Ibid, 44. As one might imagine, to this day, tension exists within the Christian Science organization between these two powerful boards though it is assiduously played down by the movement's spokespeople.

23. Ibid., 80.

24. Ibid.

25. Braden, 74.

26. Ibid., 76.

27. Quoted in Altman K. Swihart, *Since Mrs. Eddy* (New York: Henry Holt and Co., 1931), 138. Swihart's work remains the most complete study of Annie Bill's sectarian activities.

28. Quoted in Gottschalk, 176.

29. Cf. Braden, chapter 15.

30. Cf. Swihart, and Mary Sayles Moore, *Conquest of Chaos* (Indianapolis: self-published, 1954) for accounts of Mrs. Bill's early conflicts with the established Christian Science movement.

31. Annie Bill, *The Christian Science Journal* (1916, Page 16). At no little annoyance to the Christian Science hierarchy, Annie Bill published her own "authentic" journal until legal steps were taken to stop her replication of official Christian Science periodicals.

32. Swihart, 206–207.

33. Ibid., 208.

34. Ibid., 210–211.

35. Ibid., 244–249.

36. Ibid., 264–265.

37. Peel, 116–117.

38. Quoted in Swihart, 265.

39. The Christian Science organization today is by no means in great shape, but due to the strength of *The Manual* the problems are not organizational. The difficulties facing the movement arise from trying to maintain the belief in and devotion to spiritual healing in an increasingly secular society. Recently, Christian Scientist parents have been convicted of third degree murder for allowing their child to die while under the care of a Christian Science practitioner.

40. J. Gordon Melton, *The Encyclopedia of American Religions*, 3rd. ed. (Detroit: Gale Research, 1988), 876–877.

41. Mott, 23–25.

42. Melton, 877.

43. Peter Williams, *Popular Religion in America* (Englewood Cliffs, NJ: Prentice Hall, 1980), 13.

44. Cf. Stillson J. Judah, *The History and Philosophy of the Metaphysical Movements in America* (Philadelphia: Westminster, 1967).

45. Cf. William G. McLoughlin, *Revivals, Awakenings, and Reform* (Chicago: University of Chicago Press, 1978).

Chapter 8. When Prophets Die:
The Case of the Spirit Fruit Society

1. Letter from Evelyn Beilhart Hastings to author, 9 November 1984; Jacob Beilhart, *Fruit of the Spirit* (Ingleside, IL: Privately Printed, 1908), 2–13.

2. Beilhart, *Fruit of the Sprit*, 7, 9.

3. *Spirit Fruit* (Lisbon, OH), June 1899; *Spirit's Voice* (Lisbon OH), June 1899.

4. *Spirit Fruit*, June 1899; *Jacob Beilhart: Life and Teachings* (Burbank, CA: Freedom Hill Pressery, 1925), 58–60.

5. Interview with Robert J. Knowdell, Santa Cruz, CA, 21 June 1984, hereafter cited as Knowdell interview.

6. H. Roger Grant, "Prairie State Utopia: The Spirit Fruit Society of Chicago and Ingleside," *Chicago History* 12 (Spring 1983): 28–35; Kate Waters to Ruth and Robert Knowdell, 14 January 1939, in possession of Ruth Knowdell, Santa Cruz, CA.

7. *Waukegan* (IL) *Daily Sun*, 24 November 1908.

8. Letter from Robert J. Knowdell to James L. Murphy, 23 March 1980. Mr. Knowdell supplied a copy of this twenty page manuscript to the author with several additions and corrections; it will be cited hereafter as Knowdell history.

9. Waters to Knowdells, 14 January 1939; *Chicago Record-Herald*, 15 January 1911; Knowdell history.

10. Telephone interview with Evelyn Beilhart Hastings, Lawrence, Kansas, 23 April 1986.

11. Telephone interview with Evelyn Beilhart Hastings, 25 October 1985; H. Roger Grant, *Spirit Fruit: A Gentle Utopia* (DeKalb: Northern Illinois University Press, 1988), 63.

12. Telephone interview with Evelyn Beilhart Hastings, 13 April 1986; William Alfred Hinds, *American Communities and Co-operative Colonies* (Chicago: Charles H. Kerr & Company, 1980), 559.

13. Grant, *Spirit Fruit*, 129–31.

14. Knowdell history.

15. Letter from "Freedom Hill" Henry to librarian, University of California, 28 November 1925, attached to *Fruit of the Spirit*; Knowdell history.

16. Knowdell interview.

17. Knowdell history; telephone interview with Evelyn Beilhart Hastings, 25 October 1985.

18. Knowdell history.

19. Ibid.

20. Knowdell interview.

21. Knowdell history.

22. Ibid.

23. Ibid.; Knowdell interview.

24. Knowdell history.

25. Ibid.

26. This book was published in Delhi, India, in 1929 by Practical Medicine.

Chapter 9. The Rastafari of Jamaica

1. The earliest sources on Rastafari beliefs are George Eaton Simpson, "Political Cultism in West Kingston, Jamaica," *Social and Economic Studies*, Volume 4, Number 2, 1955, 133–49; and M. G. Smith, Roy Augier, and Rex Nettleford, *Report on the Rastafari Movement in Kingston, Jamaica* (Kingston: Institute of Social and Economic Research, University of the West Indies, 1961). All other sources are products of the 1960s and later years. Among them one

may mention Leonard Barrett, *The Rastafari: A Study in Messianic Cultism* (Rio Piedras: University of Puerto Rico, 1968); Rex Nettleford, *Mirror, Mirror: Identity, Race and Protest in Jamaica* (Kingston: Collins-Sangster, 1970); Joseph Owens, *Dread: The Rastafarians of Jamaica* (London, Kingston, and Port of Spain: Heinemann, 1976); and K. W. J. Post *Arise Ye Starvelings: The Jamaican Labour Rebellion of 1938 and Its Aftermath* (The Hague, Boston, and London: Martinus Nijhoff, 1978); plus several as yet unpublished doctoral dissertations: Klaus de Albuquerque, *Millenarian Movements and the Politics of Liberation: The Rastafarians of Jamaica* (Virginia Polytechnic Institute and State University, 1977); Alston B. Chevannes, *Social and Ideological Origins of the Rastafari Movement in Jamaica* (Columbia University, 1989); John Homiak, *The "Ancient of Days" Seated Black: Eldership, Oral Tradition and Ritual in Rastafari Culture* (Brandeis University, 1985); and Carole Yawney, *Irons in Babylon: The Rastafarians of Jamaica as a Visionary Movement* (McGill University, 1978). Sources within the Rastafari movement itself include: Dennis Forsythe, *Rastafari: For the Healing of the Nation* (Kingston: Zaika Publications, 1983) and I. Jabulani Tafari, "The Rastafari—Successors of Marcus Garvey," Maureen Rowe, "The Woman in Rastafari," and Leachim Semaj, "Rastafari: From Religion to Social Theory," all in a special issue of *Caribbean Quarterly*, Volume 26, Number 4, 1980.

2. See the Book of Numbers, 6:5.

3. See Maureen Rowe, "The Woman in Rastafari," *Caribbean Quarterly*, Volume 26, Number 4, 1980, 13–21.

4. Carole Yawney, "To Grow a Daughter: Cultural Liberation and the Dynamics of Oppression in Jamaica" in A. Miller and G. Finn, eds., *Feminism in Canada* (Montreal: Black Rose Books, 1983).

5. Alston Chevannes, *Social and Ideological Origins of the Rastafari Movement in Jamaica*, 280–84, 402–07.

6. See Velma Pollard, "Dread Talk—The Speech of the Rastafarian in Jamaica," *Caribbean Quarterly*, Volume 26, Number 4, 1980, 32–41.

7. Joseph Owens, *Dread*, 64–68.

8. See for example Sebastian Clarke, *Jah Music: The Evolution of Popular Jamaican Song* (London: Heinemann, 1980) and Stephen Davis, *Reggae Bloodlines: In Search of the Music and Culture of Jamaica* (New York: Anchor, 1977).

9. In Jamaica the description "coloured" refers to people of mixed European and African origin. Sometimes the word "brown" is used, referring to the colour of skin.

10. Woodville Marshall, "Aspects of the Development of the Peasantry," *Caribbean Quarterly*, Volume 18, 1968.

11. Philip Curtin, *Two Jamaicas: The Role of Ideas in a Tropical Colony, 1830–1865* Westport, CT: Greenwood Press, 1955), 173.

12. "Revival" is the name that Myal, the African-Jamaican folk religion of the peasantry, adopted in 1860.

13. See Barry Chevannes, "Religion and Black Struggle," *Savacou*, Volume 2, 1972.

14. See his *Plural Society of the British West Indies* (Berkeley and Los Angeles: University of California Press, 1965).

15. See, for example, Fernando Henriques, *Family and Colour in Jamaica* (London: Eyre and Spottiswoode, 1953).

16. Monica Schuler, "Myalism and the African Religions Tradition," in Margaret E. Crahan and Franklin W. Knight, eds, *Africa and the Caribbean: the Legacies of a Link* (Baltimore and London: John Hopkins University Press, 1979), 65–79.

17. Martha Beckwith, *Black Roadways: A Study of Jamaican Folk Life* (Chapel Hill, NC: University of North Carolina, 1929), 172–73.

18. Among the more recent books on Garveyism are Robert A. Hill, ed., *The Marcus Garvey and Universal Negro Improvement Association Papers* (Berkeley: University of California Press, 1983–1985); Rupert Lewis, *Marcus Garvey: Anti-colonial Champion* (London: Karia Press, 1987); Rupert Lewis and Maureen Warner-Lewis, eds., *Garvey: Africa, Europe, the Americas* (Kingston: Institute of Social and Economic Research, 1986); Rupert Lewis and Patrick Bryan, eds., *Garvey: His Work and Impact* (Kingston: Institute of Social and Economic Research and Department of Extra-Mural Studies, University of the West Indies, 1988); and Tony Martin, *Race First: The Ideological and Organizational Struggles of Marcus Garvey and the Universal Negro Improvement Association* (Westport, CT: Greenwood Press, 1976).

19. See Bengt Sundkler, *Zulu Zion and Some Swazi Zionists* (London: Oxford University Press, 1976), 15.

20. Post, *Arise Ye Starvelings*, 161.

21. Post, 166.

22. *The Daily Gleaner*, 9 January 1936, 23.

23. The Rastafari believe that blacks were the original "children of Israel," but regard Jesus, the Son of God, as the Messiah. Selassie, therefore, is Jesus Christ returned.

24. E. P. S. McPherson and Leahcim Semaj, "Rasta Chronology," *Caribbean Quarterly*, Volume 26, Number 4, 117.

25. The Late Vivian Durham, for example, a prominent Garveyite and attorney, called for it to be banned from Kingston, if not from the entire island *(Daily Gleaner, 6 January 1937)*, a call later echoed by at least one middle—class group (Post, 191–92).

26. "It stemmed from the evangelism of Marcus Garvey," wrote Vittorio Lanternari, *The Religions of the Oppressed: A Study of Modern Messianic Cults* (New York: Alfred Knopf, 1963), 135.

27. Chevannes, *Social and Ideological Origins of the Restafari Movement*, 175. See also Robert Hill, "Leonard P. Howell and Millenarian Visions in Early Rastafari, *Jamaica Journal*, Volume 16, Number 1.

28. Ajai and Laxmi Mansingh, "Hindu Influences on Rastafarianism," *Caribbean Quarterly Monograph* (Kingston: University of the West Indies, 1985), 112.

29. Chevannes, *Social and Ideological Origins.*

30. *Arise Ye Starvelings*, 166.

31. Barry Chevannes, "Revival and Black Struggle," *Savacou*, Volume 2, 1972.

32. Post, 165.

33. *Daily Gleaner*, 22 May 1954.

34. Chevannes, *Social and Ideological Origins*, 222.

35. *Bantu Prophets in South Africa* (London: Oxford University Press, 1960).

36. Post, 164–165; emphasis added.

37. *Social and Ideological Origins*, 242–71.

38. *Daily Gleaner*, 21 August 1948.

39. A Barrington Chevannes, "Repairer of the Breach: Reverend Claudius Henry and Jamaican Society," in Frances Henry, ed., *Ethnicity in the Americas* (The Hague: Mouton, 1976).

40. Rex Nettleford, *Mirror, Mirror.*

41. Leonard Barrett, *The Rastafarians: the Dreadlocks of Jamaica* (London: Heinemann, 1977).

42. Colin Clarke, "The Slums of Kingston," in Lambros Comitas and David Lowenthal, eds., *Work and Family Life: West Indian Perspectives* (New York: Anchor Books, 1973).

43. Carl Stone, *Electoral Behavior and Public Opinion in Jamaica* (Kingston: Institute of Social and Economic Research, 1974), 26–27.

44. Frank Jan van Dijk, "The Twelve Trives of Israel: Rasta and the Middle Class," *New West Indian Guide*, Volume 62, Numbers 1 and 2.

45. Len Garrison, *Black Youth, Rastafarianism and the Identity Crisis in Britain* (London: Afro-Caribbean Resource Project, 1979).

46. D. Hebdige, "Reggae, Rastas and Rudies: Style and Subversion of Form" (stencilled Occasional Paper, Centre for Contemporary Cultural Studies, University of Birmingham, 1975).

47. Horace Campbell, *Rastafari and Resistance: From Marcus Garvey to Walter Rodney* (London: Hasib Publishing Limited, 1985).

48. Neil Savishintsky (personal communication) found Rastafari in all six West African countries he had visited in 1989 on his doctoral research. A South African student has informed me that there are even white Rastafari in a small settlement outside Cape Town. One important tenet not shared by the Africans is apparently the belief in Selassie's divinity.

49. See John Homiak, *The "Ancient of Days."*

50. Dennis Forsythe, *Rastafari: For the Healing of the Nation.*

51. Maureen Rowe, "The Woman in Rastafari" and Leahcim Semaj, "Rastafari: From Religion to Social Theory."

52. Derek Gordon, "Race, Class and Social Mobility in Jamaica," in Rupert Lewis and Patrick Bryan, *Garvey: His Work and Impact* (Kingston: Institute of Social and Economic Research and Department of Extra-Mural Studies, University of the West Indies, 1988), 277.

53. Derek Gordon, 278.

54. Carl Stone, "Race and Economic Power in Jamaica," in Lewis and Bryan, *Garvey*, 262.

Chapter 10. The Call of the Lotus-Eyed Lord: The Fate of Krishna Consciousness in the West

1. Parts of this essay are drawn, in condensed and revised form, from my article "The Fading of Utopia: ISKCON in Transition," *Bulletin of the John Rylands University Library of Manchester* 70:3 (Autumn, 1988): 171–183.

I should point out that my assessment herein of the present state of ISKCON (and its future prospects) is slightly less sanguine than that in my earlier article, "The Future of Krishna Consciousness in the West: An Insider's Perspective," which appears in *The Future of New Religious Movements*, ed. David G. Bromley and Phillip E. Hammond (Macon, GA: Mercer University Press, 1987), 187–209; and even less so than in an earlier article, "ISKCON after Prabhupada: An Update on the Hare Krishna Movement," *ISKCON Review* 1 (1985): 7–14.

2. Kenneth Westhues, *The Religious Community and the Secular State* (Philadelphia: J. B. Lippincott, 1968), 18.

3. There are several major works in English on the Chaitanya or Gaudiya ("Bengali") Vaishnava tradition. See, for example, S. K. De, *The Early History of the Vaisnava Faith and Movement in Bengal* (Calcutta: Firma K. L. Mukhopadhyay, 1961); and Ramakanta Chakrabarty, *Vaisnavism in Bengal* (Calcutta: Sanskrit Pustak Bhandar, 1985).

4. "Interview with Thomas J. Hopkins," in Steven J. Gelberg, ed., *Hare Krishna, Hare Krishna: Five Distinguished Scholars on the Krishna Movement in the West* (New York: Grove, 1983), 114–15.

5. Quoted in Satsvarupa dasa Goswami, *Vaisnava Behavior* (Port Royal, PA: Gita-nagari Press, 1983), 72.

6. "Interview with Thomas J. Hopkins," 107.

7. Ibid., 108–109.

8. *Letters from Srila Prabhupada* (Los Angeles: Vaisnava Institute, 1987), vol. 3, page 1959.

9. Ibid., vol. 3, page 1518.

10. See, for instance, A. C. Bhaktivedanta Swami Prabhupada, *The Nectar of Devotion*, second edition (Los Angeles: Bhaktivedanta Book Trust, 1982), 116; A. C. Bhaktivedanta Swami Prabhupada, *Sri Isopanisad* (Los Angeles: Bhaktivedanta Book Trust, 1974), 68.

11. Ravindra Svarupa dasa, " 'Under my Order...': Reflections on the Guru in ISKCON" (unpublished paper, 1985), 1.

12. Ibid., 3.

13. Satsvarupa dasa Goswami, *Guru Reform Notebook* (Washington, D.C.: Gita-nagari Press, 1986), 35.

14. Ravindra Svarupa dasa, "Under My Order," 6.

15. Rohini Kumar Swami, "Some Observations on the Latter-Day Gurus" (unpublished paper, 1984), 3.

16. "Resolution to Restore Full Faith in the GBC," November, 1980.

17. For an elaboration of these aspects of the appeal of Krishna consciousness see, for example, "Interview with Thomas J. Hopkins," 115–16; and Robert Ellwood, "ISKCON and the Spirituality of the 1960s," in David G. Bromley and Larry D. Shinn, eds., *Krishna Consciousness in the West* (Lewisburg, PA: Bucknell University Press, 1989), 104–106. See also J. Stillson Judah, *Hare Krishna and the Counterculture* (New York: John Wiley and Sons, 1974), chapters 6 through 9, for a lucid explanation of why ISKCON was attractive to some young people in the late 1960s.

18. "A. C. Bhaktivedanta Swami Prabhupada and Allen Ginsberg: Conversations, Part 2." Unpublished manuscript, 47–64. A condensed, edited version of this conversation appears in Hayagriva dasa, *The Hare Krishna Explosion: The Birth of Krishna Consciousness in America—1966–1969* (New Vrindaban, WV: Palace Press, 1985), 289–94. I have based my account on both sources.

19. A. C. Bhaktivedanta Swami Prabhupada, trans. and commentary, *Srimad-Bhagavatam*, third canto, volume two (Los Angeles: Bhaktivedanta Book Trust, 1977), 308–309.

20. For a more detailed account of the ritual and contemplative regimen observed in ISKCON temples, see my article, "Exploring an Alternative Reality: Spiritual Life in ISKCON," in Bromley and Shinn, eds., *Krishna Consciousness in the West*.

21. Thomas F. O'Dea, "Five Dilemmas in the Institutionalization of Religion," in Louis Schneider, ed., *Religion, Culture and Society* (New York: John Wiley and Sons, 1964), 580–81.

22. Theodore Roszak, *Unfinished Animal* (London: Faber and Faber, 1976), 71.

23. Jacob Needleman, *The New Religions* (New York: Pocket Books, 1972), 224.

Chapter 11. Siddha Yoga:
Swami Muktananda and the Seat of Power

1. Max Weber, *The Sociology of Religion*, tr. by Ephraim Fischoff (Boston: Beacon Press, 1953), 52. For helpful recommendations, some of which could not be incorporated into the final version of this chapter, I wish to thank Dick Anthony, William Cenkner, Georg Feuerstein, Sheldon R. Isenberg, Richard D. Mann, David M. Miller, Timothy Miller, Linda E. Olds, Harry B. Partin, James E. Royster, Cari Shay, Catherine Wessinger, Charles S. J. White, and Eleanor Zelliot. And my thanks also go to many unnamed participants and former participants in Siddha Yoga, as well as to its leaders and board members.

2. A special issue of the Siddha Yoga movement's monthly magazine *Darshan*, 30–31 (October 1989), reviews Swami Muktananda's life and work in India and in the United States.

3. Joachim Wach, *Sociology of Religion* (Chicago: University of Chicago Press, 1944), 128.

4. W. H. McLeod, "On the word *panth*: a problem of terminology and definition," *Contributions to Indian Sociology*, N.S., 12, 2 (1978): 294. He was writing in response to French social theorist Louis Dumont. See *Homo Hierarchicus: The Caste System and Its Implications*, corrected tr. by Mark

Sainsbury, Louis Dumont, and Basia Gulati (Chicago: University of Chicago Press, 1980). On the *sant* tradition, with which Siddha Yoga has some affinities, see Daniel Gold, *The Lord as Guru: Hindi Sants in North Indian Tradition* (New York: Oxford University Press, 1987), 15–16, 20–21. Cf. Gold's complementary structural study, *Comprehending the Guru: Toward a Grammar of Religious Perception*, American Academy of Religion Series, 57 (Atlanta: Scholars Press, 1988).

5. On the term 'guru', which is crucial to an understanding of this movement, see: Charles S. J. White, "Hindu Holy Persons," in Keith Crim, ed., *Abingdon Dictionary of Living Religions* (Nashville: Abingdon, 1981), 300–303; Joel D. Mlecko, "The Guru in Hindu Tradition," *Numen*, 29 (July 1982): 33–61; and Swami Muktananda, *The Perfect Relationship* (South Fallsburg, NY: SYDA Foundation, 1981). For an evocative account of the process that the relationship is supposed to foster, by a member of the SYDA Foundation board, see Peter Hayes, *The Supreme Adventure: The Experience of Siddha Yoga* (New York: Delta, 1988). The Siddha Guru generally fits the "mystagogue" type proposed by Max Weber, *The Sociology of Religion*, 54–55.

"The catalyst of the *sampradāya* or teaching tradition," William Cenkner noted, "understood in the broadest sense, is the living guru....Faith experience is engendered within the context of the *sampradāya*; this always occurs, however, in direct relationship to the living guru." Cenkner, *A Tradition of Teachers: Sankara and the Jagadgurus Today* (Delhi: Motilal Banarsidass, 1983), 184. On *sampradāya* and guru see also David M. Miller, "The guru as the centre of sacredness," *Sciences Religieuses/Studies in Religion*, 6, 5 (1976/77): 527–533; and Raymond Brady Williams, *A New Face of Hinduism: The Swaminarayan Religion* (Cambridge: Cambridge University Press, 1984), xii.

6. Agehananda Bharati, *The Tantric Tradition* (Garden City, NY: Anchor Books/Doubleday & Company, Inc., 1970), 18. See also pages 9–10, 18–21, 26–27, 31–34 for further clarification of the meaning of '*sādhanā*'. On tantra, see also Paul Eduardo Muller-Ortega, *The Triadic Heart of Siva: Kaula Tantricism of Abhinavagupta in the Non-Dual Shaivism of Kashmir* (Albany: State University of New York Press, 1989); and Sanjukta Gupta, Dirk Jan Hoens, and Teun Goudriaan, *Hindu Tantrism*, Handbuch der Orientalistik, II/4/2 (Leiden/Koln: E. J. Brill, 1979).

7. On the various conventional, Hindu and Buddhist, lists of "the Siddhas" in Indian tradition, see Muller-Ortega, *The Triadic Heart of Siva*, 36–37. In Siddha Yoga the term tends to be used in two general contexts. The first refers to *a lineage (paramparā)*, which is assumed to connect the current incumbent on the Siddha Yoga *gaddi* or seat of power back to the original, essential, divine teacher and teaching—with no diminution or distortion. This usage serves to guarantee the legitimacy of authority—analogous to the theory of papal succession. The second refers to realized beings who are free from attachment and so truly free to love, wherever and whenever they might be found. Among them are the great devotional saints of Maharashtra and several

234

lesser known "great beings" whom Muktananda met in his lifetime. See his *Secret of the Siddhas* (South Fallsburg, NY: SYDA Foundation, 1980), esp. pages 38–47. On the conceptualization and study of unitive mysticism and nondual ontology, see Sheldon R. Isenberg and Gene R. Thursby, "A Perennial Philosophy Perspective on Richard Rorty's Neo-Pragmatism," *International Journal for Philosophy of Religion*, 17, 1–2 (1985): 41–65; Robert K. C. Forman, "Paramārtha and modern constructivists on mysticism: Epistemological monomorphism versus duomorphism," *Philosophy East and West*, 39, 4 (1989): 393-418; and David Loy, *Nonduality: A Study in Comparative Philosophy* (New Haven and London: Yale University Press, 1988).

8. For background on Kashmir Shaivism, see [Swami Tejomayananda], *Introduction to Kashmir Shaivism*, rev. ed. (Oakland, CA: SYDA Foundation, 1977); Gene R. Thursby, "Kashmir Shaivism in Siddha Yoga," in *Proceedings of the Eighth International Symposium on Asian Studies*, (Hong Kong: Asian Research Service, 1986), v. 4, 1227–1238; J. Gonda, *Change and Continuity in Indian Tradition*, Disputationes Rheno-Trajectinae, IX (The Hague: Mouton & Co., 1965), 429–430; Harvey P. Alper, "Śiva and the Ubiquity of Consciousness: The Spaciousness of an Artful Yogi," *Journal of Indian Philosophy*, 7 (1979): 345–407; Mark Dyczkowski, *The Doctrine of Vibration: An Analysis of the Doctrines and Practices of Kashmir Shaivism* (Albany: State University of New York Press, 1987); and especially Muller-Ortega, *The Triadic Heart of Śiva*, 1–24.

9. On body theory, see Frits Staal, "Indian Concepts of the Body," *Somatics*, 4 (Autumn-Winter, 1983–84): 31–41; and Jean Varenne, *Yoga and the Hindu Tradition*, Derek Coltman, tr. (Chicago and London: The University of Chicago Press, 1976). On *kuṇḍalinī*, see Lilian Silburn, *Kuṇḍalinī—The Energy of the Depths: A Comprehensive Study Based on the Scriptures of Nondualistic Kaśmir Śaivism*, Jacques Gontier, tr. (Albany: State University of New York Press, 1988). A summary of the Siddha Yoga viewpoint is Swami Muktananda, *Kundalini: The Secret of Life* (South Fallsburg, NY: SYDA Foundation, 1979). An interpretation of human nature that incorporates this body theory, developmental psychology, and particle physics, yet is skeptical about reincarnation, is offered by a writer closely associated with Siddha Yoga: Joseph Chilton Pearce, *The Magical Child Matures* (New York: E. P. Dutton, Inc., 1985), 208–211. See also note 15 below.

10. Published sources on Nityananda's life are heavily influenced by Indian hagiographic traditions and typologies: Swami Muktananda Paramahansa, *Bhagawan Nityananda: His Life and Mission* (Ganeshpuri: Shree Gurudev Ashram, 1972); M. U. Hatengdi, *Nityananda: The Divine Presence* (Cambridge, MA: Rudra Press, 1984); and Swami Chetanananda, "Introduction," in M. U. Hatengdi and Swami Chetanananda, *Nitya Sutras: The Revelations of Nityananda from the Chidakash Gita* (Cambridge, MA: Rudra Press, 1985), 3–27. On the regional cultural setting, see Eleanor Zelliot and Maxine Berntsen, eds.,

The Experience of Hinduism: Essays on Religion in Maharashtra (Albany: State University of New York Press, 1988), which includes extensive bibliographical references.

11. On the life-history of Muktananda, see Swami Muktananda Paramahansa, *The Play of Consciousness (Chitshaki Vilas)* (Oakland, CA: SYDA Foundation, 1974); Swami Prajnananda, *A Search for the Self: The Story of Swami Muktananda*, 3rd ed. Ganeshpuri: Gurudev Siddha Peeth, 1979); and J. Gordon Melton, *Biographical Dictionary of American Cult and Sect Leaders* (New York and London: Garland Publishing, Inc., 1986), 186–188.

12. Ram Dass is the Indian name that was given to American psychologist and spiritual leader Richard Alpert by his guru, the late Neem Karoli Baba. On Muktananda in relation to Rudi and to Rudi's two leading pupils, see John Mann, *Rudi: 14 Years with My Teacher* (Cambridge, MA: Rudra Press, 1987); Lucia Nevai, "Rudi, The Spiritual Legacy of an American Original," *Yoga Journal* (July-August 1985): 36–38, 68–71; Swami Chetanananda, "Rudi: His Life and Teachings," *Rudra* (March 1983): 8–11; Franklin Jones, *The Method of the Siddhas* (Los Angeles: The Dawn Horse Press, 1973); *The Love-Ananda Gita (The Wisdom-Song of Non-Separateness): The Simple Revelation Book of Heart-Master Da* (San Rafael, CA: The Dawn Horse Press, 1989); and Swami Chetanananda, *The Breath of God* (Cambridge, MA: Rudra Press, 1988). In a conversation reported by Swami Prajnananda, tr. and ed., *Paramartha Katha Prasang: Spiritual Conversations with Swami Muktananda (1962–1966)* (Ganeshpuri: Gurudev Siddha Peeth, 1981), 17, Rudi told Muktananda in 1963: "I had a premonition when I was young that two of my disciples would become very great and world famous." Muktananda delivered a characteristically stern rebuke to "people who claim to be Siddhas" in Swami Muktananda, *Secret of the Siddhas*, 30–37. John Y. Fenton provides a brief sketch of "The Disciples of Nityananda" on page 696 of his essay "Hinduism" in Charles H. Lippy and Peter W. Williams, eds., *Encyclopedia of the American Religious Experience: Studies of Traditions and Movements* (New York: Charles Scribner's Sons, 1988), v. 2, 683–698. Cf. J. Gordon Melton, *The Encyclopedia of American Religions*, 2nd ed. (Detroit: Gale Research Corporation, 1987), 718–719, 723. On Werner Erhard's support of Muktananda's *second* tour, see William Warren Bartley III, *Werner Erhard: The transformation of a man—The founding of est* (New York: Clarkson N. Potter, Inc., 1978), 256.

13. Ron Friedland, "SYDA: Building a Foundation," *Meditate*, 2 (1982–83): 18.

14. Charles S. J. White, "Swāmi Muktānanda and the Enlightenment through Sakti-Pāt," *History of Religions*, 13 (May 1974): 317. (Note that a typographical error on page 314 puts Muktananda's *śaktipāt* experience with Nityananda in 1957, while 1947 is the accepted date.) As White indicates, Muktananda began giving *śaktipāt* in an open fashion in the 1960s in Ganeshpuri. More controversial experiments under the direction of the late Rajneesh were taking place in the same period in nearby Pune. Even so, Muktananda's form of initiation drew

some criticism, e.g., see Robert E. Svoboda, *Aghora: At the Left Hand of God* (Albuquerque, NM: Brotherhood of Life, Inc., 1986), 25. An account of Muktananda in Ganeshpuri, prior to the first world tour, is Peter Brent, *Godmen of India* (London: Allen Lane/The Penguin Press, 1972), 230-282; and just after the second tour is Bill Simons, "Days of the Devotees: A Pilgrimage to Baba Muktananda's Indian Ashram," *New Age* (May 1977): 56–61. A telling personal memoir that evokes the flavor of the times and of Muktananda's appeal during the second tour in the United States is Sally Kempton, "Hanging Out With the Guru," *New York*, 9, 15 (12 April 1976): 36–46. She subsequently entered Siddha Yoga monastic life as Swami Durgananda.

15. On the experiences of recipients of *śaktipāt*, see I. R. Duncan, "A Western Anthropologist's Experience under One Form of Yogic Initiation," *Theoria to Theory*, 4 (1970): 78–80; Paul Zweig, *Three Journeys: An Auto-mythology* (New York: Basic Books, 1976); "Shaktipat Epilogue," by Paul Zweig, in Swami Muktananda, *Getting Rid of What You Haven't Got*, rev. ed., (Oakland, CA: SYDA Foundation, 1978); Joseph Chilton Pearce, *The Bond of Power* (New York: E. P. Dutton, 1981), 30–31; and Kanu Sandra Dunn and Paul J. Magnarella, "Siddha Yoga, Anthropology and the Human Quest," *Anthropology and Humanism Quarterly*, 8 (December 1983): 13–18. On mantra, see Harvey P. Alper, ed., *Mantra* (Albany: State University of New York Press, 1989), esp. Alper's "Introduction," 1–14, and his essay "The Cosmos as Śiva's Language-Game: 'Mantra' According to Kṣemarāja's *Śivasūtravimarśinī*," 249–294. Siddha Yoga and Alper's essay (page 277) share an assumption about effective mantra: "The utterance is directly disclosive. It is self-disclosive. One might say that it 'saves' in that, for every properly prepared adept, it is believed to disclose Śiva to himself." See also Swami Muktananda, "Mantra: Language as God," in Paul Zweig, ed., *Muktananda: Selected Essays* (New York: Harper & Row Publishers, 1976), 78–91. On meditation, see Swami Muktananda, *Meditate*, ed. with an Afterword by Sally Kempton (Albany: State University of New York Press, 1980).

16. Swami Muktananda, *Ashram Dharma* (Ganeshpuri: Shree Gurudev Ashram, 1975). Cf. Charles A. Fracchia, *Living Together Alone: The New American Monasticism* (San Francisco: Harper and Row, 1979).

17. In India the center is a response to heightened interest, especially in urban settings, in guru-oriented religion. See D. A. Swallow, "Ashes and Powers: Myth, Rite and Miracle in an Indian God-Man's Cult," *Modern Asian Studies*, 16, 1 (1982): 123; and T. N. Madan, *Non-Renunciation: Themes and Interpretations of Hindu Culture* (Delhi: Oxford University Press, 1987), 166.

18. The most recent edition of the liturgical manual that records the texts of many of the movement's devotional and ritual practices is *The Nectar of Chanting* (Ganeshpuri: Gurudev Siddha Peeth, 1987).

19. Details of the series of April-May ceremonies are reported in *Siddha Path*, Special Birthday Issue (June-July 1982).

20. A synopsis of Swami Muktananda's main activities through May is available in the Ganeshpuri ashram's annual publication *Shree Gurudev-Vani* (1982), 12–17.

21. Details of the *mahāsamādhi* and installation rituals are reported in *Siddha Path* (December–January 1983).

22. *Hinduism Today*, 8, 1 (1 January 1986), 1, 18–19. The three-year limited term as a rationale for relinquishing the position was disavowed later by all parties.

23. Nityananda formally changed his name to Venkateshwar Rao under provisions of law, notice of which was published in the Maharashtra State Government Gazette of 5 December 1985. Allegations attributed to him were in two cover stories by Sailesh Kottary, "A Stormy Succession," *The Illustrated Weekly of India* (19–25 January 1986), 6–15; and "I Was Abducted," *The Illustrated Weekly of India* (16–22 March 1986), 7–13. The retraction and apology appeared on page 5 of the issue dated 20–26 September 1987; and an article honoring Gurumayi by Namdev Riposo, "Pilgrim's Progress," appeared in the issue of 11–17 October 1987, 58–59.

24. The rejoinder, dated 23 March 1986, was issued by the SYDA Foundation in the form of "a Message from Gurumayi to All the Devotees of Siddha Yoga," photocopy, 16 pages.

25. Quoted by Peter Brent, *Godmen of India*, 275. Cf. pages 290ff. The reciprocal need for the seeker to test the guru has been affirmed in Dick Anthony, Bruce Ecker, and Ken Wilber, *Spiritual Choices: The Problem of Recognizing Authentic Paths to Inner Transformation* (New York: Paragon House Publishers, 1987). Both themes are integral to the account of another contemporary guru in Maharashtra written by Kirin Narayan, *Storytellers, Saints, and Scoundrels: Folk Narrative in Hindu Religious Teaching* (Philadelphia: University of Pennsylvania Press, 1989).

26. *Hinduism Today*, 8, 3 (May 1986): 1, 2, 10–11, 19, reports on the succession dispute, juxtaposing extracts from the *Illustrated Weekly* and from the SYDA Foundation rejoinder; and includes an interview with the SYDA general counsel. Pratibha Pachisia, "The Guru's Frolics," *The Sunday Observer* (13 April 1986) is based on the sworn testimony and corroborative interviews concerning Venkateshwar's behavior during the time when he was coguru. On his return to the role of spiritual leader: undated *Shanti Mandir News*; undated broadside "A Sad Story But True;" and personal correspondence from Venkateshwar—Nityananda, 12 April 1989. In the decision on Suit No. 664 of 1986, dated 11 December 1986, in the case of Shri Gurdev Siddha Peeth vs. Shri Venkateshwar Rao and another, Delhi High Court Justice Leila Seth found that "After having gone through the rituals and ceremonies and repeatedly reiterating that he was no longer interested in 'Sanyas' and had abdicated his position voluntarily, it is not open to him to take a different stand at this stage."

27. Joseph Chilton Pearce, "Foreword," in *Transformation: On Tour with Gurumayi Chidvilasananda*, Vol. 2 (South Fallsburg: SYDA Foundation, 1986), iii. Cf. Linda Johnsen, "Women Saints of India," *Woman of Power*, no. 12 (Winter 1989): 38–39, 88.

28. Quoted by Swami Durgananda, "Intensive at the Taj," *Siddha Path* (December-January 1983): 27.

29. Cf. Michael Gilsenan, *Recognizing Islam: Religion and Society in the Modern Arab World* (New York: Pantheon Books, 1982), 132–141.

30. Peter Hayes, *The Supreme Adventure*, 75. See also pages 5, 55, 122.

31. Personal interviews; *Hinduism Today*, 8, 3 (May 1986): 19. *Hinduism Today*, 11, 10 (October 1989): 2, estimates that twelve monks remain in service to Siddha Yoga.

32. Lawrence A. Babb, *Redemptive Encounters: Three Modern Styles in the Hindu Tradition* (Berkeley: University of California Press, 1986), 30. Cf. Daniel Gold, *The Lord as Guru*, 167: "The principle of multiple succession is indeed the norm in Hindu tantric traditions, within most of which...the appearance of a plurality of gurus is taken as a matter of course." However, Swami Muktananda's authorization of joint successors to share control of a single corporate entity and all of its resources and functions was exceptional and not an instance of the general pattern to which Gold refers.

33. Charles S. J. White's extensive body of work on Indian saints and sainthood is relevant at this point and can be regarded as a scholarly elaboration and explanation of his statement that "Hinduism finds it difficult to dismiss the claimant to divine or saintly status." White, "Indian Developments: Sainthood in Hinduism," in Richard Kieckhefer and George D. Bond, eds., *Sainthood: Its Manifestations in World Religions* (Berkeley: University of California Press, 1988), 104. Dick Anthony's work complements White's as a resource for sorting out several related issues concerning Siddha Yoga and its followers. In terms of The Anthony Typology (elaborated in Anthony, Ecker, and Wilber, *Spiritual Choices*), Siddha Yoga is an instance of "the multilevel charismatic approach as practiced in monistic frameworks." A brief summary and critique of the typology is offered by Thomas Robbins, *Cults, Converts and Charisma: The Sociology of New Religious Movements* (London: Sage Publications, 1988), 135–142. Finally, the ideal properly intended by guru and disciple in movements of the type represented by Siddha Yoga is stated with eloquence and insight by Lawrence A. Babb, *Redemptive Encounters*, 224–225.

Chapter 12. When the Prophet is Yet Living: A Case Study of the Unification Church

1. Laurence R. Iannaccone, "A Formal Model of Church and Sect." Typed manuscript at the Institute for the Study of American Religion, University of

California at Santa Barbara. I am indebted to Iannaccone's article for calling my attention to Berger's and Stark and Bainbridge's applications cited below.

2. Peter Berger, *The Sacred Canopy* (Garden City, NY: Doubleday, 1967), 138.

3. Rodney Stark and William Sims Bainbridge, "Towards a Theory of Religion: Religious Commitment," *Journal for the Scientific Study of Religion* 19 (1980): 114–128.

4. Dietrich Bonhoeffer, *The Cost of Discipleship* (New York: Macmillan, 1987).

5. See David G. Bromley and Anson D. Shupe, Jr., *"Moonies" in America: Cult, Church and Crusade* (Beverly Hills, CA: Sage, 1979), 27–29.

6. *Divine Principle,* 5th ed. (New York: HSA-UWC, 1977), 16.

7. Warren Lewis, "Hero with the Thousand-and-First Face," in *A Time for Consideration: A Scholarly Appraisal of the Unification Church,* M. Darroll Bryant and Herbert W. Richardson, eds. (New York: Edwin Mellen, 1978), 279–280.

8. See Sun Myung Moon, "A Spiritual Revolution Is Needed," *Za Rubezhom* (Moscow), 17–23 November 1989. Rev. Moon, in this interview (reprinted as paid advertisements in various U.S. newspapers), expresses his admiration for Russia's "high artistic traditions," notes the initiatives he already has undertaken in China, and asserts that "the outcome of the Soviet Union's current program of restructuring will determine the future course of history."

9. I have noted elsewhere that universalizing and ecumenical trends are apparent in later English texts. For example, whereas the earlier Korean-language editions posited Korean as the coming universal language, the first official English translation refers only to the necessity for the unity of languages, and the latest official edition drops the matter entirely. Similar development is apparent in attitudes expressed toward other religions, particularly Judaism and Islam as well as changes in terminology reflective of sensitivity to feminists. See Michael L. Mickler, *The Unification Church in America: A Bibliography and Research Guide* (New York: Garland, 1987), 63.

10. Blumer, Herbert, "Collective Behavior," in *Principles of Sociology,* A. M. Lee, ed. (New York: Barnes and Noble, 1969), 110. Quoted in John Lofland, "Social Movement Culture and the Unification Church," in *The Future of New Religious Movements,* David G. Bromley and Phillip E. Hammond, eds. (Macon, Georgia: Mercer University Press, 1987), 93.

11. Lonnie Kliever, "Unification Thought and Modern Theology," *Religious Studies Review* 8 (July 1982): 215.

12. Lofland, "Social Movement Culture and the Unification Church," 93.

13. *Divine Principle,* 9.

14. Max Weber, *The Theory of Social and Economic Orgainzation* (New York: Free Press, 1964), 398.

15. Yoshihiko Masuda, "Moral Vision and Practice in the Unification Movement," (Ph.D. diss, University of Southern California, 1987), 176.

16. Quoted in David G. Bromley and Anson D. Shupe, Jr., *Strange Gods: The Great American Cult Scare* (Boston: Beacon, 1981), 209.

17. Rodney Stark, "How New Religions Succeed: A Theoretical Model," in *The Future of New Religious Movements,* 21.

18. Max Weber, *On Charisma and Institution Building,* edited by S. N. Eisenstadt (Chicago: University of Chicago Press, 1968), 52.

19. David G. Bromley, "Economic Structure and Charismatic Leadership in the Unification Church," in *Money and Power in the New Religions,* James T. Richardson, ed. (Toronto: Edwin Mellen, 1988), 355. See also pages 336, 340–341.

20. Weber, *The Theory of Social and Economic Organization,* 364.

21. Bromley, "Economic Structure and Charismatic Leadership in the Unification Church," 342.

22. Masuda, "Moral Vision and Practice in the Unification Movement," 386–387.

23. Bromley, "Economic Structure and Charismatic Leadership in the Unification Church," 344–348.

24. Anson Shupe, "Sun Myung Moon's Mission in Retreat," *Wall Street Journal,* 1 November 1989.

25. Stark, "How New Religions Succeed: A Theoretical Model," 16.

26. Ibid., 18.

27. Masuda, "Moral Vision and Practice in the Unification Movement," 375–376.

28. Bromley, "Economic Structure and Charismatic Leadership in the Unification Church," 361.

29. J. Stillson Judah, Introduction to Mickler, *The Unification Church in America: A Bibliography and Research Guide,* 24.

30. The UC, for example, banned adherents from seeking personal and marital therapy from a Wesleyan community on Vashon Island in Puget Sound, Washington. It also has attempted to ban the utilization of certain therapeutic practices by movement counselors. At the same time, UC publications, particularly those focusing on family life and childcare, frequently cite psychological

literature. In addition, movement adherents increasingly include a number of medical doctors and psychotherapists. The therapy issue, therefore, is unresolved.

31. Bromley and Shupe, *"Moonies" in America: Cult, Church, and Crusade,* 29.

32. George Gallup, Jr., and David Poling, *The Search for America's Faith* (Nashville: Abington, 1980), 28–29.

33. See John Lofland, "The Boom and Bust of a Millenarian Movement: Doomsday Cult Revisited," epilogue in *Doomsday Cult,* enlarged edition (New York: Irvington, 1977), 289–352.

Afterword

1. Although the trend for Unitarians over several decades has been down, they seemed to turn a corner in the 1980s, growing from 139,000 to 173,000 members between 1981 and 1988. See Constant H. Jacquet, Jr., ed., *Yearbook of American Churches* (Nashville: Abingdon, 1981 and 1988 editions).